One God, One Lord

One God, One Lord

EARLY CHRISTIAN DEVOTION
AND ANCIENT JEWISH MONOTHEISM

LARRY W. HURTADO

Fortress Press   Philadelphia

To
Eldon Jay Epp
teacher and friend

Library of Congress Cataloging-in-Publication Data

Hurtado, Larry W., 1943–
  One God, one Lord.

  1. Jewish Christians—History—Early church,
ca. 30-600. 2. Jesus Christ—History of doctrines
—Early church, ca. 30-600. 3. God (Judaism)—
History of doctrines. 4. Christianity—Origin.
5. Christianity and other religions—Judaism.
6. Judaism—Relations—Christianity. I. Title.
BR158.H87 1988   231'.09'015   87–45895
ISBN 0-8006-2076-3

3220K87   Printed in the United States of America   1–2076

Contents

Preface   vii

Abbreviations   x

Introduction   1
   The Problem   1
   Early Christology and Chronology   3
   Excursus   6
   Complexity in Ancient Judaism   7
   The Historical Approach   9
   Excursus   9
   One God and Devotion to Jesus   11

1. Divine Agency in Ancient Jewish Monotheism   17
   Divine Agency Speculation   17
      Three Types • Variation of Types • Summary
   The Shape of Postexilic Jewish Religious Devotion   22
   Angelology and Monotheism   23
      A Critique of W. Bousset's View • The Data • Conclusion
   Monotheism and Other Divine Agents   35
   Summary   39

2. Personified Divine Attributes as Divine Agents   41
   Personified Divine Attributes   42
      Wisdom • Logos
   The Language of Divine Agency   49

3. Exalted Patriarchs as Divine Agents   51
   Enoch Speculations   51
      Enoch as Son of Man • Enoch as an Angel
   Exalted Moses Traditions   56
      Sirach • *Testament of Moses* • *Exagōgē of Ezekiel* • *Philo*
   Other Exalted Patriarchs   64
   Exalted Patriarchs and Jewish Religious Devotion   65

4. Principal Angels   71
   Angelology and Christology in Previous Studies   72
   Principal Angels in Ancient Judaism   75
      Principal Angels in Ezekiel and Daniel • Michael in
      Other Texts • Other Chief Angel References
   Chief Angels and God   82
      Chief Angels and the Bifurcation of God
   Summary   90

5. The Early Christian Mutation   93
   Jesus as God's Chief Agent   93
   The Christian Mutation   99
      Six Features of the Mutation
         Early Christian Hymns • Prayer to Christ •
         The Name of Christ • The Lord's Supper • Confessing
         Jesus • Prophecy and the Risen Jesus
   Causes of the Christian Mutation   114
      The Ministry of Jesus • Easter and Afterward
      Opposition to the New Movement
   Summary   123

Conclusions   125

Notes   129

Index of Ancient Sources   169

Index of Authors   175

Preface

The details of the religious innovation represented by earliest Christianity are only imperfectly preserved in the historical sources, and any attempt to organize into an orderly picture what scattered details survive runs the risk of being charged with being more clever than persuasive or, almost certainly, of suffering eventual correction or even refutation. I hope that I have not been more clever than the data warrant, but I cherish no illusion of having produced the last word on the origins of the cultic veneration of Jesus in earliest Christianity.

Barring the discovery of major new evidence, advances in the study of Christian origins will come mainly through careful refinement of the scholarly analysis of what data we have. This book contains precious little in the way of evidence not previously examined, but I have tried to advance our understanding of the origins of Christianity by the organization and analysis of the evidence considered here and by focusing on the praxis of early Christian devotion rather than on christological rhetoric such as the much-discussed christological titles. I have found it necessary to take issue with some earlier views, a few of them fairly widely shared, and naturally I hope that my investigation may constitute a contribution of some value.

Several personal acquaintances have read earlier versions of this work and discussed these ideas with me. They have shown enthusiastic interest in this project, with whose conclusions they did not always agree, and their criticisms and suggestions have produced numerous improvements. But even their disagreements have been valuable, for they have forced me to clarify my thoughts and the expression of my views as nothing else can.

Professors Martin Hengel and Peter Stuhlmacher both kindly entertained me in their homes, discussed the project with me, and gave encouragement at an early stage of the writing of this manuscript during a visit to Tübingen in November 1984. I am especially grateful to Dr. Christopher Rowland, Dr. Jarl Fossum, and Professor Alan Segal, who all kindly read the entire manuscript in an earlier draft and helped me improve it at many points. Dr. Fossum also allowed me to examine the proofs of *The Name of God and the Angel of the Lord*, prior to its publication, and arranged discussions with Professors Peter van der Horst and Gilles Quispel. Both Dr. William Horbury and Dr. Douglas DeLacy provided helpful comments on the first three chapters. Professor Saul Olyan read chapters 1 and 2, giving me some valuable insights into the nature of preexilic Israelite religion and the wider West Semitic religious atmosphere of ancient times. Professor Kent Brower reviewed the whole manuscript and helped me to improve more than a few passages. All these scholars have shown exemplary cooperation, fairness, and commitment to academic dialogue.

A good deal of the research and writing was done during a sabbatical research leave (1984–1985 academic year) spent in Cambridge, England. I am grateful to the University of Manitoba for granting me the leave and to the Social Sciences and Humanities Research Council of Canada for a Leave Fellowship and research grant which enabled me and my family to travel to England for the year. During our time in Cambridge, I was a Bye Fellow of Robinson College, a thoroughly enjoyable association for my part. I thank Professor Morna Hooker, Fellow of Robinson College, for nominating me for the Bye Fellowship, and my family joins me in expressing our thanks to the Warden, Sir Jack Lewis, the Fellowship, and the staff of the college for helping to make our time there so pleasant and memorable.

During that sabbatical leave, I presented some portions of this book at Professor Hooker's New Testament Seminar in Cambridge, Professor Barnabas Lindars's Ehrhardt Seminar, and Professor J. D. G. Dunn's New Testament Seminar, and I wish to thank these colleagues for their invitations to address these meetings. Among the benefits of these presentations, I was particularly helped by conversations in Manchester with Dr. Richard Bauckham and Dr. Philip Alexander and his wife, Loveday; in Durham with Professor Dunn; and in Cambridge with Dr. Rowland. At my Cambridge presentation, Dr. Rowland gave a prepared response, making that seminar doubly valuable for me. I also profited from several colleagues at the 1985 meeting of the Society of Biblical Literature New Testament Christology Group, where I presented a similar paper.

I wish to thank Fortress Press for undertaking the publication of this work, and particularly Dr. John A. Hollar for his many editorial improvements in my manuscript and for his general assistance in bringing the book to publication.

Through the whole process of producing this book, my wife, Shannon, has continued to endear herself to me through her patient interest in my work, her editorial assistance in clarifying numerous passages in my prose, and her warm companionship in life.

I dedicate the volume to Eldon Jay Epp, whose high standards of scholarship I admire and whose help, both during student days and subsequently, has made me his grateful debtor.

University of Manitoba   LARRY W. HURTADO
September 1987

Abbreviations

GENERAL

AGJU	Arbeiten zur Geschichte des antiken Judentums und des Urchristentums
ANET	*Ancient Near Eastern Texts Relating to the Old Testament.* 3d ed. J. B. Pritchard, ed.
ANRW	*Aufstieg und Niedergang der römischen Welt.* H. Temporini and W. Haase, eds.
AOAT	Alter Orient und Altes Testament
AOT	*The Apocryphal Old Testament,* H. F. D. Sparks, ed.
ATAbh	Alttestamentliche Abhandlungen
BA	*Biblical Archaeologist*
BHT	Beiträge zur historischen Theologie
Bib	*Biblica*
CBQ	*Catholic Biblical Quarterly*
CBQMS	Catholic Biblical Quarterly Monograph Series
ET	English Translation
ExpTim	*Expository Times*
HSM	Harvard Semitic Monographs
HSS	Harvard Semitic Studies
HTR	*Harvard Theological Review*
HTRDR	Harvard Theological Review Dissertations in Religion
HTS	Harvard Theological Studies
HUCA	*Hebrew Union College Annual*
ICS	*Illinois Classical Studies*
IDB	*Interpreter's Dictionary of the Bible*

IDBSup	*Interpreter's Dictionary of the Bible, Supplementary Volume*
ITQ	*Irish Theological Quarterly*
JBL	*Journal of Biblical Literature*
JJS	*Journal of Jewish Studies*
JSJ	*Journal for the Study of Judaism in the Persian, Hellenistic and Roman Period*
JSNT	*Journal for the Study of the New Testament*
JSS	*Journal of Semitic Studies*
JSSR	*Journal for the Scientific Study of Religion*
JTS	*Journal of Theological Studies*
LCL	Loeb Classical Library
LXX	Septuagint
NIDNTT	*New International Dictionary of New Testament Theology.* 3 vols. C. Brown, ed.
NovT	*Novum Testamentum*
NovTSup	Novum Testamentum Supplements
NT	New Testament
NTS	*New Testament Studies*
OT	Old Testament
OTP	*Old Testament Pseudepigrapha.* 2 vols. J. H. Charlesworth, ed.
PVTG	Pseudepigrapha Veteris Testamenti graece
QD	Quaestiones Disputatae
RB	*Revue biblique*
RelSRev	*Religious Studies Review*
RRR	*Review of Religious Research*
RSPT	*Revue des sciences philosophiques et théologiques*
RSV	Revised Standard Version of the Bible
SBLDS	Society of Biblical Literature Dissertation Series
SBLMS	Society of Biblical Literature Monograph Series
SBS	Stuttgarter Bibelstudien
SBT	Studies in Biblical Theology
SJLA	Studies in Judaism in Late Antiquity
SJT	*Scottish Journal of Theology*
SNTSMS	Society for New Testament Studies Monograph Series
SR	*Studies in Religion/Sciences religieuses*
ST	*Studia Theologica*

TDNT	*Theological Dictionary of the New Testament.* 10 vols. G. Kittel and G. Friedrich, eds.
TRu	*Theologische Rundschau*
TS	*Theological Studies*
TU	Texte und Untersuchungen
VC	*Vigiliae christianae*
WMANT	Wissenschaftliche Monographien zum Alten und Neuen Testament
WUNT	Wissenschaftliche Untersuchungen zum Neuen Testament
ZAW	*Zeitschrift für die alttestamentliche Wissenschaft*
ZNW	*Zeitschrift für die neutestamentliche Wissenschaft*

BIBLICAL

Gen.	Genesis
Exod.	Exodus
Num.	Numbers
Deut.	Deuteronomy
Josh.	Joshua
Isa.	Isaiah
Jer.	Jeremiah
Ezek.	Ezekiel
Mal.	Malachi
Ps.	Psalms
Prov.	Proverbs
Dan.	Daniel
Matt.	Gospel of Matthew
Rom.	Epistle to the Romans
1 Cor.	First Epistle to the Corinthians
2 Cor.	Second Epistle to the Corinthians
Gal.	Epistle to the Galatians
Eph.	Epistle to the Ephesians
Phil.	Epistle to the Philippians
Col.	Epistle to the Colossians
1 Thess.	First Epistle to the Thessalonians
1 Tim.	First Epistle to Timothy
2 Tim.	Second Epistle to Timothy
Heb.	Epistle to the Hebrews
1 Pet.	First Epistle of Peter

2 Pet.	Second Epistle of Peter
Rev.	Revelation of St. John

EARLY CHRISTIAN LITERATURE

Comm. Joh.	*Commentary on John*, Origen
Dial.	*Dialogue with Trypho*, Justin Martyr
Strom.	*The Strommata*, Clement of Alexandria

APOCRYPHA AND PSEUDEPIGRAPHA

Apoc. Abr.	*Apocalypse of Abraham*
Apoc. Zeph.	*Apocalypse of Zepheniah*
Ascen. Isa.	*Ascension of Isaiah*
Bar.	*Baruch*
2 Bar.	*Second (Syriac) Baruch*
Bib. Ant.	*Biblical Antiquities of Pseudo-Philo*
Jub.	*Jubilees*
4 Macc.	*4 Maccabees*
Paral. Jer.	*The Paraleipomena of Jeremiah*
Sir.	*Ben Sirach (Ecclesiasticus)*
Tob.	*Tobit*
T. Abr.	*Testament of Abraham*
T. Ash.	*Testament of Asher*
T. Benj.	*Testament of Benjamin*
T. Dan	*Testament of Dan*
T. Judah	*Testament of Judah*
T. Levi	*Testament of Levi*
T. Mos.	*Testament (Assumption) of Moses*
T. Naph.	*Testament of Naphtali*
T. Sim.	*Testament of Simeon*
T. Sol.	*Testament of Solomon*
T. Zeb.	*Testament of Zebulon*
Wis.	*Wisdom of Solomon*

PHILO OF ALEXANDRIA

Conf. Ling.	*De Confusione Linguarum*
De Agr.	*De Agricultura*
Cherub.	*De Cherubim*
Det.	*Quod Deterius Potiori insidiari solet*
Fug.	*De Fuga et Inventione*

Gig.	De Gigantibus
Leg. Alleg.	Legum Allegoriae
Migr. Abr.	De Migratione Abrahami
Mut.	De Mutatione Nominum
Opf. Mun.	De Opficio Mundi
Post.	De Posteritate Caini
Prob.	De Quod Omnis Probus Liber sit
Quaest. Exod.	Quaestiones et Solutiones in Exodum
Quaest. Gen.	Quaestiones et Solutiones in Genesin
Sac.	De Sacrificiis Abelis et Caini
Somn.	De Somniis
Spec. Leg.	De Specialibus Legibus
Vit. Mos.	De Vita Mosis

QUMRAN TEXTS

1QH	1Q Hodayot (Hymn Scroll)
1QM	1Q Milchamah (War Scroll)
11QMelch	11Q Melchizedek

RABBINIC TEXTS

t. Hul.	Tosephta Hullin
b. Abod. Zar.	Aboda Zara
m. Hul.	Mishnah Hullin
b. Sanh.	Sanhedrin
b. Ber.	Berakot
Midr. Ber. R.	Midrash Bereshit Rabbah

Introduction

THE PROBLEM

Although there may be so-called gods in heaven or on earth—as indeed there are many "gods" and many "lords"—yet for us there is one God, the Father, from whom are all things and for whom we exist, and one Lord, Jesus Christ, through whom are all things and through whom we exist. (1 Cor. 8:5-6)

In these lines, written only slightly more than twenty years after the crucifixion of Jesus, Paul the Apostle summarizes the distinctive nature of early Christian devotion. At the same time he identifies the problem to be investigated. First, Paul distinguishes Christian devotion from other varieties in the Greco-Roman world of his day. He does so by rejecting the plurality of deities otherwise almost universally accepted in varying ways among his pagan contemporaries as legitimate manifestations of "the divine," insisting that for Christians there can be only "one God." In doing this, Paul and early Christians were not entirely alone, nor were they the first ones to take this position. This rather strict monotheistic stand—indeed, offensively strict in the eyes of virtually all pagans of that time—was nothing but the common position taken by Judaism, something to which Paul the Jewish Christian would have pointed happily as proof that he was truly serving the God of his fathers.[1]

Paul's statement also distinguishes early Christian faith from the Jewish background by his reference to Jesus in the same breath, so to speak, as the mention of the one God, linking Jesus with God and conferring on him what is here to be seen as a title of divine honor, "Lord."[2] Although we do not actually have first-century Jewish documents that tell us directly what Jewish religious leaders thought of Christian devotion,

1

there seems to be every reason to assume that the attitude was probably very much like the one reflected in slightly later Jewish sources, which apparently reject cultic devotion to Jesus as constituting an example of the worship of "two powers in heaven," that is, the worship of two gods.[3]

We may have indirect evidence of this suggestion in the apostle Paul. It is, in my view, likely that Paul's persecution of Jewish Christians (Gal. 1:13-14; 1 Cor. 15:9) prior to his conversion experience was occasioned partly by the reverence they gave to Jesus. Paul describes his change of heart as brought about because God "was pleased to reveal his Son to [or "in"] me" (Gal. 1:16), which suggests that the experience forced Paul to embrace a view of Jesus' relationship to God that he, as one "so extremely zealous . . . for the traditions of [his] fathers," had been unable to accept previously.[4]

Our starting point is the fact that, although their devotion to Jesus may have caused other Jews to regard them as having violated the uniqueness of God, early Jewish Christians, like Paul after his Damascus road experience, apparently felt thoroughly justified in giving Jesus reverence in terms of divinity *and* at the same time thought of themselves as worshiping *one God*.

The problem to be investigated in this book is therefore precisely this: How did the early Jewish Christians accommodate the veneration of the exalted Jesus alongside God while continuing to see themselves as loyal to the fundamental emphasis of their ancestral tradition on one God, and without the benefit of the succeeding four centuries of Christian theological discussion which led to the Christian doctrine of the Trinity? As an answer to this problem, I propose that early Christianity drew upon important resources in ancient Judaism and also developed a somewhat distinctive "mutation" or innovation in this monotheistic tradition.

The origin of this "binitarian shape" of early Christian devotion reflected in 1 Cor. 8:6, which involved the veneration of Jesus alongside God and a refusal to venerate all other divine figures, constitutes a major historical problem.[5] But, given the investigation already carried out on the origins of Christology, whoever dares to contribute anything further has the double responsibility of demonstrating familiarity with the previous work and of advancing the discussion in some way. The endnotes will show how indebted I am to the work of others. In what follows, I shall try to indicate why I offer this contribution to the literature on early Christology.

EARLY CHRISTOLOGY
AND CHRONOLOGY

Conscious of the distinctive binitarian shape of early Christian devotion over against the monotheistic emphasis of early Judaism and also that Christianity began as a kind of Jewish sectarian movement, scholars have sought to explain the veneration of Jesus as due to the influence of the veneration of a wide variety of divine figures in Greco-Roman paganism.[6] But, given the general antipathy of ancient Judaism toward pagan religion, it has often been claimed that the influence described here could have had its effect only at a secondary stage of early Christianity, when significant numbers of Gentiles had been converted (who are portrayed as remaining open to the worship of more than one divine figure) and in a cultural and geographical setting somewhat removed from Palestine and traditional Jewish devotion.[7] Thus the veneration of Jesus is seen as merely a particular example of the syncretistic tendencies characteristic of Greco-Roman religion and as an early stage of the Hellenization of Christianity that proceeded much further in the first several centuries of the church.

However plausible this view appears at first glance, and however "comfortable" to particular historical schemes and theological preferences, a careful consideration of the evidence available to us concerning the earliest stages of Christian tradition makes such a view virtually untenable, at least as it has characteristically been expressed.[8] That is, the question of how the veneration of Jesus began in early Christianity cannot be answered by invoking the influence of pagan polytheism in Christian circles insufficiently familiar with the monotheistic tradition of the first Jewish Christians. The chronological data concerning early Christian belief and devotion do not easily permit this approach.[9]

Among scholars who study the origins of Christianity, it is agreed that the earliest Christian writings we possess are the letters of the apostle Paul, sent to various churches in the course of his missionary travels (approximately 50 to 60 C.E.), which take us back almost to the beginning of Paul's mission to the Gentiles and to within twenty years of the beginning of Christianity. Later I shall more closely examine passages in these letters that tell us what Paul believed about Christ and that reflect the reverence Paul approved. Here I want to anticipate this later discussion by emphasizing two points.

First, Paul regarded the resurrected Jesus as occupying a unique position of heavenly authority and honor, and he wrote of the exalted Christ and reverenced him in ways that seem to require us to conclude that Paul treated him as divine. Second, although Paul had clashes with people who troubled his churches and whose view of Christian faith he found seriously defective, and although he had differences with the Jerusalem church over matters connected with the mission to the Gentiles, nothing in Paul's letters indicates any awareness that his fundamental view of Christ was unique or that he had made any serious innovation in the way Christians before him had regarded the exalted Jesus, however much he may have had his own emphases in the articulation of his message.[10] Indeed, the Pauline letters may enable us to catch glimpses of Christian belief and devotion from the first few years of the church.

Although Paul insisted that the basis for his Christian faith and apostleship lay in the direct call of God and in a divine revelation to him of Jesus as the Son of God (Gal. 1:11-17), he also wished to associate his message and the beliefs and practices he urged upon his converts with the faith of other Christians, including those who were not a part of his own mission work (e.g., 1 Cor. 11:23-26; 15:1-8). In Paul's letters there are a number of passages that reflect the devotion of Christians of the period prior to Paul's gentile mission, which began no later than the 40s C.E.: credal statements (e.g., Rom. 1:3-4; 10:9-10); fragments of church prayers (e.g., Rom. 8:15; 1 Cor. 16:22; Gal. 4:6); and possibly some hymns (e.g., Col. 1:15-20; Phil. 2:5-11). Some of these fragments of early church tradition may take us back to churches of a Palestinian setting and to Christians whose native language was Aramaic (e.g., the untranslated Aramaic prayer fragment in 1 Cor. 16:22, "Maranatha").[11]

Thus we seem to be afforded glimpses of Christian devotion from what must include Jewish Christian groups very close in time, culture, and geographical setting to the origin of Christianity. And the indications are that already in these groups the exalted Jesus had begun to play a significant role as the object of religious devotion, indeed as an object of cultic veneration. In the gatherings of the Christians with which Paul was familiar, it appears that they sang "hymns" honoring and celebrating Christ,[12] baptized converts "in the name of Jesus,"[13] and very likely had rituals of "calling upon" Jesus and "confessing" him as "Lord" (e.g., Rom. 10:9-10; 1 Cor. 12:3). In all of this they seem to have seen themselves as reflecting the heavenly and eschatological veneration of Jesus anticipated in Phil. 2:9-11 (cf. Rev. 5:1-14).[14]

Further, when we recall the dramatic experience that caused Paul to become a follower of Jesus and a preacher of the gospel (ca. 32-34 C.E.)

and that from this point he began his association with Christians in Damascus, Jerusalem, and Antioch (Gal. 1:17–23), it becomes evident that the Christian tradition with which Paul was familiar was impressively broad in geographical extent and went back to within a few years of the beginning of the church.[15] Actually, we must conclude that Paul's acquaintance with Christian beliefs went back even earlier than his Damascus road experience, for he must have obtained some familiarity with Jewish-Christian devotion in order to have been moved to persecute Jewish Christians for their beliefs (Gal. 1:13; 1 Cor. 15:9). In Paul, then, we have not only an important Jewish Christian in his own right but also one who was familiar with, and discloses aspects of, the devotion of Jewish-Christian groups of the most primitive period of Christianity.[16] Paul, whose own faith was decisively shaped within the very first few years of Christianity, and in contact with believers familiar with the earliest Christian groups in Palestine, gives the impression that the exalted status he accorded to the risen Jesus was reflective also of the faith of those who "were in Christ before" him (Rom. 16:7).

Thus Paul's own letters, the earliest literary access to Christianity afforded to us, provide strong evidence that the period in which to seek the decisive beginnings of the veneration of Jesus is not at all late but extremely early, easily within the first decade of the Christian movement. They also indicate that the setting for the origin of Jesus veneration is within Christian groups led by, and at least initially comprised mainly of, Jewish Christians, including Aramaic-speaking groups in Palestine. This in turn means that a historical inquiry into the origins of Jesus veneration that seeks to take into account the religious background must give primary attention to ancient Judaism and cannot easily resort to hypotheses involving the direct influence of pagan cults. For this reason I concentrate on the Jewish religious background.

Certainly ancient Judaism was not immune to the larger Greco-Roman environment. Both Philo of Alexandria and Paul himself, to take but two examples, show the adaptation of concepts and literary conventions circulating in their time. But both authors also show strong reserve toward the specifically religious beliefs and practices of the pagan world and illustrate the tendency of most Jews in the Greco-Roman setting to hold themselves aloof from and superior to other religious groups. It is therefore appropriate to think of Judaism as distinguishable in some ways within the Greco-Roman setting. And on account of the evidence concerning the origin of the Christian veneration of Jesus mentioned above (cf. chap. 5), it is proper to insist that the correct history of religions approach is to see ancient Judaism as the most immediately relevant religious background for this phenomenon, especially in its early stages. Exploring general connections of Jewish and early Christian traditions with pagan thought and religious practices is a legitimate inquiry, of course, but it is the topic of another book to be written by a specialist on that complex issue.[17]

EXCURSUS

My focus on the Jewish background may cause some readers to wonder whether I am not subject to the charge of arbitrarily and incorrectly ignoring the pagan religious traditions of the Greco-Roman period, the sort of criticism directed by C. R. Holladay against J. D. G. Dunn's *Christology in the Making*.[18] There is a certain similarity between Dunn's book and mine, in that we both investigate the historical origin of a feature of early Christianity and both concentrate on the Jewish background. There are, however, also some significant differences.

First, Dunn's failure to discuss more fully the pagan evidence was particularly puzzling because he dated the emergence of the Christian doctrine of the incarnation late in the first century C.E., when there would have been several decades during which Christian doctrines could have been directly influenced by pagan cults and myths. If the cultic veneration of the exalted Christ, the subject of my investigation, were only a feature of gentile Christianity appearing after several decades had elapsed, the pagan evidence would be much more relevant. Such is not the case. I am concerned with a characteristic of early Christian piety that has its origins within the very first few years of Christianity, when it was thoroughly dominated by Jews and functioned as a sect of ancient Judaism.[19]

Second, given Dunn's concern to show that the early Christian doctrine of the incarnation of Christ did not find a parallel anywhere in the ancient world, his choice not to discuss more thoroughly the apparent similarities to pagan ideas of divine beings appearing on the earth in human form or as humans was a mistake. For our problem the pagan evidence does not help us. There is simply no comparable tradition of exclusivist monotheism in the pagan religions of the Greco-Roman period. That Gentiles were able to accommodate numerous gods in their theologies and religious practices is interesting but does not tell us how those concerned for the uniqueness of the God of Israel became functionally binitarian in religious practice. When scholars refer to ancient pagan monotheism they refer to ideas of one god manifested through the many or one god high above the many other divinities. And such ideas did not involve exclusivist devotion to one god such as distinguished Judaism and early Christianity.

I am specifically concerned with the question of how pious Jews, who, like Paul, show a commitment to a rather exclusivist monotheism, were able to accommodate a second figure alongside God as an object of religious devotion. Since I want to see what precedents or stimuli for this Christian binitarianism there may have been in Jewish monotheistic tradition, choosing to omit discussion of Greco-Roman pagan religions is not arbitrary, nor a sign of some sort of bias, but seems only logical.

Since I hope to show that the emergence of early Christian binitarian devotion to God and Jesus can be explained on the basis of the Jewish background and the religious experiences of the early church, a fuller discussion of pagan religions of the Greco-Roman period would simply be beside the point. I agree with Holladay's view that a comprehensive description of early Christianity would require detailed consideration of all aspects of religiosity in the Greco-Roman period. But the purpose of this book is much more modest, and the evidence that is directly relevant is therefore much more limited in scope.

COMPLEXITY IN ANCIENT JUDAISM

One reason that the older history of religions approach to the origin of the cultic veneration of Jesus resorted to the hypothesis of direct pagan influence is that exponents of this view seem to have been bedeviled by a simplistic and inaccurate view of ancient Judaism. Scholars in this school were certainly aware of the evidence mentioned above that suggests that the origin of Jesus veneration was in a Palestinian and Jewish setting. But it appears that they felt compelled to explain this evidence in other ways because they could not imagine Christians of a very traditional Jewish background being able to take the step of bestowing upon the risen Jesus the exalted status clearly reflected in the Pauline letters.[20] The attempts to deal with this evidence by representatives of this point of view show that no attempt was satisfactory and that strong notions about the nature of ancient Judaism (especially Palestinian Judaism) thoroughly controlled their investigation. Here I want to summarize how our understanding of ancient Judaism has been enhanced, especially in relation to the study of the origins of Christianity. I also want to indicate why the older notions about ancient Judaism must now be regarded as erroneous.

The origins of Christianity lie in the context of Palestinian Judaism, to be sure, but Palestine too had been in contact with Greek language and culture for more than three hundred years by the time of Jesus' crucifixion. Although there were Palestinian Jewish attempts to oppose this influence, they met with only partial success. Therefore the overly rigid distinctions between Hellenistic Judaism and Palestinian Judaism common in some past studies must be avoided.[21] Greek language, for example, was apparently used throughout Palestine, even among local Jews, and not just among Jews who adopted Greek culture.[22] Further, the Judaism of Palestine was much more diverse culturally than has sometimes been recognized.

Jewish travel between Diaspora locations and Palestine was steady, and at the time of the origin of Christianity Jews frequently moved from Diaspora locations to Palestine, bringing with them the use of Greek language and other aspects of their Diaspora culture.[23] In the first Christian community in Jerusalem there were apparently such Greek-speaking Jews as well as Palestinian-born Jews whose primary language was Aramaic. Thus Christianity was probably from the beginning a bilingual community.[24] So, if we use the term "Palestinian Judaism" to mean the religion and culture of Jews living in Palestine of that time, it designates a bilingual phenomenon which included within it significant variations.[25]

Even in Palestinian Judaism, there was much ferment in beliefs and practices, including notions about God and other heavenly figures. This means that previous ideas about what could or could not have been included in Palestinian Jewish monotheism may need to be reexamined[26] (see chap. 1). There is some indication that Jewish belief in the uniqueness of God was able to accommodate surprising kinds of reverence for and interest in other heavenly figures such as chief angels and exalted patriarchs as well as personified attributes or powers of God. Interest in the role of these divine agents was apparently widespread and probably of some importance in understanding how early Jewish Christians were able to accommodate the exalted Jesus without feeling that they had violated the uniqueness of God.[27]

In short, the more complex picture of ancient Jewish monotheism in the first century may assist us in understanding that early Jewish Christians could think of themselves as holding to belief in "one God" while also viewing the risen Jesus in the most exalted of categories. I shall argue later that the early Christian veneration of Jesus involved somewhat new and distinctive developments beyond the reverence characteristically given to divine agents in ancient Judaism. But these Jewish-Christian developments are probably to be understood as historically related to, and indebted to, the complex nature of monotheism in the Jewish context.[28] If previous scholars thought it impossible to account for the beginnings of the cultic veneration of Jesus in a Jewish monotheistic setting, this may now be regarded as partly due to an incorrect and rigid view of what Jewish faith in one God could accommodate, even in a Palestinian setting.

To some degree, the error just described is simply the result of doing historical work, which is always in danger of being shown to be erroneous by later discoveries of evidence or by revised critical opinions on the use of evidence. Of course, historical work is a complex interaction among available evidence, critical opinions and methods, and the interpreters conducting the historical investigation. This is especially the case when the topic is religion. Since I have elsewhere discussed these matters as they pertain to the study of Christian origins,[29] I will summarize the matter here in order to illuminate the approach I take here and why it may advance the discussion beyond previous studies.

THE HISTORICAL APPROACH

All historical investigations of Christian origin today are influenced in varying ways by the scholars who are often described as forming the history of religions school, which came to prominence in the early decades of this century.[30] Dissatisfied with previous historical studies of early Christianity, ones basically concerned with the development of Christian doctrines, this school of thought sought to deal with the whole of early Christian religion, including cultic practices and devotion. Furthermore, concerned to treat early Christianity in a truly historical way, they sought to disclose the relationship of Christian beliefs and practices to the surrounding Greco-Roman world. Current historical study of Christian origins at its best still embodies these aims and draws upon the work done by these scholars. I must, however, lodge certain criticisms of their work in order to show the need for further investigation. Precisely because their work is still so influential, I believe that my criticisms are relevant to current scholarly discussions also.

First, although the attempt to place early Christianity in its historical setting produced valuable studies of the religious environment of the Greco-Roman world, the attempt to find parallels for early Christian beliefs and practices was sometimes insufficiently critical in attempt and therefore erroneous in result. There seems to have been the assumption that all characteristics of early Christianity (all beliefs, ethics, practices, and concepts) must have been borrowed from the surrounding religious environment. That is, the religious influences were seen as coming only *from* the surrounding world *into* early Christianity. There was insufficient readiness to entertain the question of whether influences might ever have run in the other direction.[31] Nor was much consideration given to the possibility that the early Christians might have developed genuinely distinctive ideas and practices. To some degree this is understandable in that these scholars were reacting against descriptions of early Christianity that paid little or no attention to the religious context out of which it developed. But, with the advantage of hindsight, their own approach must be seen as an overreaction.

EXCURSUS

Because some apologists for Christian faith have tried to make what they understand as the distinctiveness of Christian ideas and practices a basis for arguing for the superiority of Christianity, and because some scholars, aware of this type of apologetic, have then become chary of anyone referring to distinctive developments in early Christianity, I wish to make my own position clear. (1) I refer to "distinctiveness in early Christianity" because I think that the historical evidence leads to such a conclusion. (2) Indeed, although religious groups of the Greco-Roman world had much in common, many of them also had distinctive practices or ideas, so I do not imply that Christianity was the only Greco-Roman religious movement that developed distinctive characteristics. (3) To speak of something as distinctive does not mean that it is therefore better or more likely to be valid than something that is common to more than one religious group. My emphasis upon the need to look for and do justice to the distinctive developments in early Christianity is based upon a concern for detailed and accurate historical understanding, apart from one's personal religious response to Christianity.

It is a reasonable assumption that early Christian beliefs and practices were conditioned in varying ways by the ancient religious and social environment, an assumption that can be verified by many examples and an assumption operative in the present study also. But a genuinely historical investigation of any religious movement must also account for the particular ways in which each religious movement modifies and converts terms, ideas, and practices for its own purposes, and even fills them with significantly new meaning. Just as modern linguists recognize that the same words can acquire different meanings in the context of different sentences, so historians of religions must pay careful attention to the different meanings acquired by terms, rites, and even concepts in different religious movements and must avoid committing a kind of "etymological fallacy" by uncritically reading the meaning of a phenomenon from one religious setting into another setting.[32] Or, to borrow E. P. Sanders's language, one must always study a particular religious phenomenon in the overall "pattern" of each religious movement, for the overall pattern may give to the phenomenon very different significance and meaning.[33]

In addition to their somewhat one-sided approach to Christian origins, some early history of religions scholars seem to have been heavily influenced in their historical work by their own religious preferences. The pioneers of this school were adherents of the "modern" religious attitudes and preferences of their day, the theological liberalism of the late nineteenth century so uncomfortable with traditional Christian theology, including, quite significantly, the traditional view of Jesus as divine.[34] Additionally, they seem to have been uncomfortable with religious intensity, preferring what they saw as a more urbane and dignified devotion that emphasized ethical principles over doctrine. It is perhaps not entirely coincidental that these scholars preferred to explain the origin of the cultic veneration of the risen Jesus as essentially happening at a secondary stage of the Christian movement and as due to the influences of pagan syncretism. One senses that they regarded the cultic veneration of Jesus as a thoroughly understandable but somewhat unfortunate development in the Christian tradition.[35]

ONE GOD AND DEVOTION TO JESUS

This investigation is prompted by the fact that the cultic veneration of Jesus as a divine figure apparently began among Jewish Christians, whose religious background placed great emphasis upon the uniqueness of God. It is evident that their devotion had its own distinctive shape, a kind of binitarian reverence which included both God and the exalted Jesus. Also it is obvious that these Christians did not have the benefit of the prolonged and intricate developments and discussions that led to the theology reflected in the Nicene Creed and that one must refrain from reading these later developments back into the earlier period with which we are concerned.[36] But the evidence suggests strongly that, well before these later developments, within the first two decades of Christianity, Jewish Christians gathered in Jesus' name for worship, prayed to him and sang hymns to him, regarded him as exalted to a position of heavenly rule above all angelic orders, appropriated to him titles and Old Testament passages originally referring to God, sought to bring fellow Jews as well as Gentiles to embrace him as the divinely appointed redeemer, and in general redefined their devotion to the God of their fathers so as to include the veneration of Jesus. And apparently they regarded this redefinition not only as legitimate but, indeed, as something demanded of them.

Just as we cannot read the later theological developments in Christianity back into this earlier period, so we cannot anymore resort to older history of religions theories about the direct influence of pagan polytheism to account for the rise of the veneration of Jesus as a divine figure. If a precritical view is forbidden to us in doing serious historical study of Christian origins, so is what once passed as the critical approach to this important feature of early Christianity. Two factors in particular remain for explaining the origin of the veneration of Jesus: (1) The Jewish background of the earliest Christian communities may have provided precedents and resources for accommodating the exaltation of Jesus. (2) Owing to the particular nature of their religious experiences, the primitive Christian groups may have generated what was for Jews a somewhat novel and distinctive redefinition of devotion to God that allowed for cultic reverence of the exalted Jesus. It is the thesis of this book that a historical understanding of the rise of Jesus veneration must include *both* factors. In the following chapters, I argue two main points: (1) that ancient Judaism provided the first Christians with a crucial conceptual category for accommodating the exaltation of Jesus to God's "right hand," through the traditions I label "divine agency"; and (2) that early Christian religious experiences produced a somewhat distinctive modification of these traditions involving the cultic veneration of God's chief agent, in this case the risen Christ.

In our time there has been an explosion in the scholarly investigation of early Christology. Unfortunately much of it is vitiated by dependence upon outworn assumptions and hypotheses, such as a dubious and overly sharp distinction between "Hellenistic" and "Palestinian" Judaism or that chimera of modern New Testament scholarship, the notion that "the Son of man" was a widely known title for an apocalyptic figure prominent in ancient Jewish eschatological expectations.[37]

Much of the work in New Testament Christology has been concerned with particular christological titles given to Jesus in early Christianity, "Son of man" receiving by far the most attention. But the other main titles, "Lord," "Christ," and "Son of God," have by no means been neglected.[38] Also, christological concepts such as the idea of Jesus' preexistence have been the subject of detailed investigation.[39] But, to my knowledge, the precise question of how the cultic veneration of Jesus began in the earliest Jewish-Christian groups has not received the focused or sustained attention it deserves.[40] I am concerned here not to trace the usage of a particular christological title or to study the development of a particular doctrine (e.g., preexistence). Rather, I wish to examine what is the more fundamental and historically prior matter—the origin of the binitarian shape of early Christian devotion and its relationship to the religious context in which it first appeared, ancient Judaism.

This matter is more fundamental than the use of particular christological titles, for the basic conviction that Jesus had been exalted to a heavenly and divine status and that this demanded the cultic veneration of him in early Christian gatherings does not seem to have been generated by the adoption of any one title. Rather, the veneration of Jesus probably generated a new and deeper connotation for such titles as "Lord," which is attested with special frequency in connection with liturgical formulae of the early decades (e.g., 1 Cor. 12:3; Rom. 10:9-10). The veneration of Jesus also explains in part why other titles (e.g., "Christ/Messiah") quickly underwent a redefinition in early Christian circles, coming to be used for a figure regarded as holding a heavenly and divine status, although not characteristically connoting such a figure in pre-Christian usage.

The conviction that the risen Jesus held a heavenly and divine status helps to explain the development of christological concepts (e.g., preexistence). On the basis of analogies in ancient Jewish thought, we know that preexistence was predicated of various entities (e.g., angels, the Torah, Wisdom) without these entities finding a place as objects of worship.[41] But, given the conviction of the early Christians that Jesus held a kind of divine status and was to be the eschatological redeemer, it is easier to understand that they came to view him as having had some sort of role in connection with creation also, especially in the light of the frequently attested connection in ancient Jewish thought between eschatological redemption and creation.[42] That is, given the cultic veneration of Jesus, the development of the concept of his preexistence is not such a big step; but it is more important to explain the place of Jesus in early Jewish-Christian worship.

Further, the cultic veneration of Jesus in early Christian circles is the most important context for the use of the christological titles and concepts. This context indicates what they signified and gives us insight into the pattern of the religion in which they functioned. For example, "lord" either in Greek (*kyrios*) or in Aramaic (*marêh*) was used with a variety of connotations in the ancient world. But once we see this title in the context of the early Christian cultic actions of prayer and hymn, it acquires a much more specific connotation. The term "lord" in either language does not automatically connote divine status. But the use of the title in such cultic actions implies much more than simple social superiority of or respect for the figure to whom it is given.

The notion that the crucified Jesus had been sent by God, or that he was the promised Messiah, was no doubt offensive to Jews who had found his ministry objectionable or puzzling to those who could not see the basis for such a notion. But I suggest that it was the practice of according Jesus a place in the cultic activities of early Christian groups, together with the underlying conviction that he held a heavenly and divine status, which must have appeared to ancient Jews as an even more problematical aspect of the devotion of these Christian groups. This cultic veneration of Jesus was the most visible distinction of the devotion of early Christians. More than anything else, it demonstrated the fundamental conviction that distinguished "Christian devotion" from the other forms of religious devotion of the time. The conviction that Jesus was worthy of such veneration could have been the major change in the religious viewpoint of the Jews (e.g., Paul) who joined the early Christian communities. Above all other features of the Christian message and practice, this conviction probably called for the greatest modification of the devotion inherited from their ancestors.[43]

All evidence indicates, however, that those Jewish Christians who made such a step remained convinced that they were truly serving the God of the Old Testament. This fact begets the questions with which we are concerned: Was there anything in the religious heritage of the first Jewish Christians that furnished them with resources for accommodating the exalted position of the risen Jesus, in heaven and in their devotion? Can we determine with any precision how these Jewish Christians viewed Jesus' status alongside God, a status that both merited Jesus the kind of cultic devotion characteristic of early Christian groups and yet also did not apparently threaten God's uniqueness and importance in their faith and life?

In chapters 1 through 4 I address the first question. In chapter 5 I address the second question. First, I want to examine the nature of the Jewish monotheism in which devotion to Jesus first developed by investigating how ancient Jews accommodated reverence for other heavenly figures alongside God without seeing themselves as having violated God's uniqueness. In short, I shall attempt to trace the extent to which Jewish monotheistic faith could stretch to accommodate reverence for additional figures without breaking.

The judgment about whether monotheistic commitment was significantly modified will be settled basically by discernment as to whether, in a specific case, another figure was given corporate cultic reverence in actions normally reserved for God. But if the ancient Jews whose writings we examine regarded themselves as still safeguarding the uniqueness of God, and if their religious devotion seems to have been essentially directed toward this unique God, then whatever honorific status they accorded to other beings will have to be taken as examples of the way ancient Judaism was able to include additional heavenly figures without ceasing to be exclusivist monotheism.

Also I want to show whether there appear to have been limits on the kinds of reverence that were accommodated. Thus I will search for the sorts of reverence given *and* the sorts of reverence withheld from the figures to be considered. Once these matters have been plotted, then I will be in a better position to interpret the reverence given to the exalted Jesus in the earliest Christian groups: Was it related to the reverence given to other figures in ancient Jewish circles? How did it represent a distinctive mutation in the commitment to one God broadly characteristic of Greco-Roman Judaism?

I have tried to avoid the simplistic approach to the background of early Christianity criticized earlier. I do not work here with a model of Christian origins that involves accounting for features of early Christianity by a simple borrowing from the religious background of the time. I also have tried to avoid making facile contrasts between Christianity and its religious matrix. Instead, I seek to portray a complex interaction between the background (especially the Jewish tradition) and the religious experiences of early Christians. I shall argue that their religious experiences provided the early Jewish Christians with the cause and the standpoint for appropriating and reinterpreting their religious tradition, producing the beliefs and practices that characterized them and sometimes distinguished them from other religious groups. The first Christians, as well as other Jewish groups of the time (e.g., the Qumran sect), formed their beliefs and practices on the basis of a broad and variegated Jewish tradition. Each group reinterpreted and modified that tradition in the light of its own distinctive religious and social experiences. As I examine the early Christians' veneration of Jesus, I will show not only how this is related to the Jewish reverence of other heavenly beings but also how it is distinctive.

1
Divine Agency in Ancient Jewish Monotheism

We now proceed to examine the phenomena in ancient Jewish tradition that in all likelihood assisted the first Christians in framing the earliest understanding of the position of the exalted Christ.

DIVINE AGENCY SPECULATION

It is of course known that the literature of postexilic Judaism contains many references to various heavenly figures who are described as participating in some way in God's rule of the world and his redemption of the elect. In particular, there are heavenly figures described as occupying a position second only to God and acting on God's behalf in some major capacity. It is these figures which are most relevant for the historical problem of the origin of the cultic veneration of Jesus. My view is that the references to these particular figures all reflect an interest in what may be termed "divine agency," although the motives behind the interest varied and the interest manifested itself in a variety of forms. Scholars have often focused their attention on specific examples of divine agency figures (e.g., Philo's Logos or personified Wisdom). But I submit that ancient references to these specific figures reflect the more fundamental idea that God might have a chief agent prominent over all other servants of God and associated with him particularly closely.

Three Types

We may classify examples of divine agency speculation under three types: (1) interest in divine attributes and powers (e.g., Wisdom or Philo's Logos); (2) interest in exalted patriarchs (e.g., Moses and Enoch); and (3) interest in principal angels (e.g., Michael, Yahoel, and [probably] the Melchizedek of the Qumran fragment *11QMelch*). This classification is not intended to be taken rigidly, and I do not suggest that ancient Jews worked with such an analysis of their thought. But this schema is offered as a helpful tool for modern analysis of the texts and phenomena.

Of course, ancient Jewish tradition pictures a wider variety of figures acting as agents of God, such as prophets, priests, kings, and Messiah(s), as well as the angelic host, but the types of figures I have enumerated here can be distinguished in certain ways. (1) They are all pictured either as heavenly in origin or as exalted to a heavenly position, thus resembling more closely than the earthly figures mentioned the status associated with the risen Jesus in the early church. (2) Although the vast angelic host is likewise heavenly in origin, nevertheless these chief agent figures are described as bearing more fully than the earthly agents or the angelic host the properties associated with divinity. Moreover, the figures emphasized are each described as representing God in a unique capacity and stand in a role second only to God himself, thus being distinct from all the other servants and agents of God.

Variation of Types

The variation in the names and types of the figures viewed as occupying this position next to God is interesting for three reasons:

1. The variation shows that a number of Jewish groups worked with the idea of God having such a chief agent who was second only to God in rank. This is important because it means that, wherever the idea may have come from originally, by the Greco-Roman period it was widely shared and cannot be described as the exclusive property of any one type of Judaism. As we shall see, both Diaspora Jews, such as Philo, and Palestinian Jews were familiar with the idea, though they employed it in varying ways according to their purposes.

The relevance of this for the study of the origin of the veneration of the exalted Jesus is clear: we do not have to postulate the direct influence of one particular type of Judaism. Why? Because it appears that a wide spectrum of Jewish groups reflects what is termed here "divine agency." These groups were able to accommodate this or that chief agent in quite exalted terms without feeling that commitment to one God had been compromised.

2. The variation indicates a variety of religious motivations behind the descriptions of the figures and also varied religious needs to which the positing of this or that chief agent spoke. I will suggest what appear to have been these motivations and needs when we examine the individual

types of chief agent figures later (see chaps. 2—4). While I refer to the concept of divine agency, here I wish to emphasize that we are not dealing with purely intellectual developments but rather with conceptual developments in a religious tradition. Thus a full understanding of these developments requires that we ask about the religious factors that provoked them and to which these conceptual developments were linked.

One frequently asserted view is that in the postexilic period God was seen as less accessible than in earlier times, and so Jewish piety populated the heavens with various intermediary beings to make up for the religious distance that Jews felt between themselves and God. In favor of this view one can say that it does involve an attempt to relate the conceptual developments in question to the religious life of ancient Judaism, but I shall proceed to show why I think this attempt fails.[1]

3. The variation also shows that no one figure or type of figure ever acquired an unquestioned and uniformly held position next to God across the diverse Jewish tradition. That is, although the concept that God might have a chief agent who stood far above all other servants of God seems to have been widely shared in ancient Judaism, nevertheless no one particular figure was generally agreed upon as this chief agent. Further, even though the writings of this period describe this or that chief agent in quite exalted language, it is not at all clear that the persons who produced these writings believed that Jewish piety demanded the recognition and veneration of a particular figure as God's chief agent.

The importance of these observations is that—however interesting the divine agency concept is in understanding ancient Jewish tradition and however important it may have been for other developments, such as the veneration of Jesus, or, as A. F. Segal and J. E. Fossum have argued, for gnostic demiurgical traditions[2]—we must be careful not to exaggerate what it represented in postexilic Judaism. As I shall argue, the concept of divine agency did not originally represent a major mutation in ancient Jewish monotheism comparable to the cultic veneration of the exalted Jesus. Segal has shown that rabbinic traditions of the second century C.E. and later seem to indicate that some Jewish "heretics" were accused of going too far in the reverence given to God's chief agent and were accused of holding the idea that there were "two powers" in heaven.[3] In the surviving literature of the pre-Christian period, however, it is not clear that any of the chief agent figures were seen as sharing the unique veneration due to God alone or that Jewish monotheism was fundamentally modified by the interest shown in these figures.

My use of "divine agency" is an attempt to label the basic conception that seems to me to lie behind the description of the various figures in question, in which a chief agent is associated with God in a unique capacity in the manifestation of his sovereignty. But, in addition to the variation in the identity and nature of this chief agent, there is also variation in the specific nature of the role exercised. For example, in some texts God's creation and ordering of the world is the focus, and here the chief agent is pictured as participating prominently in these matters. This is the sort of role ascribed in the *Wisdom of Solomon* to Wisdom (*sophia*), who is described as "fashioner of all things" (7:22), the one who "reaches mightily from one end of the earth to the other" and who "orders all things well" (8:1), who is "an associate in his works" (8:4; cf. 9:9, 11). Somewhat similarly, Philo of Alexandria describes the Logos as God's administrator of the world and chief steward (*kybernētēs kai oikonomos*, *Quaest. Gen.* 4.110–111).[4]

In other texts, the focus is on God's eschatological redemption of the elect, and consequently the chief agent figure is shown prominently involved in this action. For example, *1 Enoch* portrays a figure who serves as God's agent in bringing eschatological judgment upon the wicked and mercy upon the elect (46:1–8; 48:4–10; 51:3–5; 52:4–9; 61:8–9; 62:7–16). Similarly, *11QMelch* refers to a Melchizedek who seems to act on God's behalf in eschatological triumph.[5] In these texts, the chief agent figure is not connected with creation or with governance of the world, and in the texts cited in the preceding paragraph Wisdom and Logos are not connected with eschatological redemption.[6]

In still other texts, the chief agent figure is not clearly linked with God's act of creation or with eschatological redemption but rather seems to function more or less as God's grand vizier or chief representative in terms of general authority and power. In the *Testament of Abraham*, the angel Michael is described as God's "commander in chief" (*archistrategos*, 1:4; 2:1), probably an allusion to the mysterious figure of Josh. 5:13–15 and an indication that the writer saw Michael as God's chief heavenly agent. Or, there is the angel Yahoel in the *Apocalypse of Abraham*, in whom God's name dwells (an allusion to Exod. 23:20–21) and who consequently exercises quite impressive powers in the administration of God's rule (10:1–14).[7] Philo's exalted description of Moses does not clearly link him with creation or with eschatological hopes but rather portrays Moses more generally as God's partner (*koinōnos*), the one man worthy to be called "god" (*theos*) by God himself (alluding to Exod. 7:1;

see, e.g., *Vit. Mos.* 1.155–58), the mortal to whom all the world was made subject, and the human made worthy to share God's own nature (*tes heauton physeōs*; Philo, *Post.* 28).[8]

The various chief agent figures play different roles. But common to all the descriptions of these figures is the basic idea that there is a chief agent who has been assigned a unique status among all other servants of God. Nevertheless the variation in the roles of the figures described as God's chief agent indicates further that this idea was interpreted differently across the spectrum of ancient Judaism.

The variation in the sphere of activity of these chief agent figures is interesting in comparison with the more comprehensive role of the exalted Jesus in early Christian literature. To cite only a few of the more well-known passages and themes, Jesus is described as the agent of creation (1 Cor. 8:6; John 1:1–3) and redemption (1 Cor. 1:30; 15:20–28; Rom. 3:23–26; 4:24–25; 1 Thess. 1:10), the one whom all creation is to acknowledge as "Lord," with a status far above all others in any sphere of creation (Phil. 2:9–11), the eschatological judge to whom all must answer as to God (2 Cor. 5:10).

One last passage serves to illustrate my point. In Heb. 1:1–14, Jesus is described as the heir of all things (v. 2), the agent of creation (vv. 2, 10), who reflects the glory and nature of God (v. 3), has made purification for sins (v. 3b), and is to preside in eschatological triumph (v. 13; cf. 2:5).

This placing of Jesus at the center of virtually all aspects of God's activity, this rather comprehensive way in which Jesus functions as God's chief agent, is not fully paralleled in the roles assigned to other chief agent figures in the Jewish literature of the early Greco-Roman period. This is further evidence that the interest in God's chief agent apparently did not, in our period of concern, represent a fundamental modification of Jewish monotheism.

Summary

1. The literature of postexilic Judaism exhibits an interest in various figures who are each described as holding a position next to God in honor and power, and behind the interest in these various figures was what we designate "divine agency."[9]

2. This concept may have been important in giving early Jewish Christians a conceptual framework into which to begin fitting the exalted Jesus, their religious experiences having communicated the conviction that Jesus had been given a position "at the right hand" of God.[10]

3. Although the concept that God had a chief agent seems to have been widely shared in the Judaism of this period, the variation in the names and descriptions of the figures placed in this position shows that Jews employed the concept to serve a variety of religious interests. Further, notwithstanding the exalted position of such figures, the interest in them did not amount to a fundamental "redrawing" of the nature of Jewish monotheistic faith, when contrasted, for example, with the more thoroughgoing way that the exalted Jesus was made chief agent of all God's activities in early Christian devotion. In taking this position, I am at odds with some other interpreters of the evidence who argue that the ancient Jewish interest in divine agency indicates that postexilic Jewish devotion was no longer "pure" monotheism (e.g., W. Bousset) or was already incipiently binitarian (e.g., Fossum). To this question we now turn.

THE SHAPE OF POSTEXILIC JEWISH
RELIGIOUS DEVOTION

The classic presentation of the view that postexilic Judaism was marked by a weakening of an earlier and purer monotheism is found in the widely cited and influential book by W. Bousset, *Die Religion des Judentums im späthellenistischen Zeitalter.*[11] The frequent citation of Bousset's book in subsequent studies shows that the case presented in it is basically representative of the views of a number of scholars on down to the present time. We therefore begin by summarizing Bousset's case.

In what follows, I will argue that there is no basis for the idea that postexilic Judaism represents a weak stage of exclusivist monotheism. Instead, particularly after the Hellenistic crisis of the Maccabean period, postexilic Judaism shows signs of a fairly healthy commitment to the uniqueness of God. I do not intend to minimize the very real differences among Jewish groups of that period. Nor do I overlook the indications of some Jews assimilating to the gentile culture even in the religious realm. But the crucial question is whether, among Jewish groups who still wished to be identified as loyal to their ancestral religion, there are indications of significant exceptions to the exclusivist monotheism that we identify with ancient Judaism.

Bousset's now classic work was intended as a comprehensive study of ancient Jewish religion; it appeared in a series for students of the New Testament. In more recent years, it has become apparent that Bousset's appreciation for and grasp of important aspects of ancient Judaism were deficient.[12] I want to concentrate on his discussion of the ancient Jewish interest in divine agents and what it meant for Jewish monotheism.[13]

Bousset's discussion deals with three undercurrents of postexilic Jewish religious thought, which he regarded as erosive of an earlier and purer form of monotheistic Jewish faith: (*a*) angelology; (*b*) "dualistic tendencies"; and (*c*) speculation concerning "hypostases." He did not here discuss the interest in exalted patriarchs, and it is really his understanding of the meaning of Jewish angelology and the personification of divine attributes that concerns me. Bousset was not particularly innovative or groundbreaking in his views on these matters, but his book became widely cited because it articulated well the views of many scholars of his own and subsequent times.

Jewish postexilic literature gives names to several angels (e.g., Michael and Gabriel, Dan. 8:16; 10:13; 12:1; Raphael, *Tob.* 5:4), bestows upon them certain specific tasks, and classifies them in various ranks (angels, archangels, angels of the presence, etc.). From these data, together with the presence of personified Wisdom and other hypostases in Jewish writings of the same period (e.g., *Wis.* 6:12—10:21), Bousset concluded that postexilic Judaism was characterized by a growing interest in "intermediary beings" (*Mittelwesen*).[14] This interest in turn he attributed to a growing sense of God's transcendence, which involved the notion that God had distanced himself from the world and was less available, having turned his rule of the world over to angels and other intermediaries.[15] In Bousset's view, although these figures were messengers of God and executors of his will, nevertheless they represented a threat to Jewish monotheism, and the interest in them was linked with a certain softening of monotheism characteristic of Jewish piety of the period in question.[16] For Bousset, this weakened monotheism was the background of early Christianity. This helped to explain how it was that the exalted Jesus came to be viewed as a heavenly, preexistent being very early in the Christian movement. To Bousset's religious tastes, this veneration of Jesus was an unfortunate development which itself represented a defective monotheism; he regarded the Jewish interest in angels and hypostases as a less than healthy influence upon Christianity.[17] With this as a brief but initially sufficient summary of his position, I should now like to take up some of his specific points in more detail and indicate why I find this sort of presentation unsatisfactory.

ANGELOLOGY AND MONOTHEISM

Here I wish to deal with the more general questions of the meaning of the angelic host in ancient Jewish religious thought and their place in religious practice vis-à-vis Bousset's point of view.

A Critique of W. Bousset's View

In Bousset's view, the angelic hierarchy featured in postexilic literature was a self-evident indication that Jewish religion of the period had a weakened sense of God's availability to the pious. He seems to have assumed that the interest in angelic beings could only indicate a decline in the intensity of devotion to God as the living center of piety. Thus he portrayed the role of angelic messengers of the revelations given to seers in the apocalyptic literature, in contrast to the claim of Old Testament prophets to speak a message given to them by God himself, as evidence that in the period in which the apocalyptic writings appeared God was perceived as removed from the world. Thus the Jewish piety of this time was less thoroughly monotheistic in emphasis.[18]

Similarly, pointing to the intercessory role of angels in postexilic texts (e.g., *Tob.* 12:12; *Jub.* 30:20; *T. Dan* 6:1-2; *T. Ash.* 6:6; *T. Levi* 5:5-7), Bousset argued that this too indicates a blurring of the central importance of God and suspected that in Jewish "popular piety" the interest in angels in all likelihood even led to the cultic veneration of them.[19] Citing passages in apocalyptic texts where messenger angels forbid the seers to worship them (Rev. 19:10; 22:8; *Ascen. Isa.* 7:21; 8:5), Bousset insisted that these prohibitions must indicate that the worship of angels was practiced in Jewish circles, finding additional evidence in Col. 2:8, 18, and Hebrews 1, which he took to be polemic against cultic veneration of angels.[20] Finally, he referred to the criticisms of Jews as worshipers of angels in pagan and Christian polemic as further proof that such a cultic practice was a known part of Jewish piety of the time.[21]

I contend, however, that Bousset's interpretation of this evidence is incorrect. First, while it is true that postexilic interest in the heavenly host apparently involved some new features (e.g., angels with names and specialized functions), Bousset's claim that there developed "a systematic doctrine of angels (*eine Engeldogmatik, eine Angelologie*)," implying a formalized and fixed teaching, is simply an exaggeration.[22] P. Schäfer's verdict that "the early Jewish idea of angels is in no way uniform" is more accurate.[23] S. F. Noll's description of the angelology of the Qumran texts as "not a carefully worked out system but a more impressionistic portrayal of the heavenly world" does seem to be fairly representative of the references to angels in the whole body of postexilic Jewish literature.[24]

Bousset did not try to demonstrate the *Engeldogmatik* he ascribed to postexilic Judaism, and no one else to my knowledge has produced it either. One can prepare a list of the things said about various angels and classes of angels in the literature of that period. But those who have done this work point out the impossibility of organizing such data into a systematic doctrine of angels, a conclusion supported by my own reading of the literature as well.[25]

In view of the studies by H. Bietenhard, H. B. Kuhn, Noll, and Schäfer, it would be superfluous for me to give a detailed survey of ancient Jewish references to angels. But one should observe that certain themes appear with some frequency: for example, the angelic host is organized into ranks or classes (the descriptions of these ranks vary); there are certain angels, often called archangels, in a special class above the rest (the number and names of these angels vary); angels act as messengers for God. Other themes are less frequent: for example, angels carry the prayers of the elect before the throne of God; a group of angels (seventy or seventy-two) are assigned to supervise the various nations of the world. The entire collection of things said about angels is evidence of a general belief in angels and a widely shared interest in angels, but the data hardly constitute a doctrine of angels and certainly do not represent a systematic doctrine of angels.[26]

Given the unsystematic, even conflicting, nature of the treatment of angels in the literature of postexilic Judaism, it is difficult to connect interest in them to a particular theological program or shift in religious belief. Bousset's misleading claim, echoed by many others subsequently—the texts present the angelic hosts as intermediaries between a distant God and an elect who felt a growing sense of alienation from him and who assigned to the angels greater importance than in earlier times because God seemed so remote and inactive—must be rejected. The angelic hosts do not function in these texts as substitutes for God but as his servants, as vehicles of his power and will.[27]

In his analysis of the "heavenly world" in Greco-Roman Judaism and Christianity, Bietenhard properly rejected Bousset's view, insisting that the descriptions of angels set over various areas of nature in the Jewish texts were the writers' attempts to show that God's power reaches to all areas of the world and that all operations of the world are under his control.[28] Further, the description of the heavenly hosts as a gigantic hierarchy of many ranks with numerous specialized duties is quite easily understood as an attempt to defend the power and significance of Israel's God. The point of these descriptions is to say, "Do you see how great our God is, who has such a vast and powerful retinue to do nothing but serve him?"

In view of the historical situation of ancient Israel, this emphasis and the imagery employed are both quite logical. From the exile onward, Israel was under the domination of a succession of imperial powers, with only brief interludes. Israel's significance seemed marginal. The most powerful realities were the might and structure of the empires that dominated Israel's world. In ancient Jewish thought, Israel's God was so closely tied to the nation that the apparent insignificance of the latter must have raised questions about the significance of the former as well, especially from Hellenistic times onward when so many cultures and religions met and made their claims. It should not be surprising, therefore, to find that in this same period Jews portrayed their God as the great heavenly king with a massive and many-tiered hierarchy of heavenly servants.

Over against the apparent earthly insignificance of Israel, God's elect, God is shown to be the true king of all in the sphere of ultimate reality—the heavenlies. God's might and awesomeness are portrayed by means of the most impressive model of earthly power known to the writers of these texts, the imperial court and its hierarchy of powerful officers and servants. In other words, the image of the angelic hierarchy was intended as a way of relativizing the earthly structures of authority and power with which Israel had to contend in this period. This is not evidence of a distant God at the center of Jewish religion but the opposite!

This judgment is reinforced when one observes that the attention given to angels in the postexilic literature *is not* accompanied by indications that God was viewed as inaccessible or remote. On the contrary, as H. J. Wicks pointed out, in each century of the postexilic period "the clear doctrine of the majority of the authors, whatever their angelology, is that of a God who is in unmediated contact with His creation."[29] It should be noted that in the same writings where the angelic hosts are referred to the writers characteristically show mortals praying directly to God and being heard.

To cite one example, in *2 Bar.* 48:1-24 there is a long prayer of Baruch, who describes God's control over his creation (vv. 2-9) and mentions the "innumerable hosts" which serve God "according to their positions" (v. 10) but appeals directly to God, "Hear your servant, and regard my appeal" (v. 11), invoking God's mercy and grace as the hope of Israel (v. 18) in his petition (vv. 11-24). In response to this prayer God answers directly (48:25-41). A conversation between God and the seer follows (48:42—52:7). That is, the writer pictures God as having a mighty host of heavenly servants who act at his bidding in various tasks, including the delivery of messages (e.g., 6:5-9; 55:3—74:4). But this document also regularly portrays Baruch addressing God directly and shows God answering equally directly (e.g., 1:2; 3:1; 4:1; 5:1, 2; 15:1; 17:1).

This is also the case in *Tobit*. It describes the angel Raphael as the vehicle of

God's healing power (3:17) and refers to "seven holy angels who present the prayers of the saints and enter into the presence of the glory of the Holy One" (12:15). It always shows mortals in the story praying directly to God alone in the most familiar and direct way (3:1-6; 4:11-15; 8:5-7, 15-17; 13:1-18) and their prayers being instantly heard by God (3:16).

We are at an advantage over some of our predecessors. The actual texts themselves can easily be consulted, thanks to the recent English editions of the pseudepigraphical literature.[30] There is simply no clear basis in the texts for the view that the descriptions of the activities of angels indicate a declining confidence in God's concern for the world, God's power and willingness to act directly upon it, or God's accessibility to the elect. The view may be comfortable for those, such as Bousset, whose attempt to magnify the significance of Christianity involves the portrayal of ancient Judaism in a very negative way.[31] To others it may simply seem logical to assume that descriptions of the activities of angels must mean that God was seen as less active.[32] But whatever may make such an assumption seem plausible at first, the data do not warrant it.

By all indications, the postexilic interest in angels went hand in hand with a vigorous and lively monotheistic piety. The descriptions of the angelic hosts and their many activities, including such things as intercession on behalf of the elect (e.g., *T. Levi* 3:5-7; 5:6; *T. Dan* 6:2; *1 Enoch* 9:3; 40:6; 47:1-2; 104:1), were all intended to make vivid God's concern for his people and God's control over the world, with a view toward strengthening the faith of the readers. That God employed many angelic servants in carrying out his will did not make God more remote. Rather, this showed God to be great and able to enforce his will at all times and in all places. The prayers and praises described in the same writings in which the activities of angels are elaborated show that the angelic retinue did not make God seem less available; the texts do not offer any indication that the interest in angels was tied to a softening of monotheistic emphasis in Jewish piety of the time.[33] The God of Israel remained the living center of Jewish devotion.

What then of the claim that the worship of angels was a feature of Jewish piety in the early Greco-Roman period? If the cultic veneration of angels was practiced in Jewish circles of this period, this would certainly seem to constitute a significant modification of the emphasis upon the exclusive worship of the God of Israel which distinguished Jewish religion. Having summarized the data cited by Bousset and others as evidence of a Jewish angel cultus, I now reexamine the data before I answer the question.[34]

The Data

Aside from the supposition, already rejected above, that the emphasis upon the activity of angels in postexilic literature must in itself indicate a tendency in the direction of angel veneration, there are basically three groups of data used to support the claim that angels were worshiped in Greco-Roman Jewish circles.[35]

1. There are texts that mention appeals made to angels (e.g., *T. Levi* 5:5; *Paral. Jer.* 3:4) and other indications that in magical incantations Jews (and/or Christians and even pagans) pronounced the names of angels as vehicles of power (e.g., *T. Sol.* 2:5, 7; 14:8; 15:7; and 18:1–40 with its list of thirty-six demons and the spells that thwart them).[36]

2. There are prohibitions against the worship of angels, both in apocalyptic writings (e.g., *Apoc. Zeph.* 6:14–15; *Ascen. Isa.* 7:21–23; Rev. 19:10; 22:8–9) and in rabbinic literature.[37]

3. Finally, there are the accusations in the writings of Aristides, Clement of Alexandria, and Origen that Jews worshiped angels.[38]

Appeals made to angels. This category of data does not seem to serve very well as evidence that angels were worshiped in Jewish cultic settings. The example in *Paral. Jer.* 3:4–14 (also known as *The Rest of the Words of Baruch*) has Jeremiah pleading with the angels who are about to destroy Jerusalem that they not act before he has a chance to pray to God to save the sacred things of the temple. In the passage, Jeremiah then prays to God, and from that point on God deals with Jeremiah directly, giving him instructions about what to do with these sacred objects. This is hardly evidence of angel worship.[39] Nor is *4 Macc.* 4:10–14 an example of prayer to angels, for, although the pagan Apollonius implores the Jews to "pray for him and propitiate the wrath of the heavenly army" (the angelic hosts who appeared to him in a vision in the temple area), the passage gives no hint that Onias the high priest does anything but offer prayer to God (4:13).[40]

I reject E. R. Goodenough's proposal that the invocation of both "the God Most High, the Lord of the spirits and of all flesh" and the "angels of God" found on a grave inscription from Delos is evidence of Jewish prayer to angels.[41] The invocation requests that divine vengeance be visited upon the murderers of the young girls whose grave is marked by the stone on which the inscription appears. As A. Deissmann accurately noted, the inscription "keeps well within the bounds of the Biblical creed,'' citing Ps. 103:20 as an analogy. Neither reference constitutes evidence of what can fairly be called "prayer" to angels as part of a cultus devoted to them jointly with God.[42]

The appeal to the angel in *T. Levi* 5:5—"I beg you, Lord, teach me your name, so that I may call on you in the day of tribulation"—does not look like evidence of a Jewish cultus devoted to angels. The *Testaments of the Twelve Patriarchs* has obviously passed through Christian hands, receiving a number of Christian additions and emendations in the process. In such a passage as *T. Levi* 5:5 it is not entirely clear whether we are encountering Jewish ideas or Christian ones.[43] Even if the passage as it stands has not suffered from Christian redaction, it is not clear what sort of appeal to the angel is involved. The text refers only to an appeal to be made "in the day of tribulation." This may indicate that the writer has in view the eschatological time of trial when he expected the elect to summon their divinely designated angelic protector to come to their rescue.[44]

Although *T. Dan* 6:2—"Draw near to God and to the angel who intercedes for you, because he is mediator between God and men for the peace of Israel"—is often cited as another example of Jewish angel worship, nevertheless it is not clear that the text will bear this interpretation.[45] Here again we may be dealing with a text that has undergone Christian editing, for the description of the "angel" as "mediator between God and men" is found verbatim in 1 Tim. 2:5, from which it was perhaps taken.[46] If this is the case, then the "angel" mentioned may in fact be a Christian reference to the preincarnate Christ.[47] But whoever the angel is and whoever wrote the text in question, it is by no means a reference to angel worship, for the following verses (6:3-11), which are entirely concerned with urging the readers to maintain faithfully the "righteousness of the Law of God" (v. 10), seem to be the writer's explanation of what it means to "draw near to God and to the angel who intercedes for you." At most, the passage shows that a principal angel figure was prominently associated with God's care of the elect. It does not indicate a cultus devoted to such a being in place of or alongside God.

The use of angelic names in exorcisms and spells in the *Testament of Solomon* (esp. chap. 18) very likely reflects Jewish magical practices of the early Greco-Roman period and earlier.[48] But such practices can hardly be termed "worship" of angels in any ordinary sense of the word, for they do not furnish evidence that angels were invoked by name or otherwise in the cultic gatherings of any known Jewish group of that period.[49] Whatever experimentations in technique were undertaken by enterprising

exorcists of Jewish background (see Acts 19:13–16), this is not the same
thing as evidence of the organized veneration of angels in gatherings of
Jewish sects of the time.

Prohibitions against the worship of angels. These data consist of prohibitions against undue reverence for angels. In apocalyptic texts (*Apoc.
Zeph.* 6:15; *Ascen. Isa.* 7:21–22; *Rev.* 19:10; 22:8–9), the angel who
delivers the revelation prohibits the human recipient from worshiping
him or any heavenly power other than God alone. But are these prohibitions evidence that some Jewish groups were in the habit of worshiping
angels? Or are they only intended to warn against such deviations from
monotheistic piety ever taking place? Whether the writers only feared the
possibility of such undue reverence of angels or knew of actual cases, we
cannot decide with certainty on the basis of these references. The texts,
however, offer clear evidence that those who produced the literature in
which angels figure so prominently were firmly set against the cultic
veneration of these beings. And if these circles rejected the worship of
angels, then I find it difficult to suggest other Jewish groups in which
such practices might have been a part of their cultic activities. Other
scholars seem to have experienced the same difficulty. Simon, for example, could only refer vaguely to the possibility of cultic veneration of
angels in "marginal conventicles" which he was unable to identify with
confidence.[50]

There are also passages in rabbinic literature, incorporating traditions
mainly from the second century C.E. and later, in which we find prohibitions against the making of images: of the sun, the moon, stars, angels,
cherubim, and other heavenly beings.[51] In a passage prohibiting sacri-
fices to the sun, the moon, stars, and planets, sacrifice to "the great
prince Michael" is also forbidden (*t. Hul.* 2:18; cf. *b. Abod. Zar.* 42b; *m.
Hul.* 2:8). In a debate with a "heretic" (*min*), Rav Idit (or Idi) rejects the
suggestion that worship should be given to an angelic figure named Metatron (*b. Sanh.* 38b). Schäfer takes these passages as indirect indications
that the sorts of things prohibited occurred in some Jewish circles contemporary with the rabbinic traditions in which the prohibitions appear.
He also suggests that such practices may have developed under the influence of Gnosticism.[52] I am not so sure that the texts are necessarily evidence that the worship of angels was a part of Jewish religious life, and I
will explain my reservations.

First, we note that the worship of angels is not at the center of the
prohibitions that deal with the making of images or the offering of sacri-

fices. Angels are listed as only one of several items, along with the sun, the moon, planets, and stars, as well as "the names of mountains, hills, seas, rivers or waste places." Are we then to assume that the worship of all these items was also a known part of Jewish piety? On the basis of the evidence, this seems to be a highly dubious assumption, and I am not aware that those scholars who use these passages as evidence of Jewish worship of angels have suggested that Jews worshiped all these other items as well.

Second, the prohibitions seem intended as attempts to make more specific the meaning of such Old Testament texts as Exod. 20:4. That is, the prohibitions seem more clearly prompted by the homiletical need to interpret Old Testament prohibitions against the cultic veneration of anything but the God of Israel than by a desire to stop purported Jewish practices that the rabbis found unacceptable. The inclusion of angels in these midrashic statements may simply have been meant to show that nothing, including the heavenly beings well known in Jewish tradition, was to be given the honor and worship due to God alone.

For these reasons, I am not as inclined as Schäfer to see the inclusion of angels in these general prohibitions as evidence per se that the worship of angels was practiced in ancient Jewish circles.

Finally, if the worship of angels was actually a Jewish practice known to the rabbis who clearly opposed the idea of such a thing, then I find it strange that we do not have a much more emphatic and direct handling of the question in the rabbinic materials. The rabbinic prohibitions, like the prohibitions in the apocalyptic literature, do not demand the existence of Jewish worship of angels to explain them and may be simply expressions of opposition to the possibility of such a thing arising. Given the polytheistic climate in which postexilic Jews had to exist as a subject people, I do not find it difficult to think that the rabbis and the apocalypticists warned their fellow religionists (who held God's angels in high honor and accorded them many important roles, including intercession for the elect as in *1 Enoch* 40:5-7; 47:2; 104:1) to keep respect for and interest in such beings within the bounds of traditional Jewish concern for the uniqueness of God. And such warnings may have been given, not because there were Jewish groups who worshiped angels as part of their cultic activities, but out of a strong concern to distinguish Jewish devotional practice from pagan practices.

But even those who do not share my reservations about the rabbinic prohibitions as evidence of the Jewish cultic veneration of angels must admit that these traditions may at the most tell us what the rabbis regarded as unacceptable practices in the second century C.E. and later.

(Schäfer gives such a date for the practices he sees as being attacked.)[53] In any case, then, the rabbinic prohibitions are hardly to be used in determining the nature of Jewish religious devotion in the earlier centuries of the postexilic period, before the interaction with Christian and gnostic developments.

As for the passage in *b. Sanhedrin* 38b where a rabbi and a "heretic" debate the question of whether worship is to be given to a second figure other than God (referring to Exod. 23:20–21), here too the question is how much earlier than the third century C.E. (the period of Rabbi Nahman, the rabbi to whom the report of the debate is ascribed) this sort of debate can be placed with confidence. Although Segal tries to argue that such a debate may go back to the first century C.E., he admits that the "heretic" in this passage is probably a Christian and that the dispute as described in the passage must come from the amoraic period (third century).[54] Note also that the only first-century support that Segal supplies for Jewish sects worshiping a second figure alongside God is the early (Jewish) Christian devotion to the exalted Jesus as indicated in the New Testament.[55]

Segal is correct in arguing that the interest in heavenly beings, including a principal angel figure, goes back to the first century and earlier, but an interest in angelic beings is one thing and the worship of them another. The latter may have grown out of the former under the impact of various factors, but the two are not the same thing.[56] I am prepared to agree that the argument about worship of a second heavenly figure may also go back to the first century and may reflect the impact of the binitarian devotion of early Jewish Christians. But, as we shall see, the evidence at hand suggests that Christian cultic devotion to Jesus was a somewhat distinctive mutation in Jewish monotheism.

As a first-century hint that Jews worshiped angels, one sometimes encounters references to Col. 2:16–18, where Paul warns against preoccupation with various ritual concerns (v. 16, food, drink, festivals, the new moon, or the Sabbath), which appear to be Jewish in derivation, and where Paul also criticizes those who make much of "self-abasement" (RSV) or "humility" (*tapeinophrosynē*) and "worship of angels" (*thrēskeia tōn angelōn*, v. 18). The last phrase is the key item. Frequently it is taken to refer to the cultic veneration of angels, sometimes without recognition that a good case has been mounted for a different interpretation of the phrase.[57]

I refer to F. O. Francis, who presents a persuasive argument that the phrase refers to the heavenly liturgy conducted by angels: the phrase concerns, not the worship of angels by humans, but the worship that angels perform. The context of the passage warns against a preoccupation with an ascetic mysticism that involved techniques for heavenly visions and pride in the heavenly visions experienced.[58] I am not aware of a refutation of Francis, and in view of his work citation of Col. 2:18 as evidence of a first-century Jewish cult of angels must be considered a misinterpretation of the passage.[59]

Accusations in early Christian writings.[60] First, there is the statement of Celsus that Jews "worship the heaven and the angels who dwell therein," quoted by Origen.[61] Two points in particular render this accusation less than compelling as evidence of a Jewish angel cultus.

An examination of Celsus's full statement shows that he wanted to portray the Jews as inconsistent and foolish in showing interest in heavenly beings that he regarded as inferior, while ignoring and failing to honor the sun, the moon, and other heavenly bodies, which he regarded as the "truly heavenly angels" of the divine. Given his polemical purpose, it is likely that Celsus either deliberately exaggerated the Jewish interest in angels for the purpose of trying to make Jews seem inconsistent or clumsily misunderstood their interest in angels as the worship of them. This suggestion is supported by the second point: Origen rejected the accusation. Of Celsus's assertion that it is a "Jewish custom to bow down to the heaven and the angels in it," Origen says, "Such a practice is not at all Jewish, but is a violation of Judaism." We are left then with an accusation made by a hostile outsider to Judaism, whose claim is rejected as unfounded by a person with no particular reason to defend Judaism but who had sufficient familiarity with the actual practices of Jews to know that the claim that they intend to worship angels is foolishness.

This brings us to the references to the *Kerygma Petrou* found in Clement of Alexandria (*Strom.* 6.5.39) and in Origen (*Comm. Joh.* 13.17) as well as the statement in the *Apology of Aristides* 14. The *Kerygma Petrou* passage referred to by Clement and Origen expresses an attempt to distinguish the Christian worship of God as alone truly valid over against the practices of pagans and Jews. Of the Jews, the passage as it appears in Clement says, "They also who think that they alone know God (*epistasthai theon*), do not know him (*agnoousin auton*), worshiping angels and archangels, the months and the moon." The statement goes on to describe Jewish practices concerning the Sabbath, the new moon, the Feast of Unleavened

Bread, the Feast of Tabernacles, and the Day of Atonement.[62] Similarly, the passage in the *Apology of Aristides* says of the Jews, "In the methods of their actions their service is to angels and not to God, in that they observe sabbaths and new moons and the passover and the great fast, and the fast, and circumcision, and cleanness of meats."[63] As Simon has shown in his discussion of these passages, they are not the proof of Jewish angel worship that some have taken them to be.[64]

First, note that the accusations are not directed against Jewish marginal groups, the sort of circles usually posited as practicing angel worship. Instead, they seem to be intended as characterizations of Judaism in its entirety. Second, the accusations appear to be concerned primarily with the ritual practices of Jews, for the statements in *Aristides* and in the *Kerygma Petrou* both list examples of Jewish ritual occasions as illustrations of the things being criticized. Taken together, these two factors strongly suggest that these condemnations of Jews as worshiping angels are not simple descriptions of actual Jewish practices but instead are theologically motivated interpretations of Jewish ritual observances. That is, the statements tell us much more about the sort of Christian polemic directed against Jewish rituals than they do about the actual nature of the cultic observances of Jews of the ancient period.[65]

The polemic seems to be similar to the sort of criticism of Jewish ritual observances found in the *Epistle to Diognetus* 3—4 and is probably based on the Pauline texts where certain Jewish rituals are rejected (Gal. 4:1-11; Col. 2:8-23). In these texts Paul seems to say that for his gentile converts to take up these practices is equivalent to putting themselves under servitude to powers inferior to Christ (*stoicheia tou kosmou*, Gal. 4:9-10; Col. 2:8, 20). Elsewhere Paul specifically describes the law of Moses as delivered through the mediation of angels (Gal. 3:19).[66] With these Pauline texts in view, it is not at all difficult to see how the sort of polemic against Judaism represented in the statements from *Aristides* and the *Kerygma Petrou* may have arisen. Nor is it difficult to conclude that the statement that Jews worship angels is simply a theological critique of Jewish religion.

This conclusion seems to be supported by the very nature of the charges in the *Kerygma Petrou* and *Aristides*. Both statements imply that, although Jews intend to worship God and think that they alone do so correctly, Christians understand that their ritual practices show that Jews render service to angels and not to God. That is, the charge that Jews worship angels is presented as an insight of the Christian authors and is not intended as a simple description of the intentions of the Jews themselves.

Conclusion

We have observed that angels figured prominently in the Jewish under-standing of God's rule of the world and care of the elect. We have evidence that apocalypticists and rabbis were concerned to warn Jews against giving undue reverence to angels, but there is no proof that these warnings were prompted by an actual cultus devoted to angels in Jewish groups. Finally, in Clement, Origen, and Aristides we have interesting examples of a theological critique of Judaism made by Christians of the early centuries of the common era. In short, the data do not offer the evidence needed to justify the claim that the worship of angels was a regular part of ancient Jewish cultic practice.

I am not so foolish as to assume that in the entire period of the ancient world no Jew ever wandered into the sort of religious practices forbidden in the apocalyptic and rabbinic prohibitions cited here, especially in view of the indications that Jews as well as others involved themselves in the ancient quasi-religious phenomena commonly called magic.[67] But the existence of professional Jewish exorcists who expelled demons by means of pronouncing over the afflicted person the names of angels, and the use of the names of angels in charms and spells and on amulets worn for protection against demonic affliction, all fall considerably short of constituting the worship of angels in a Jewish cultic setting. Of course, it is possible that the data available to us may not give a fully representative picture of what ancient Jewish religion involved and that angels may have been worshiped among Jewish groups concerning which we have no direct evidence. But until clear indication of the existence of such groups and practices is furnished, the claims that postexilic Jewish monotheism was seriously compromised on a wide scale by the worship of angels, either in a Palestinian or in a Diaspora setting, are not well founded.

MONOTHEISM AND OTHER
DIVINE AGENTS

To those scholars (e.g., Bousset) who hold the view that Jewish mono-theism underwent a significant alteration in the postexilic period, the purported evidence of Jewish worship of angels is extremely important. It is easy to see why. For if their interpretation of the data were correct, we would have the only clear indication that any of the heavenly agents that appear in the ancient Jewish sources were actually worshiped in Jewish religious groups. We do not have evidence that might be used to claim that the exalted patriarchs or the personified divine attributes ("hypostases") were worshiped by Jews. For example, there are no prohibitions against the worship of Wisdom or Moses. Nor do we have accusations in the polemical writings of Christians of the ancient period that Jews worshiped such figures.

But even though the interest in exalted patriarchs and personified divine attributes had no serious effects upon the actual practice of Jewish devotion to God, these figures, especially personified divine attributes, are portrayed by some scholars as significant conceptual modifications of Jewish monotheism (so Bousset).[68] Thus, rejecting the work of G. F. Moore[69] and of H. L. Strack and P. Billerbeck,[70] Bousset insisted that the Aramaic term *memra* was not just a mode of speech but was a theological concept which, along with personified Wisdom and other such figures, became *Zwischenwesen* (intermediary beings), for which "hypostasis" is the best term.[71] Bousset defined these Jewish "hypostases" as "intermediate entities (*Mitteldinge*), something in between personalities and abstract beings," and regarded them as representing the concepts of a type of thinking "not yet capable of fullscale abstraction."[72]

The reader will recall that the personified divine attributes, such as Wisdom, form one category of what I term "divine agency" figures featured in the postexilic Jewish literature. In chapter 2 I will examine these so-called hypostases, what they seem to have signified, and the motivations behind the interest shown in them in the ancient sources. Here it is necessary to anticipate that discussion briefly in view of the present question of whether the interest in these figures represented a conceptual weakening of postexilic Jewish monotheistic devotion.

First, at least some of the items referred to as "hypostases" are in fact not to be so understood; careful analyses of *memra* and *shekinah* have shown this to be the case.[73] The notion of a proliferation of intermediate beings rests partly upon a misunderstanding of certain phenomena of ancient Jewish discourse.

Second, the importance of the hypostases has also been greatly exaggerated. In his survey of postexilic Jewish literature, G. Pfeifer concluded that the items referred to as hypostases seem to have played no important role in Jewish theology of that period, with the possible exception of Philo of Alexandria.[74]

Third, if we are to conclude that the references to Wisdom, the divine Word, and so forth, in language that pictures them as personal beings and actual entities are to be taken as evidence for the belief in such items as "hypostases," then surely Pfeifer is correct in pointing out that such concepts are found in all periods of Judaism. It is therefore incorrect to think that hypostasis concepts developed only in the postexilic period and indicate a new sense of greater distance from God in Jewish piety.[75] Just as the concept of the heavenly host appears to be a genuinely venerable part of Jewish tradition, found in preexilic as well as postexilic layers, so does it seem that the language regarded by some scholars as signifying a hypostasis concept was hardly a postexilic development. Rather, from ancient times such language seems to have been frequently used to describe God's activity.

Finally, in reference to hypostases, I find the attempts to define or justify the use of this term as a description of personified attributes of God in Jewish tradition neither very clear nor compelling. For example, just what are we to make of something defined as "a quasi-personification of certain attributes proper to God, occupying an intermediate position between personalities and abstract beings"?[76] The use of descriptions of such items as divine Wisdom for evidence of a belief in actual quasi-divine entities distinct from God is a failure to understand the language used by ancient Jews to describe God's activities and powers, taking literally what is in fact best understood as a vivid idiom of ancient Jewish religious expression.[77]

Even in the instance of Philo, the case has not been made successfully for the view that his employment of categories such as "Logos" or the "powers" (*dynameis*) really amounted to anything more than an attempt to uphold the reality of God's actions in the world and maintain that God is far greater than any of his actions indicate. In short, I do not share the view of some that the Jewish interest in personified divine attributes reflected or amounted to a significant modification of Jewish monotheistic practice and belief.

Especially in recent years some scholars have suggested that within pre-Christian Judaism there were certain elements of religious thought that amounted to an incipient binitarianism. These scholars tend to emphasize the postexilic interest in the principal angel figures as especially important evidence of such a theological tendency[78] (see chap. 4, "Principal Angels"). Although I have learned much from these scholars, I do not fully share their understanding of the religious developments in question. I am not persuaded that a postexilic Jewish binitarianism has been demonstrated.

Perhaps the most ambitious recent attempt to argue that the postexilic Jewish interest in heavenly agents reflected a major theological development is that by Fossum.[79] He defends the theory "that the concept of the gnostic demiurge was forerun by Jewish ideas about the creative agency of the hypostasized divine Name and of the Angel of the Lord."[80] That is, he attempts to show that there was what can be described as at least an incipient binitarianism in Jewish and Samaritan religious thought of the first century C.E. and perhaps earlier and that this was a major source for the gnostic doctrine of the lesser (creator) god, the demiurge.

Fossum appeals to a large volume of data, the dating and relevance of some being debatable, offers many controversial interpretations and assertions, and addresses many complex issues, some of which I do not think he handles with sufficient caution. With reference to the major issue with which he is concerned, the origins of Gnosticism, I will not pass judgment. His case for an ancient Jewish tendency toward binitarianism is another matter. Here I object.

First, I agree with R. Bauckham: "In the exclusive monotheism of the Jewish religious tradition, as distinct from some other kinds of monotheism, it was worship which was the real test of monotheistic faith in religious practice."[81] That is, assertions about substantial developments in Jewish tradition away from monotheism must be measured by the evidence for the cultic veneration of figures alongside the God of Israel. The case for Jewish worship of angels, as I have tried to show, rests on very tenuous grounds. As for the view that there were binitarian tendencies in ancient Jewish thought, I ask what evidence is there that a second "divine" being—hypostasis, exalted patriarch, or principal angel—was worshiped alongside God as part of the devotional practice of Jewish religious groups?[82] The absence of such evidence, I suggest, should make us cautious about claiming major modifications of Jewish monotheism as characterizing the postexilic period. In fact, it seems that concern for the uniqueness of God became more broadly and solidly characteristic of Jewish religion in the postexilic centuries than it had been earlier.[83] There were, of course, Jews who attempted to facilitate a full-scale assimilation with Hellenism, and there were other Jews who mixed Judaism and elements of other religions of the Hellenistic period.[84] Nevertheless, with due allowance for the undeniable diversity in postexilic Judaism, the evidence indicates that concern for the uniqueness of God commonly characterized Jewish sects that differed on many other matters.

Second, in studying the development of religious ideas we must beware of reading later developments into earlier stages of religious traditions. It seems to me that Fossum is not always sufficiently cautious about this matter. For example, he confidently uses heresiological texts from the second century C.E. and later, as well as Samaritan sources from the fourth century C.E. and later, to describe the beliefs and practices of first-century religious groups.[85]

There may well be connections between the divine agency figures of Judaism and the gnostic demiurge, but I do not think that Fossum has shown that a second divine being (actually divine and an actual being) was an object of Jewish religious devotion in the immediate pre-Christian period. In the following chapters I present another interpretation of the relevant Jewish data, and readers will have the chance to judge for themselves.

SUMMARY

I have now introduced the concept of divine agency, in which God is understood as having given a unique place and role to this or that heavenly figure who becomes something like the grand vizier of the imperial court. Second, I have argued that this concept operated within the traditional Jewish concern for the uniqueness of God. Thus I have tried to show that postexilic Judaism, with all its variations, remained essentially monotheistic in belief and practice and that assertions to the contrary (e.g., that Jews worshiped angels) are not well substantiated. Greco-Roman Judaism was by no means a monolithic unity and I have no intention of collapsing the diversity evident in Jewish groups of that period. I contend only that the emphasis upon God's uniqueness was a broadly shared characteristic of this diverse religious tradition by this point in its development.

In the next three chapters, I will examine the major types of chief agent figures in ancient Jewish tradition in order to evaluate the contention that this divine agency tradition may have been drawn upon by the first Christians in framing their understanding of the exalted Jesus.

2

Personified Divine Attributes as Divine Agents

We now turn to the three types of figures portrayed as agents of God, beginning with examples of divine attributes. These items, especially personified Wisdom and Logos, have already received attention from scholars interested in tracing the Jewish background of early Christology.[1] In some studies Wisdom and Logos are described as the most important factors in the Jewish tradition as far as understanding the development of the belief in the exalted Jesus as a divine being is concerned.[2]

It is quite clear that early Christians, Paul (e.g., Col. 1:15–20) and the author of the prologue to the Gospel of John (1:1–4), for instance, seem to have drawn upon the language used by Jews to describe Wisdom, Logos, and Torah in articulating the significance of the exalted Jesus (cf. also Heb. 1:1–4).[3] But there remain questions as to what this represents. For W. Bousset, the personified divine attributes were hypostases, divine beings semidistinct from God, and the ancient Jewish interest shown in them constituted an erosion of genuine monotheism.[4]

I contend, however, that the personified divine attributes were basically vivid ways of speaking of God's own powers and activities and were not characteristically perceived by Jews as constituting an erosion of their commitment to one God. The "weakened monotheism" of postbiblical Judaism described by Bousset and others is an erroneous construct.

Moreover, I argue that the language used to describe the activities and roles of divine attributes often reflects divine agency. That is, the description of divine attributes as chief servants of God does not really indicate major modifications of Jewish theology but instead shows the metaphorical use of language used in other contexts to describe chief angels or exalted patriarchs.

PERSONIFIED DIVINE ATTRIBUTES

Wisdom

The description of divine attributes as personified beings is a well-known feature of ancient Jewish religious language. Wisdom is the most familiar example, with roots deep in the history of ancient Israel.[5] Although it might be argued that such passages as Job 15:7-8 and 28:12-28 dimly reflect the personification of Wisdom, scholars agree that it is in the Book of Proverbs where we encounter the first clear example of Wisdom personified as a personal being (see Prov. 1:20-33; 3:13-18; 8:1—9:12). Here Wisdom, a female figure, addresses the readers, inviting them to commune with her. Of particular interest is the passage in Prov. 8:22-31, where Wisdom speaks of herself as present at the creation of the world as God's companion, indeed, as his "architect" or "master workman" (RSV).[6]

In later Jewish writings, this personification of Wisdom continues, as demonstrated in *Wis.* 6:12—11:1. Here Wisdom is "the fashioner of all things" (7:22), "an associate in his [God's] works" (8:4), the one by whom God "formed man" (9:2), her influence reaching to all things (8:1). She is closely associated with God as "a pure emanation of the glory of the Almighty," "a spotless mirror of the working of God, and an image of his goodness" (7:25-26), and is pictured as sitting by God's throne (9:4). Similarly, in *Sirach* (*Ecclesiasticus*), Wisdom is pictured as a member of God's heavenly council (24:2) with eternal existence (v. 9), who appeals to the readers in intimate terms to learn from her (vv. 19-22; cf. also 4:11-19).

Jewish texts also demonstrate the identification of Wisdom with Jewish religious life in general and with the law of Moses (*tôrāh*) in particular. For example, even in Proverbs there is the linking of Wisdom with the fear of God and obedience of his commands (e.g., Prov. 1:7, 29; 2:1-6). In *Sir.* 24:8, the command to Wisdom, "Make your dwelling in Jacob, and in Israel receive your inheritance," can only be a reference to the giving of the law through Moses. This link of Wisdom with Torah is made unambiguously clear in *Sir.* 24:23: "All this is the book of the covenant of the Most High God, the law which Moses commanded us as an inheritance for the congregations of Jacob."[7] Similarly, in the mediation on Wisdom in *Bar.* 3:9—4:4, the same connection is made explicit (esp. in 4:1; note the allusion to Deut. 30:11-12 in *Bar.* 3:29-30).

Evidently the point of this identification is to glorify the obligations of

Torah by making them the essence of heavenly Wisdom, thus making the Jewish religious "life style" the earthly embodiment of the divine plan and the living out of divine truth. Here is certainly a polemic against challenges to Jewish religious distinctives in the ancient world. Perhaps scholars are also correct in suggesting that the Jewish treatment of the female figure of Wisdom may have been influenced by and intended partially as a polemic against the descriptions of certain goddess figures of pagan religions.[8] But whatever the possible sources of the imagery employed, the link of Wisdom with the religious obligations of Judaism (Torah) and the description of the figure of Wisdom as an agent of the God of ancient Israel show that we are dealing with a category of thought that was contextualized into and was governed by the fundamental religious commitments of Jewish faith.[9]

In *Wisdom of Solomon*, which is commonly thought to have come from a Diaspora setting, although the explicit link of Wisdom and Torah is not made, it is nevertheless clear that the writer's meditations on Wisdom are motivated primarily by his Jewish faith. This is evident from the way that the author connects Wisdom with the sacred history of Israel. After warning the kings of the earth to keep God's law and "walk according to the purpose of God" (*Wis.* 6:1-11), apparently alternate terms for divine Wisdom, the author promises to trace the course of Wisdom "from the beginning of creation" (6:22). Then follows the story of Solomon, who is given Wisdom (7:1-22), and a prolonged meditation on Wisdom's nature and role in God's creation and rule of the world (7:22—9:18) which includes the most elaborate personification and the most lofty praise of Wisdom found in ancient Jewish literature. Thereafter, the author links Wisdom with major events in biblical history, beginning with the creation of Adam (10:1-2) and extending through Abraham (10:5), Lot and Sodom (10:6-8), Jacob (10:9-12), Joseph (10:13-14), and the exodus/wilderness/conquest story (10:15—12:11), the last receiving the most elaborated treatment. To be sure, this author demonstrates some familiarity with Greek thought, but for him the key manifestations of Wisdom and the index of its content are given in the Jewish scriptures with their testimony to the acts of God. The vivid personification and exaltation of Wisdom in this book also must be seen in the context of the author's firm commitments to the uniqueness of God and the special election of Israel which are made clear in *Wis.* 12:12—19:22.

Thus it appears that in the later stages of postexilic Wisdom thought, as evidenced in *Sirach, Baruch,* and *Wisdom of Solomon,* there is also the most emphatic and explicit link of Wisdom with the God of Israel and with the revelation of God and God's will in the Jewish scriptures. This definition of Wisdom as Torah continues into the rabbinic literature in which the personification of Wisdom is replaced by the vivid personification of *tôrāh*, which assumes much of the significance and role of Wisdom (e.g., *Midr. Ber. R.* 1:1, 4).[10]

For my purposes, however, the most important aspect of the personification of Wisdom is the description of her as *God's chief agent*, where the language of divine agency is used to refer to an attribute of God. Although Prov. 8:22-31 presents Wisdom mainly as God's companion in the creation of all other beings, the more active role given to her in *Wisdom of Solomon* (e.g., 7:22; 8:2) seems to reflect the idea of God's use of a chief servant in carrying out God's work. Note again the description of Wisdom: as having dominion over the whole earth (8:1), God's "associate in his works" (8:4), the one seated by God's throne (9:4; cf. v. 10) who is given knowledge of all divine purposes (9:9-11). The previously cited language of 7:25-26 ("a breath of the power of God," "a pure emanation of the glory of the Almighty," "a reflection of eternal light, a spotless mirror of the working of God, and an image of his goodness") both subordinates Wisdom to God and elevates her to a position of great prominence in comparison with all other creatures, such as the sun and stars (7:29-30).

Although *Sirach* 24 (unlike *Wisdom of Solomon*) does not describe Wisdom as the agent of creation, the prominence given to her in God's heavenly assembly (v. 2), her exalted position enthroned in heaven (v. 4), and her connection with all of creation (vv. 5-6) certainly convey a priority among God's entourage. The divine command to Wisdom to make Israel her dwelling place and "inheritance" (v. 8) and to have "dominion" in Jerusalem (vv. 10-12) suggests that Wisdom is portrayed here as God's viceregent for the guidance and care of his elect people.

Logos

In addition to Wisdom, there are other important examples of the personification of divine attributes to be considered. Philo of Alexandria is a major source, giving us perhaps the most elaborate discussions of not one but several. His emphasis upon the role of the divine "Word" (*Logos*) is well known among students of antiquity, but in some passages he portrays God as acting upon the world by means of the divine Logos and as many as five other attributes which he terms collectively the *dynameis* ("powers"), which he sometimes arranges in a kind of hierarchy. Philo's imagery is rich and somewhat diverse, and his treatment of these matters, not always easy to arrange in a systematic form, has been expounded at length by specialists.[11] Here I will present a few examples of Philo's discussion of Logos and other divine attributes and briefly outline what these items seem to represent in his thought.

The frequency of the term *logos* in Philo's extant writings (over fourteen hundred occurrences!) and the difficulty in systematizing his use of the term are both well known. His thought involves a bold attempt to draw upon the thought of the Jewish Wisdom tradition as well as Platonic and Stoic philosophy in order to present a religious point of view loyal to traditional Jewish religious concerns but sensitive to philosophical questions of his day. Certainly in some passages Philo's language could easily be taken to imply the belief that the Logos is an actual intermediary being, a lesser god, through whom God conducts his relationship with the world. Indeed, in *Quaest. Gen.* 2.62, Philo calls the Logos "the second god" (*ton deuteron theon*) and states that the "God" in whose image Adam was created in Gen. 1:27 is actually the Logos, which the rational part of the human soul resembles. It is impossible (according to Philo) to think of anything earthly being a direct image of God himself. In *Quaest. Exod.* 2.13, Philo seems to identify the Logos with the "angel" sent by God to lead Israel in the wilderness (referred to in Exod. 23:20–21), and here Philo also calls the Logos "mediator" (*mesitēs*).

Philo also uses a wide array of other honorific terms to describe Logos: "first-born" (*prōtogonon*), "archangel," "Name of God" (*Conf. Ling.* 146), "governor and administrator of all things" (*kybernētēs kai oikonomos*, see *Quaest. Gen.* 4.110–11). Philo also describes the full complement of divine attributes, which includes, in a descending order of priority, "the creative power" (*hē poietikē*), "the royal power" (*hē basilikē*), "the gracious power" (*hē hileos*), then the two "legislative" powers (*nomothetikē*) by which God prescribes and prohibits acts; and over all these is placed the "Divine Word" (*theios logos*), the chief of God's "powers" (*dynameis*; see, e.g., *Fug.* 94–105, where the "powers" are discussed in connection with the Old Testament images of the cities of refuge [94–99, 103–105] and the furnishings of the tabernacle of Moses [100–102]).[12]

In *De Confusione Linguarum*, Philo discusses at some length a notion of God as the heavenly sovereign who has surrounded himself with innumerable "powers" which are employed in his rule of the created order (168–175). Philo also refers to the angels who wait upon these heavenly powers. The full heavenly host is thus like an "army" with "contingents" and "ranks." Here we have clear evidence of the phenomenon in which God's rule of the world is patterned after the ancient imperial court. Over this court God is "King." On the basis of other references in Philo (e.g., *Conf. Ling.* 146, where the "first-born Logos" is said to hold the "eldership among the angels, their ruler as it were," *tōn angelōn presbytaton, hōs an archangelon*), we conclude that he pictured the divine Logos as God's vizier or chief steward over the heavenly assembly. In *Fug.* 101–102, Philo likens the relationship of the Logos and the five chief "powers" to that of a charioteer wielding the reins of his horses, with God himself as the master, seated in the chariot and giving directions to his charioteer, who wields "the reins of the Universe."[13]

I suggest then that these texts concerning divine Wisdom and the Logos reflect two ancient Jewish linguistic practices: (1) the personification of divine attributes, a practice observed in connection with many divine attributes; and (2) the description of particular personified divine attributes, especially Wisdom and Logos, as the chief servant of God, his viceregent. It is the second practice which is of most relevance to my case. The personification of divine attributes is an interesting phenomenon that seems to have been characteristic of ancient Jewish religious thought of all periods and appears to be the result of reflection upon God's nature and activities.[14] As I have already indicated (see chap. 1), this language of personification does not necessarily reflect a view of these divine attributes as independent entities alongside God. Hypostasis is not particularly helpful in trying to describe how personified divine attributes were understood by ancient Jews of the Greco-Roman period.[15] The personification of God's attributes is of course often vivid, and, especially in the case of Wisdom, mythic imagery from the surrounding religious world is employed. Such language would seem to justify the conclusion of some scholars that divine attributes such as Wisdom were seen as actual beings in God's service, if the language is taken literally. I am persuaded, however, that this conclusion is a misunderstanding of this particular type of ancient Jewish religious language.[16]

Although my position puts me in conflict with other major studies,[17] I am not alone. J. D. G. Dunn's investigation of the Jewish background of the doctrine of the preexistence of Christ takes a similar position with regard to the meaning of personified divine Wisdom and Logos.[18] In my judgment, Dunn properly insists that the personification of Wisdom and the Logos must be understood within the context of the ancient Jewish concern for the uniqueness of God, perhaps the most controlling religious idea of ancient Judaism. E. Schüssler Fiorenza has also emphasized the necessity of interpreting the sort of mythic imagery employed to portray divine Wisdom with due regard for the theological concerns and religious convictions and needs of ancient Judaism. She points out that the meaning of the imagery can be understood only by inquiring into its function in specific religious contexts.[19] In a thoughtful discussion of H. Ringgren's classic study *Word and Wisdom*, R. Marcus made a similar point, warning against the fallacy of equating imagery used in various religions without sensitivity for the functional meaning of the imagery in the setting of particular religious cultures.[20]

Thus, for example, J. E. Fossum's claim that in such texts as Prov. 8:22–30 and *2 Enoch* 30:8 Wisdom is to be taken as "an independent deity" is in my judgment simply unwarranted and imports into such passages connotations never intended by the writers.[21] Similarly, although he is correct to emphasize that in ancient Judaism the name and word of God are redolent with significance, Fossum's view that they "seem to have a kind of substantive existence" and that each amounts to a kind of "independent entity" (citing Isa. 30:27; 55:10–11; Jer. 10:6; Pss. 20:1; 54:6; 143:13; Joel 2:26; Prov. 18:10; Mal. 1:11; *Wis.* 18:15–16) strikes me as a failure to appreciate the character of ancient Jewish religious language.[22] That the divine Name, divine Wisdom or Word, and other divine attributes are referred to in ancient texts in language of personification is not sufficient reason to conclude that these items were understood by ancient Jews as personal beings or as things somewhere in "between personalities and abstract beings" (e.g., hypostases). While personified divine attributes behave in the linguistic world of ancient Jewish texts as personal beings, this is not necessarily indicative of the function of divine attributes in the conceptual world and religious life of the people who created the texts.[23]

To illustrate my point, I cite an example from *Joseph and Asenath* (a first-century Jewish composition). Here we have an elaborate personification of Penitence (15:7–8), an essentially human action, as "the Most High's daughter . . . the mother of virgins . . . a virgin, very beautiful and pure and chaste and gentle." She entreats God on behalf of the repentant and "has prepared a bridal chamber for those who love her." We are told that "God the Most High loves her, and all his angels do her reverence." It is unlikely that Penitence is to be taken as a real "intermediary," yet the personification language is just as rich as for Wisdom and similar figures. Surely this text shows the prevalence of personification in the religious language of ancient Jews and is a warning against much that has been concluded on the basis of such vivid rhetoric.[24]

Nor is it determinative for the meaning of such items in ancient Judaism that in other ancient religious groups there were gods of Wisdom, Justice, and so forth, and secondary gods who acted on behalf of the high gods. Such information may shed light on the possible origin and influences upon the language and imagery used by ancient Jews in describing divine attributes, but the actual significance of the language must be determined by the function of the language in the religious life of ancient Jews. Much history of religions work can be characterized as zealous but misguided in its use of alleged parallels and sources involving the equivalent of the "etymological fallacy"—religious terms and symbols are assumed to carry the same meaning and function anywhere they appear.

Even in the case of Philo, whose discussion of personified divine attributes is perhaps the fullest in Jewish antiquity, it is doubtful that Logos and other divine powers amount to anything more than ways of describing God and his activities. Thus, when Philo calls the Logos "god" or "second god," he seems to mean only that the Logos is God as apprehended in his works of creation and redemption by means of human reason. Philo's discussions of the divine attributes are, in part, designed to say that the creation and the sacred history in the Old Testament really do reveal God but do not and cannot ever reveal God fully. The hierarchy of divine powers is also used by Philo as a teaching device to urge his readers to seek an ever more lofty understanding of God and to recognize the ultimately ineffable nature of God.[25]

The important question, however, is not whether the personification of divine attributes represents a vivid way of describing God's nature and actions, or a conception of these attributes as quasi-personal entities, or a view of them as extensions of God's nature, so to speak, out into the world. Instead, the important matter is that these personified attributes do not seem to have acquired a place in the cultic devotion of Greco-Roman Judaism. That is, there is no indication that these figures functioned as the objects of prayer and adoration in the religious life of Jews of that period. We read nothing of Jewish sects in which Wisdom, Logos, the Name, or other divine attributes were adored alongside God.[26] In *Wisdom of Solomon* 6—10 we find a lengthy recitation of the significance of divine Wisdom, in rhetoric that seems almost hymnic. But there is no indication that such rhetoric reflects religious devotion to the figure of Wisdom, as an object of cultic veneration alongside God. Thus, whatever the personification of divine attributes represented for ancient Jews, it did not involve a threat to the uniqueness of God or a modification to the shape of ancient Jewish devtotion.[27]

THE LANGUAGE OF DIVINE AGENCY

In addition to the linguistic practice of personification, the ancient Jewish texts cited earlier also reflect the description of certain divine attributes as the chief agent of God. I have already given some examples of why this is so and I will examine a few more here. The description of divine attributes as if they were God's viceregent or grand vizier is interesting because to some extent it corresponds to and reflects an aspect of the conceptual background of the understanding of the role of the exalted Jesus in earliest Christianity. There are differences, of course: (1) These divine attributes were not thought of as real entities alongside God, as I have argued; and (2) at a very early point the exalted Jesus did come to function as an object of religious devotion in the life and cultic setting of Christian groups. This role of the exalted Jesus in the devotional life of earliest Christianity marked the Christian binitarian mutation in ancient Jewish piety and gave Christian devotion its distinctive binitarian shape.

This mutation was not, however, unrelated to factors in the Jewish religious matrix in which it developed, and an important factor to be reckoned with is what I have termed the concept of divine agency. Although personified divine attributes were not real beings alongside God, ancient Jewish texts employ divine agency language in referring to them. This shows that divine agency was a familiar element of Jewish tradition.

Of course, the ultimate background of this language of divine agency is the ancient royal court, as E. R. Goodenough pointed out with reference to Philo's description of the "powers."[28] But the description of divine attributes as God's grand vizier drew not only upon the earthly model of the royal court but also upon Jewish traditions about the heavenly court. The figurative description of Wisdom or the Logos as God's chief agent invoked not only the political experience of ancient Jews but also their religious thought. It should not be seen in isolation from the larger pattern of the divine agency concept which was a feature of their religious thought. This is made clear in *Sir.* 24:2, for example, where Wisdom is made prominent among the heavenly host, and in Philo where the Logos is linked with the principal angel of Exod. 23:20–21 who is said to bear the name of God (e.g., *Quaest. Exod.* 2.13; *De Agr.* 51; *Migr. Abr.* 174).

The personification of divine attributes was intended to focus attention upon particular aspects of God's nature and (e.g., in Philo) occasionally to magnify God by emphasizing that he is greater than any of his works indicate. The appropriation of the language of divine agency to describe particular personified divine attributes was intended to highlight even more the significance of the attribute so described. Thus when *Wisdom of Solomon* describes Wisdom as God's "associate in his works" (8:4), the one who sits by God's throne (9:4, 10), and "knows and understands all things" (9:11), the intention is to make Wisdom the direct expression of God's nature and purposes. The same point is made by means of different imagery in 7:24–26 where Wisdom is described as God's "breath," "emanation," "reflection," and "image." The variation in imagery makes all the figurative language used secondary to the main point symbolized: adherence to Israel's God and the way of life he has ordered is the way of true Wisdom with assurance of great reward.[29]

Similarly, Philo's references to the Logos employ a variety of figurative terms: "High Priest" (*Migr. Abr.* 102; *Fug.* 108–18; *Somn.* 2.183), "image of God" (*Fug.* 101), "first-born" (*Conf. Ling.* 63), and others drawn from the Old Testament and the cultural life of his readers, as well as general terms such as "model" (*Somn.* 1.75), to emphasize the importance of the Logos as a revelation of God. In the variety of symbolic language there is also the language of divine agency, in which the Logos is described as God's chief agent who is above all other servants of God: he "who holds the eldership among the angels, their ruler as it were" (*Conf. Ling.* 146), God's "governor and administrator of all things" (*Quaest. Gen.* 4.110), God's "viceroy" (*hyparchos, De Agr.* 51). Philo several times refers to Exod. 23:20–21, with its description of a principal angel in whom the name of God dwells, to describe the importance of the Logos. This shows that Philo also was familiar with the tradition of a heavenly chief servant of God; the same text is alluded to by other ancient Jews where other figures (especially principal angels) are placed in such a role. In Philo's case, however, this tradition is appropriated to describe the Logos as the highest revelation of God perceptible to the intellect.[30]

The description of personified divine attributes as God's chief agent thus offers interesting linguistic parallels to the description of the exalted Christ in the New Testament. More important, it is one indication among others that the Jewish tradition was familiar with the concept that God's rule might include such an office. Wisdom and the Logos, portrayed in the language of divine agency, in part form the Jewish background of the early Christian understanding of the exalted Jesus, but they also point to the more fundamental conceptual background from which the language was borrowed. This concept, that God has a chief agent in heaven above all other divine servants, served the early Christians in their attempt to accommodate the exalted Jesus alongside God. In the next two chapters I shall examine additional evidence of this conceptual background.

3

Exalted Patriarchs as Divine Agents

The glorification of Old Testament patriarchs is standard fare in post-exilic Judaism.[1] Prominent figures include Adam, Seth, Enoch, Abraham, Jacob, and especially Moses. Perhaps the best example we have of this is *Sirach* (*Ecclesiasticus*) 44—49, which apparently distills and adapts an elaborate body of traditions about some of the figures mentioned there. Here I only want to focus on some examples of the ones who are exalted to a heavenly position as God's chief agent. As I have indicated (chap. 1), interest in certain exalted patriarchs constitutes one of three categories of divine agency thought. Along with the other two categories of divine agency thought (personified divine attributes and chief angels), the patriarchs reflect the ability of ancient Judaism to accommodate exalted figures alongside God. This may have enabled the first Christians to come to grips with their conviction about the exaltation of Jesus.

So far I have argued that the descriptions of divine attributes as God's chief agent were a figurative use of divine agency language (chap. 2). But when we turn to the descriptions of the exalted patriarchs, we are dealing with real figures distinct from God, who are pictured as having a glorious place of heavenly power and honor. These patriarchs were in this way real precursors of the exalted Jesus and, like Jesus, were figures who led an earthly, historical existence. Unlike Jesus, however, they were all from the distant past.[2] I shall now proceed to illustrate the way certain Old Testament heroes are described, especially as God's chief agent.

ENOCH SPECULATIONS

Among the patriarchal figures to whom great attention was given in ancient Judaism is Enoch. Mentioned only briefly in Gen. 5:18-24, he became a figure of great importance in postexilic literature, and from the brief biblical reference there grew an elaborate tradition concerning him.[3] For example, in *Jubilees* (2d century B.C.E.),[4] Enoch is described as the first man "to learn to write and to acquire knowledge and wisdom" (4:17) and he is credited with a book about "the signs of heaven" (i.e., the calendrical matters with which *Jubilees* is so concerned). Further, according to *Jubilees*, Enoch was given a "vision in his sleep" in which he saw everything that is to happen "till the day of judgement," and wrote all this too (4:18-19). While spending "six jubilees of years" with the angels of God, he learned "everything on earth and in the heavens" (4:21). He was finally taken away and conducted into the Garden of Eden "in majesty and honour," where he records all human deeds until the day of judgment (4:23-24) and where "he burned the incense of the sanctuary" (4:25), apparently indicating that he was seen as having a priestly role in his glorified state. *Jubilees* 4:17-26 also indicates that a significant body of Enoch lore was already established at the time the book was written. The passage contains several basic themes associated with Enoch in a number of other ancient sources.[5]

The tradition that Enoch wrote books is reflected also in *Jub.* 21:10. In the *Testaments of the Twelve Patriarchs* there are many references to writings bearing his name (see *T. Sim.* 5:4; *T. Levi* 10:5; 14:1; *T. Judah* 18:1; *T. Zeb.* 3:4; *T. Dan* 5:6; *T. Naph.* 4:1; *T. Benj.* 9:1).[6] Indeed in *2 Enoch* 10:1-7, we are told of 360 books (or 366) written by Enoch! His heavenly scribal activity as recorder of human deeds is referred to in *T. Abr.* 13:21-27 and in *2 Enoch* 11:37-38; 13:57, 74 (cf. also *Jub.* 10:17). In this capacity he witnesses against evildoers in the last judgment (*Jub.* 10:17).[7]

In keeping with the tradition of Enoch as the writer of books, we possess writings attributed to him. There is the well-known *1 Enoch* (*Ethiopic Enoch*), which appears to be a composite of material ranging from the early second century B.C.E. to any time from the first to the third century C.E.[8] There is also *2 Enoch* (or *Slavonic Enoch*), another apparently composite work dating from the first or second century C.E.[9] These sizable writings are composites of the work of various persons writing in Enoch's name over several centuries, a further indication of the significance of Enoch, especially for those wishing to disclose information about the heavenly world or about the last days.

Apparently, on the basis of the statement in Gen. 5:24, "Enoch walked with God," there developed the tradition of "righteous Enoch," whose great righteousness qualified him to act as the impartial recorder of human deeds and as witness against human sins at the last judgment.

That "he was not, for God took him" (Gen. 5:24) may have given biblical justification for the tradition that Enoch ascended into the heavens and saw all the heavenly secrets. Of course, we must reckon with other influences, apart from the Old Testament text, which helped to shape the body of Enoch tradition at various stages.[10]

My main concern is with the ways in which Enoch came to be described as God's chief agent. There are two variations: (1) the apparent identification of Enoch as the "Son of man" of *1 Enoch* 37—71, a figure who carries out messianic tasks in connection with the manifestation of eschatological redemption and judgment; and (2) the tradition that Enoch was transformed into a glorious heavenly being like an angel, which reached its zenith in the identification of Enoch with Metatron, the heavenly prince, in *3 Enoch*.

Enoch as Son of Man

The "Son of man" figure appears in several passages in the section of *1 Enoch* often called the Parables or Similitudes (chaps. 37—71).[11] He is clearly a figure of great importance, for we are told of his righteousness, familiarity with divine secrets, triumphant position (46:3), victory over the mighty of the earth and judgment of the wicked (46:4-8; 62:9; 63:11; 69:27-29), preordained status in God's plans (48:2-3, 6; 62:7), and salvific role on behalf of the elect (48:4-7; 62:14). Further, it appears that this figure is the same one described in these chapters as the "Chosen One" (or the "Elect One") and as the "Messiah" (or the "Anointed One"), for practically identical functions are attributed to all three figures (see, e.g., 49:2-4; 51:3-5; 52:4-9; 55:4; 61:4-9; 62:2-16). In all these references, this figure is clearly messianic in function and stature, and passages from the Old Testament are alluded to in portraying his significance as the fulfillment of redemptive hopes (e.g., note 48:4 with its allusion to Isa. 42:6; 49:6, describing the "Son of man" in terms like the "Servant of the Lord" of Isaiah).

This figure seems to act as judge on God's behalf ("in the name of the Lord of Spirits," e.g., *1 Enoch* 55:4) and in this capacity sits upon a throne that is closely linked with God: "On that day the Chosen One will sit on the throne of Glory" (45:3; see also 51:3; 55:4; 61:8; 62:2, 3, 5-6; 70:27).[12] The meaning of this is not that the figure rivals God or becomes a second god but rather that he is seen as performing the eschatological functions associated with God and is therefore God's chief agent, linked with God's work to a specially intense degree.

The association of this figure with God's throne is also similar to the conception of the Davidic king in some Old Testament passages, who likewise is pictured as ruling in God's name and whose throne is likened to God's (e.g., Ps. 45:6; or *Sir.* 47:11, where we are told concerning David that God "exalted his power for ever" and gave him "a throne of glory in Israel"). Therefore one must recognize that the descriptions of the Chosen One (and of Metatron in later tradition) on a "throne of glory" may very well be drawing upon traditional imagery once associated with the Jewish monarchy and that sitting on such a throne does not involve deification but more accurately designates the figure as supreme over all others in God's service.

The effects of the heavenly divine agent concept may be seen especially in *1 Enoch* 46:1-3, where, employing imagery from Dan. 7:9-14, the writer pictures the "Son of man"/"Chosen One" in a heavenly scene, prominently associated with God, possessing an angelic aspect, and privy to all heavenly secrets.[13] In this theophanic scene, the writer pictures God and "another," manlike in appearance, whose face was "full of grace, like one of the holy angels," who "will reveal all the treasures of that which is secret."[14] The writer of *1 Enoch* 46 apparently saw the figure in Dan. 7:13-14 as a real being bearing heavenly (angelic) qualities and as God's chosen chief agent of eschatological deliverance. Whether this interpretation reflects the meaning intended by the author of Daniel 7 or was a later development, in either case I suggest that such an interpretation is evidence of the concept of a heavenly divine agent, a figure next to God in authority who acts as God's chief representative.[15]

In addition to blending together features of the manlike figure from Dan. 7:13-14, the "Servant" of Isaiah 40—55, and the Davidic Messiah, the Parables of *1 Enoch* (chaps. 37—71) conclude by indicating that Enoch was apparently designated the powerful figure called "that Son of man" and "the Chosen One." In *1 Enoch* 71, Enoch ascends into the heavens (71:1, 5), where he encounters the heavenly inhabitants (71:1, 7-9) and God himself (71:2, 10-13). Enoch is informed that he is in fact the prominent figure mentioned in the previous chapters (71:14-17). This indicates clearly a tradition that the Enoch of Gen. 5:18-24 had been exalted by God to the position of chief agent for the salvation and preservation of the elect.[16] Even if this tradition is no earlier than the late first century C.E. (the probable period for the composition of chaps. 37—71),[17] the description of Enoch as God's chief agent is an example of the ability of ancient Judaism to accommodate this or that figure in a position in God's rule like that of vizier of the royal court.

Enoch as an Angel

The other variation on Enoch as God's chief agent is the idea that at his ascent he was transformed into an angelic being and made head over all the heavenly court. This is unambiguously attested only in *3 Enoch* (about the fifth century C.E.),[18] which identifies Enoch as "Metatron" (4:2-3), a powerful heavenly being referred to in other ancient Jewish texts as well.[19] In 4:8-9, God tells the heavenly host that he has chosen Enoch to be "a prince and a ruler over you in the heavenly heights" (cf. also 10:3-6). In *3 Enoch* 9, we are told of Enoch's transformation into a gigantic being from whom "no sort of splendor, brilliance, brightness, or beauty" was missing, and in *3 Enoch* 10—12 we read of Metatron/Enoch's throne "like the throne of glory" (10:1), his majestic robe (12:1-2) and crown (12:3-4), and we are told that God orders Metatron/Enoch to be called "the lesser *YHWH*," with a clear allusion made to Exod. 23:20-21 ("my name is in him," 12:5).

Given the late date of *3 Enoch*, we must be cautious about taking the ideas in it as indicative of Enoch traditions in the pre-Christian period. The earlier Enoch materials have references to some sort of powerful experience of Enoch in connection with his ascent into heaven but do not explicitly say that he was transformed into an angelic being. For example, in *1 Enoch* 71:11, when Enoch sees God in heaven he says, "My whole body melted, and my spirit was transformed."[20] Also, in *2 Enoch* 22:5-10 we read that God calls Enoch to "stand in front of my face forever" (vv. 5-6). God tells Michael to "extract Enoch from his earthly clothing," to "anoint him with my delightful oil, and put him into the clothes of my glory," after which Enoch looks at himself and comments that he "had become like one of his glorious ones" (vv. 8-10). In *2 Enoch* 24:1-3, God invites Enoch to sit on his left and says that secrets left unexplained even to angels are to be made known to him.[21] It is therefore possible that those whose speculations are reflected in *3 Enoch* took such references as the basis for the idea that Enoch was transformed into a principal angelic being and, for reasons we cannot trace with confidence, identified this being as Metatron. The Metatron speculations may be too late to be of direct importance for the background of earliest Christology. I cite the tradition of Enoch as Metatron only to illustrate an example of speculations about exalted patriarchs in ancient Judaism, with no necessary implication that this tradition was drawn upon by the earliest Christians.

However, this tradition about Enoch as Metatron is worth noting for three reasons.

1. The description of Enoch as God's chief agent, Metatron, may be compared with and may be a development partly from the identification of Enoch as the "Chosen One"/"Son of man" in *1 Enoch* 71. The latter is a chief agent whose primary work and authority appear to be exercised upon the earth, although he is described in heavenly scenes. Metatron's authority and role are primarily heavenly.

2. The idea of Enoch's transformation into a heavenly being may have drawn upon the sort of tradition reflected in the passages in *1 Enoch* and *2 Enoch* cited, where Enoch undergoes some sort of change experience in connection with his ascent. If so, then it may be proper to think of these passages as reflecting an earlier tradition of Enoch as not just ascended but also exalted and given some sort of heavenly glory.

3. The idea that Enoch was made a heavenly being and was given authority second only to God's is also to be seen in connection with the speculations circulating in ancient Judaism about other patriarchal figures. Thus the Enoch/Metatron idea, though possibly late in origin, may be only a variation of the sort of interest in exalted patriarchs that was a part of pre-Christian Jewish tradition.[22]

EXALTED MOSES TRADITIONS

Another Old Testament patriarch in whom a good deal of interest was shown is Moses. Indeed, W. A. Meeks has concluded that "Moses was the most important figure in all Hellenistic Jewish apologetic." [23] Given these extensive investigations of Moses in ancient Jewish sources,[24] I want to give special emphasis to indications that Moses was sometimes portrayed as God's chief agent.

Sirach

Notice the reference to Moses in *Sir.* 45:1-5, originally in Hebrew by a Palestinian Jew in the early second century B.C.E.[25] In 45:2, the Greek text says that God made Moses "equal in glory to the holy ones [angels]."[26] The Hebrew text is defective in this verse but appears to compare Moses to *'elôhim*, a term used in the Hebrew Bible often with reference to God (e.g., Gen. 1:1) and sometimes with reference to angels (e.g., Ps. 82:1). The ancient Greek translator has clearly taken the term in the latter sense here (as was also done, e.g., in the LXX at Ps. 8:5), but it is probable that the original writer meant to allude to Exod. 4:16 and 7:1, where Moses is said to be as "a god" to Aaron and Pharaoh respectively.[27] Also, Moses is said to have been chosen "out of all mankind" (*Sir.* 45:4), and, in the Mt. Sinai ascent, received the law from God "face to face" (v. 5). These statements are hints that a body of tradition glorifying Moses in such superlative terms was familiar to the writer. This tradition seems to have included the idea that Moses' Mt. Sinai ascent involved a direct encounter with and vision of God, perhaps a heavenly ascent such as appears to be attributed to him in Pseudo-Philo (11:14; 13:8-9), where we are also told that Moses "was covered with invisible light—for he had gone down into the place where is the light of the sun and moon."[28]

Testament of Moses

In the document called the *Testament* (or *Assumption*) *of Moses* he is described as chosen and appointed "from the beginning of the world, to be the mediator [Latin: *arbiter*] of his covenant" (1:14; cf. 3:12). Moses is also celebrated as "that sacred spirit, worthy of the Lord . . . the lord of the word . . . the divine prophet throughout the earth, the most perfect teacher in the world," the "advocate" and "great messenger" whose prayers on earth were Israel's great security (11:16-19). The idea of Moses as chosen before the creation of the world is similar to the way the "Son of man"/"Chosen One" is described in *1 Enoch* 48:2-7. This shows that the motif of foreordination could be applied to various figures who were seen as of central importance in God's redemptive work. The description of Moses as specially foreordained and as "mediator" of the covenant between God and Israel certainly seems to reflect a view of him as God's chief agent.

Exagōgē of Ezekiel

Moses is also featured in the fragmentary *Exagōgē of Ezekiel*. It was a play written in Greek by a Jewish poet called Ezekiel, originally written in the second century B.C.E.[29] The play seems to have been concerned with the deliverance of the Jewish people from Egypt described in Exodus 1—15. The most important passage for us (H. Jacobson's lines 68–89) pictures Moses relating a dream to his father-in-law, Raguel, who then offers an interpretation.

Moses says that he saw on Mt. Sinai "a great throne" which reached "the fold [or "layers"] of heaven" and on it a "noble man" wearing a crown with a scepter in his left hand. In answer to the beckoning of the enthroned man, Moses approached him, whereupon he was given the scepter and the crown and was instructed to sit on the throne, which the humanlike figure then vacated. Once seated on the throne, Moses saw "the whole earth all around" and "beneath the earth and above the heavens" as well. Further, a "multitude of stars (*plēthos asterōn*)" fell before him and passed in front of him as if in battle order, and he "counted them all," thereafter awaking (lines 68–82). Then there follows an interpretation of the scene by Raguel (lines 83–89), who says that the vision prefigures a day when Moses will set up a "great throne" and "will judge and lead mortals (*brabeuseis kai kathēgēsē brotōn*)." Moses' vision of the whole earth and regions above and below is said to signify that he "will see what is, what has been and what shall be (*ta t' onta ta te pro tou ta th' hysteron*)."

Because the text is only a fragment of the original work, and because Moses' vision is composed of symbolic items requiring interpretation, it should not be surprising to find that the scholarly discussion of this passage has produced major disagreements. It is clear that the dream and Raguel's interpretation both include the themes of Moses as ruler/leader and as prophet/seer.[30] But the more precise significance of the passage is disputed. Some interpreters see it as reflecting a view of Moses as God's viceregent (Meeks), or even as implying a deification of Moses (P. W. van der Horst), and draw upon Moses traditions in Philo, rabbinic literature, and other sources to illumine the text.[31] On the other hand, another recent interpreter argues that the passage is to be seen as a deliberate critique of, and contrast with, the very same themes of mystical ascent and quasi-deification which Meeks and van der Horst see as the interpretive key![32] From still another standpoint, C. R. Holladay has argued that Jewish apocalyptic and mystical traditions are not the background of the scene but rather classical Greek traditions of the relationship of Zeus and Apollo and that the writer intended to present Moses in the image of a *mantis* ("seer").[33] Here I restrict myself to a few comments relevant to my concerns.

First, although Holladay rightly has pointed to the wider literary and thematic background with which the writer and audience (especially pagans) may have been acquainted, in my opinion, the Jewish tradition about Moses cannot be dismissed as a likely influence upon Ezekiel.[34] As Meeks has shown, this tradition presented Moses in the roles of king and prophet, the two themes emphasized in the vision and Raguel's interpretation.[35] Given the other evidence of interest in the exalted Moses in the Hellenistic period, it is altogether likely that the author knew of the tradition of the exalted Moses and drew upon it in his construction of the dream scene, although he seems to have exercised some freedom in the way he did so.

Second, as to the disagreement over whether Ezekiel intended to affirm

(Meeks, van der Horst) or modify (Jacobson) the tradition of a Mosaic heavenly ascent and exaltation, in either case the text is further evidence that there was such a tradition at the time Ezekiel wrote. Representatives of both positions agree that Ezekiel was familiar with such a Moses tradition and emphasize either similarities or differences between this text and other ancient Jewish texts.

Thus it seems that the *Exagōgē of Ezekiel* can be taken as another indication of a pre-Christian Jewish presentation of Moses in terms of divine agency. Whether the enthroned figure in the vision is God or a heavenly figure, such as a principal angel, representing God,[36] in either case Moses is given a divinely appointed position as ruler, together with the appropriate symbols of such status, the scepter and the crown. His exalted position is also reflected in the deference shown to him by the "stars," which bow to him and parade for his inspection.[37] The stars could be taken as symbolic of the people over whom Moses is to be placed as leader and judge (alluding perhaps to Gen. 37:9–10, the dream of Joseph). Or, more likely in my judgment, they may represent the acceptance by the heavenly hosts of Moses' appointed place as God's chief agent. Stars are a familiar symbol for angelic beings in Jewish tradition (e.g., Job 38:7) and are linked with divine beings in other religious traditions as well.[38]

The seating of Moses on a divinely appointed throne is paralleled in the description of the "Chosen One" of *1 Enoch*, who is to be seated similarly in the eschatological judgment (e.g., 45:3; 51:3; 55:4; 61:8).[39] The cosmic insight given to Moses (lines 77–78, "the whole earth . . . beneath the earth and above the heavens") is similar to the descriptions of the revelation of heavenly secrets given to Enoch (e.g., *Jub.* 4:21; *1 Enoch* 14—36; 72—82). This is a further indication that the vision reflects a view of Moses as divinely chosen and equipped to take a prominent role in God's rule of the creation. Even if Jacobson is correct that Ezekiel wished to reject the idea of Moses as given cosmic rule and insight, and intended to reduce Moses' place to that of divinely appointed earthly leader and prophet, the *Exagōgē* is at least indirect evidence of a tradition that Moses was viewed as God's chief representative in heaven.[40]

Philo

The fullest witness to a pre-Christian interest in Moses as God's exalted agent, however, is Philo of Alexandria (approximately 50 B.C.E. to 50 C.E.). Not all of Philo's witness is directly relevant to my concerns, and very full treatments have already been produced.[41] Thus I will focus on Philo's portrayal of Moses as God's chief agent.

The best place to begin is in Philo's writing on the life of Moses (*Vit. Mos.* 1.155–159).[42] In this passage Philo writes that, on account of Moses' rejection of the advantages of Pharaoh's palace, God rewarded him by appointing Moses "partner (*koinōnon*) of His own possessions" and "gave into his hands the whole world as a portion well fitted for His heir" (1.155). As his evidence, Philo says that "each element obeyed him [Moses] as its master," no doubt alluding to the signs and wonders in the biblical account done at Moses' command (1.156). Then Philo makes one of a number of allusions in his writings to Exod. 7:1, where Moses is called "god" (*'elôhîm* in Hebrew and *theos* in Philo's Greek Bible; cf. also Exod. 4:16), and says that Moses entered "into the darkness where God was, that is into the unseen, invisible, incorporeal and archetypal essence of existing things," there beholding "what is hidden from the sight of mortal nature" (1.158).[43] Philo appears to have known of a tradition in which Moses' ascent on Mt. Sinai involved some sort of direct encounter with God, perhaps a heavenly ascent.

The context of this passage makes it fairly clear, in my judgment, that in Philo's thought the major significance of Moses' position as God's "partner" is that Moses is the perfect "model" (*paradeigma*) for all others who would aspire to godliness (1.158–59). But it is also likely that this represents his own particular interpretation of the image of Moses as God's chief agent and that he is drawing upon a tradition of divine agency in which Moses was the featured figure and was regarded as God's viceroy or grand vizier.[44]

This is perhaps substantiated when Philo refers to Deut. 5:31. After the Israelites are told, "Return to your tents," God distinguishes Moses by inviting him to "stand here by me," and makes him the spokesman of the divine commands. Philo's references to Deut. 5:31 indicate that he took the words to Moses as constituting an invitation to be associated with God in some special capacity. Again, in each case the context of each reference shows that Philo interprets this association with God in terms of the spirituality which he advocates, presenting Moses' "place" with God as an example of the acquisition of the divine characteristics which he commends to his readers. But it seems likely that Philo is once more adapting to his own purposes a tradition of Moses in a special role before God and that Philo was not the first to fasten upon the reference in Deuteronomy as justification for regarding Moses as occupying a divinely appointed position of authority.

For example, Philo refers to Deut. 5:31 in proof of his view that certain people are distinguished by God to advance even higher in knowledge of

God and in manifestation of his purposes than such Old Testament heroes as Abraham or Isaac (*Sac.* 8). God appoints some special people to be stationed "beside himself," that is, to share in God's own unchanging perfection. Philo continues his discussion of Moses (*Sac.* 9) by saying that God gifted him above the sort of special excellence found in kings and rulers: "He appointed him as god" (*eis theon*, alluding to Exod. 7:1). Then (*Sac.* 10) Philo finds further evidence of Moses' special status in the scriptural tradition that "no man knows the place of his grave" (alluding to Deut. 34:6). Philo takes this as an indication that Moses did not undergo the same sort of change as ordinary mortals do at death, just as God does not change.

In discussing types of human character in *Post.* 27–31—Moses is the supreme example of the highest kind of attunement to God—Philo draws upon Deut. 5:31 and other Old Testament passages to make his point. Philo takes Deut. 5:31 to mean that God makes "the worthy man (*ho spoudaios*) sharer of His own Nature (*tēs heautou physeōs*), which is repose (*eremias*)" (*Sac.* 28). A similar point is made in *Gig.* 49, also by reference to Deut. 5:31. Clearly Deut. 5:31 was a favorite text of Philo's both for exalting Moses and for presenting his view of spirituality.

The ethicizing nature of Philo's interpretation of Moses' exalted status must not be overlooked. For Philo, Moses was deified in the sense that Moses was blessed with a special measure of the divine qualities such as true tranquillity and with special knowledge of God's nature and purposes. This special knowledge is embodied in the law given through Moses as a heritage to Israel. Philo can describe Moses as so endowed by God with these qualities that he became a living embodiment of them, "like some well-wrought picture, a piece of work beautiful and godlike, a model for those who are willing to copy it" (*Vit. Mos.* 1.158), or as "chief prophet and chief messenger" (*archiprophētēs kai archangelos*, e.g., *Quaest. Gen.* 4.8) and "man of God" (*anthrōpos theou*, e.g., *Mut.* 125–129). Moses never really becomes anything more than the divinely endowed supreme example of the religious life commended by Philo. Moses' participation in divine qualities as "partner" offers encouragement to others to "imprint, or strive to imprint, that image in their souls" as well (*Vit. Mos.* 1.159). If his endowment with divine qualities can be thought of as a transformation, it is a transformation to which Philo exhorts his readers also.[45]

In the larger context of the references to Moses in other Jewish documents, Philo's interpretation of the figure of Moses may indicate that Philo has adapted to his purposes a tradition of Moses as God's appointed and honored agent. In short, Philo may be taken as further evidence for the divine agency concept in ancient Judaism (applied to Moses), although Philo has apparently given the tradition of Moses as divine agent his own hortatory and philosophical twist, as other evidence suggests.[46]

Another of Philo's favorite Old Testament texts in his discussions of Moses is Exod. 7:1. This text may be alluded to in the Hebrew of *Sir.* 45:2, where Moses is compared to *'elôhim*, which seems to reflect a tradition of Moses as specially favored by God and given special status. Since Philo refers to Exod. 7:1 in ten instances, it is proper to conclude that in the linking of Moses to the title "god" Philo found an important basis for his own presentation of Moses as the divinely set forth model of godliness and insight into the divine nature.[47]

Holladay[48] shows that Philo's use of Exod. 7:1 is always governed by his fundamental conviction that it is improper for any human to be thought of literally as a god and by his desire to present Moses as the model of the virtues Philo affirms. These virtues are influenced heavily by Hellenistic philosophical traditions of the wise and virtuous king.[49]

The fullest indication of how Philo took the term "god" as applied to Moses is in *Det.* 161-162. After citing the phrase from Exod. 7:1 that Moses was appointed "a god unto Pharaoh," Philo quickly notes that "he did not become such in reality" (161) and gives as the meaning "that the wise man is said to be a god to the foolish man," for when compared with a foolish man (e.g., Pharaoh) the wise man (e.g., Moses) "will turn out to be one conceived of as a god, in men's ideas and imagination, not in view of truth and actuality" (162).

E. R. Goodenough acknowledged that in some passages Philo expressly repudiated the idea that Moses was really deified but argued that Philo was inconsistent and that in other passages he really meant to ascribe deity to Moses (e.g., *Sac.* 9-10; *Prob.* 43; *Quaest. Exod.* 2.29, 46; *Mut.* 19, 24-26, 127-28; *Post.* 28-30).[50]

But when the passages cited by Goodenough are examined in context, his interpretation does not hold. In every case the language of deification is thoroughly controlled by Philo's allegorical approach in which Moses is used as the model of the benefits of godliness and the philosophical virtues that were so important in his thought, as Holladay has cogently demonstrated.[51] Philo's thought is complex, but it is an unwarranted exaggeration to impute to him a doctrine of the real deification of Moses along the lines of pagan deification of heroes.

No more persuasive is Goodenough's argument that the sheer frequency with which Philo referred to Moses as "god" must show "that it really represents one of his attitudes toward Moses.'' [52] The frequency of Philo's use of the language of divinity in describing the significance of Moses is better accounted for by factors described by Meeks.

Meeks has shown that Philo's treatment of Moses blends the motifs of the Hellenistic conception of the ideal "divine" king and Jewish traditions of the exalted Moses as "the divine viceroy, the envoy of God"; the Jewish traditions involved speculations about Moses' ascent on Mt. Sinai as a mystical ascent to God.[53] Meeks has also given an important reason for the blending of these Hellenistic and Jewish traditions in his discussion of Philo's polemic against the aspirations of pagan rulers to be regarded as divine beings.[54] That is, the prominence of Philo's treatment of Moses in the language of divinity is heavily accounted for by the social and political situation of Jews in Philo's time.

Philo engages in a careful attempt to counter the claims to divinity by pagan rulers by offering the true example of kingship in Moses, who alone was properly qualified to be given the title "god" on account of his superlative embodiment of the virtues of the wise ruler. This attempt was motivated not only by the need to give reason for the Jewish reluctance to assent to the divinity of human rulers—widely accepted in the eastern regions of the Roman world—but also by the desire to show his fellow Jews that their own tradition provided the only hero truly worthy of being seen as an ideal man.

Therefore the meaning of the language of divinity as applied to Moses is governed by Philo's fundamental refusal to grant real divinity to any human, including Moses, and by his thorough reinterpretation of such language in terms of the virtues he lauds. Deification language was commonly used in his time to promote religious and political practices he could not accept. Philo desired to reply to these practices by reinterpreting the language to show that it could properly be applied only in an ethicized sense and only to Moses—the paradigmatic leader and lawgiver of his own people.

Philo's emphasis upon Moses as specially favored by God with a unique status was not his own invention. Instead, Philo was able to draw upon Jewish tradition in which Moses was portrayed as God's "viceroy, the envoy of God" (Meeks), an example of divine agency. Although Philo's treatment of Moses was conditioned by the factors in his own social setting just described, the major place of Moses in Philo and the easy way he was able to draw upon the biblical texts about Moses as God's chosen instrument suggest strongly that a Moses tradition was already at hand.[55]

OTHER EXALTED PATRIARCHS

Other Old Testament patriarchs were of course pictured in similar honorific categories in pre-Christian Judaism (e.g., Adam and Abraham).[56] For my purpose I turn to one last example and piece of evidence for my case. It is a document quoted by Origen under the title the *Prayer of Joseph,* and the passage quoted deals with the patriarch Jacob.[57] What survives is only a portion of a much larger document,[58] and we cannot be sure of the exact date or larger intent of the original work, but the available portion certainly gives a fascinating portrayal of Jacob.

Jacob says that he is "an angel of God and a ruling spirit (*angelos theou kai pneuma archikōn*)" and thereafter refers to himself as "he whom God called Israel, a man seeing God," "the firstborn of every living thing (*prōtogonos pantos zoou*)." Then Jacob relates an encounter with the angel Uriel (probably alluding to the episode in Gen. 32:24–30, where Jacob strove with "a man") and says that Uriel claimed that "his name and the name of him that is before every angel" was superior to Jacob's name. To Uriel's assertion Jacob replies by telling him "his [Uriel's] name and what importance he held among the sons of God," stating that Uriel was the eighth after Jacob in rank (*ogdoos emou*) and that Jacob was "Israel, the archangel (*archangelos*) of the power of the Lord and the chief captain (*archichiliarchos*) among the sons of God," the "first minister before the face of God (*ho en prosopō theou leitourgos prōtos*)."

The passage also appears to describe Jacob/Israel as having "descended to earth" and "tabernacled among men."[59] In his discussion of this text, J. Z. Smith has emphasized this motif and has claimed the text as evidence of what he calls "*the* fundamental pattern of hellenistic Mediterranean religious," a myth of a descending-ascending heavenly figure, like that reflected in gnostic sources.[60] I simply want to comment on the significance of the titles claimed by the figure of Jacob in this document.

Whatever the origin and significance of the idea of a descending angelic being who then dwells among humans as one of them, the aforementioned titles seem to be clear examples of divine agency language, here applied to a major Old Testament patriarch. "Chief captain" and "first minister" place Jacob in the role of God's principal agent. The title "firstborn" also clearly carried a sense of prominence as well as temporal priority. (Smith has collected references from ancient Jewish sources to all the self-descriptive terms used by Jacob in the passage.[61]) While we are dealing only with a fragment of a document of an uncertain provenance, I contend that this is another example of the fascination with certain Old Testament patriarchs which has been influenced by divine agency thinking. That is, Jacob appears to be placed in a role roughly similar to that ascribed elsewhere to Enoch and Moses.

The representation of Jacob as an archangel can be compared with the transformation of Enoch into the heavenly being Metatron. In *Prayer of Joseph*, however, it appears that Jacob is thought of as a preexistent angelic being who came down to earth; the descent motif is new. Nevertheless, both cases show that the three categories of divine agency speculation I have described (see pp. 17–18) are somewhat fluid and that some figures could be labeled as exalted patriarchs or as principal angels.[62] My three categories are of value only as a means of organizing the material. The more important matter is that the wide assortment of figures pictured as God's chief agent indicates the popularity of the tradition that God's rule involved some exalted figure in such a role.

EXALTED PATRIARCHS AND JEWISH RELIGIOUS DEVOTION

With this survey of important examples of exalted patriarchs portrayed as God's chief agent in view, I want to offer some final observations about the meaning of the data on two fronts: (1) the religious significance for ancient Jews of portraying their patriarchal figures in such a role; and (2) the effect of such glorified figures upon the practical religious devotion of ancient Jews.

The fascination with Old Testament patriarchs was no doubt promoted by and served a variety of religious concerns, as has been shown in studies of Moses traditions (Meeks) and Enoch traditions (P. Grelot).[63] For example, the stories of heavenly ascents and revelations of heavenly secrets may have been intended to give assurance of the validity of the teaching conveyed in the documents that present the stories. But I am concerned here mainly with the motif of a patriarch described as God's chief agent, as enthroned and/or in other terms given priority over all the rest of God's creation. This theme, I suggest, was prompted by at least two major concerns, both of which can be inferred from the representative significance of the figures in question.

1. The Old Testament patriarchs represented for ancient Jews the roots of their religious tradition and heritage. Thus the exaltation of such a figure to the role of God's chief agent would have signified that, in the veritable cafeteria of religious options in the ancient world, the Jewish tradition represented the highest, the most authentic, revelation of God's

purposes—indeed, the only genuinely valid tradition. Although this supremacy might not be demonstrable in the earthly realm, ancient Jews would have seen the heavenly exaltation of their representative heroes as signifying that in the highest realm of reality, ultimate reality, their religious tradition had been given prominence. In the eyes of earthly rulers, Judaism might be only one peculiar religion among others, but for God, the heavenly king over all, to appoint Moses, Jacob, or Enoch as his honored viceroy or vizier surely meant that the religious tradition they represented was in fact the divinely endorsed truth, above all other claims to truth. Our discussion of Philo's treatment of Moses offers but one example of how this representative significance of a patriarchal figure was important.

2. I suggest that the exalted patriarchs served for some Jews as assurance of the eschatological reward for which they themselves hoped. I have already noted *T. Mos.* 10:9, which promises that the elect will be set "above the stars where he [God] himself dwells," no doubt representative of the aspirations of many Jews of the postexilic period. Similarly, Dan. 7:27 promises the "saints of the Most High" that they will receive "the kingdom and the dominion and the greatness of the kingdoms under the whole heaven," "an everlasting kingdom," to which all will give obedience. In Dan. 7:13-14 the enthronement of the humanlike figure in heaven—an angelic being or a purely symbolic figure or an earthly Messiah—is clearly connected with this exaltation of the elect. In similar fashion it seems likely that the installation of Moses or other patriarchs was seen as prefiguring, and giving assurance of, the ultimate vindication of the Jewish faithful.[64] This is very likely the reason why the exaltation of patriarchal figures to heavenly rule and honor is especially emphasized in ancient texts that reflect a strong eschatological hope.

If the exalted patriarchs functioned mainly as representative figures, their exalted status validating the religious tradition they represented and prefiguring the reward of the elect who followed their righteous example, then what can we say about the effect of the interest in these exalted figures upon Jewish religious devotion? Although the portrayal of patriarchal figures in the role of God's chief agent is an interesting aspect of postexilic Judaism, the evidence does not indicate that the accommodation of such figures involved a substantial modification of the shape of Jewish devotion to one God.

The most thorough attempt to present a contrary view of these matters was Goodenough's argument that Philo is evidence of "an elaborate transformation of Judaism into a mystic philosophy," a Judaism "so thoroughly paganized that its postulates and its objectives were those of Hellenistic mysteries rather than those of any form of Judaism we have hitherto known."[65] I have already referred briefly to Goodenough's notion that Philo was not always consistent with his Jewish monotheistic background and occasionally drifted into an attitude that represented a real deification of Moses. Indeed, Goodenough thought he had found a prayer to Moses in Philo (*Somn.* 1.164–165).[66] Here Philo urges his readers to develop a keen sense of the allegorical meaning of "the most sacred oracles" and appeals to Moses to assist in this endeavor:

> O Sacred Guide (*hierophanta*), be our prompter and preside over our steps and never tire of anointing our eyes, until conducting us to the hidden light of hallowed words thou display to us the fast-locked lovelinesses invisible to the uninitiate.

Subsequent scholarship has tended to reject Goodenough's theory that Philo represents a Jewish "mystery cult,"[67] but the claim that Philo saw Moses as a "god" and that the passage quoted here is a genuine prayer to Moses persists in recent literature.[68] It seems to me, however, that to take such a passage in isolation, ignoring the overall evidence of Philo's attitude toward claims of deified humans and without regard for the strong indications of his commitment to the uniqueness of God is to import into the text a sense foreign to Philo's mind.[69] The appeal to Moses is in all likelihood a rhetorical flourish, the actual meaning of which is that Moses, through his "sacred oracles" (the Torah), has the power to overcome human dullness and awaken the insensitive to the deeper significance of what he wrote.[70] In any case, this single appeal to Moses is itself hardly evidence of real prayer to Moses in the practical religious life of Philo or any other Jew of his time.

Given the significance of the exalted patriarchal figures as representatives of the righteous, I see no reason for thinking that interest in these figures and their exalted status reflected any substantial modification in Jewish devotion to God. There is no evidence that these exalted patriarchs functioned as objects of worship in Jewish groups. As I have previously noted (see chap. 1), the studies of Jewish piety in the postexilic period indicate that it was essentially directed toward God alone. The use of divine agency language to portray exalted patriarchs further shows the fluidity and wide acceptance of the idea that God might have a chief agent figure in his service. Apparently, however, this idea did not significantly

compromise the exclusive devotion to one God that generally characterized and distinguished Judaism in the pre-Christian centuries of the postexilic period.

Finally, one should note that the portrayal of Old Testament patriarchs
as God's chosen agent has some similarity to the way the exalted Jesus was
seen in earliest Christianity. However, Jesus was obviously not a venerable figure of established representative significance for Jews. Thus the
conviction that God had appointed Jesus as his chief agent did not arise
simply from the Jewish tradition. It did not represent simply another
example of an attempt to portray the vindication of the Jewish elect by use
of a figure with obvious connotations. Instead, however much the early
Christian notion of the exaltation of Jesus drew upon and was related to
the kind of traditions we have been considering, it also represents a religious development with features of its own. The Jewish tradition sup-
plied the language and conceptual models for articulating Jesus'
exaltation by God as chief agent of the divine will. But the impact of
Jesus' ministry and the religious experiences of early Christians were the
impetus for this conviction.

Further, the conviction that Jesus had been made God's chief agent did
not arise from a concern to affirm the significance of Israel and her tradition over against competing claims or from the desire to give assurance
that the exaltation of the elect was a reliable hope. Jewish tradition
already had adequate figures who could be made to serve these concerns,
and claims of their exaltation would not have constituted the sort of controversial and audacious claim put forth by the early Christians. Unlike
exaltation of Old Testament heroes whose general worthiness was well
accepted, the identification of the crucified Nazarene in divine agency
language must have flowed from a religious development as much concerned with him as with traditional religious aspirations.

It is an interesting question as to whether there may have been other
Jewish groups in which a contemporary figure received the sort of veneration given to the exalted Jesus in early Christian circles. Based on the
available evidence, the most probable answer seems to be a negative one.
There are first-century figures such as Dositheus and Simon Magus, but
investigations of the traditions concerning these figures seem to demand
great caution in describing the early first-century religious developments
that may have been connected with them. For example, Dositheus may
have been a miracle worker and may have claimed to have prophetic
authority for his message which may have involved new interpretations of

the Mosaic law, but we can claim almost nothing else with any confidence as to what any first-century following of him may have involved.[71]

Similarly, the several major investigations of Simon Magus traditions show that almost every question associated with this figure remains open. It appears that there may have been some sort of cultic veneration of Simon in second-century circles, but claims that such veneration of Simon characterized a first-century following and that such a group is indicative of Samaritan spirituality must be treated as speculative.[72]

As far as these two figures are concerned, we have nothing like the unambiguous evidence in the New Testament that the exalted Jesus quickly acquired a place as an object of cultic veneration alongside God in Christian circles of the first century. There may have been other Jewish sects in which other contemporary figures received the same sort of veneration, but such a possibility is best treated as hypothetical. In sum, it is likely that the cultic veneration of Jesus was not only a mutation in the divine agency tradition but it was also a mutation of a somewhat singular nature at the time of its origin.

4

Principal Angels

That angelic beings seem to have had a prominent place in the religious thought of postexilic Judaism hardly requires demonstration.[1] The many references to angels in the New Testament further demonstrate that belief in such beings was a well-accepted aspect of Jewish and early Christian religion.[2] Although the "heavenly hosts" are a part of Old Testament tradition too (e.g., Gen. 32:1-2: Josh. 5:14; and the numerous references to the "Lord of hosts"), the late postexilic period seems to have been characterized by a comparatively greater interest in specifying the ranks and duties of God's angelic retinue and in assigning names to prominent members of it. Especially in the texts that describe the heavenly ascents of Old Testament heroes, we are informed about these matters.[3]

Accompanying the more explicitly organized view of the angelic hosts characteristic of the postexilic period, there is the tendency to postulate a chief angel set by God over the entire heavenly hierarchy. In spite of the variations in the name of this figure and the way he is described, it is clear that many ancient Jews were prepared to accept the idea that God might have a principal angelic servant, honored with a position far above all other angels, perhaps second only to God in heavenly rank and power. I suggest that this principal angel tradition should be viewed alongside the data discussed in the preceding chapters and that the interest in principal angels is further evidence of the concept of divine agency. As with personified divine attributes and exalted patriarchs, so with the principal angel, we see a particular figure described as God's grand vizier or chief servant, distinguished from all other creatures and closely associated with God.

It may well be that the principal angel figure is the earliest form of divine agency thought and that the descriptions of exalted patriarchs and personified divine attributes as God's chief agent were indebted to, and evolved from, the idea of a particular angel set above the heavenly hierarchy.[4] The important matter for me is that all three forms of divine agency speculation, including interest in principal angels, were current in the Jewish tradition that was the religious background of the first Christians. If the initial accommodation of the exalted Jesus next to God began among Jewish Christians and was facilitated by the divine agency concept, then we need to examine the data illustrating the ancient Jewish interest in principal angels.

ANGELOLOGY AND CHRISTOLOGY IN PREVIOUS STUDIES

In his 1898 study of Jewish and Christian interest in the archangel Michael, W. Lueken argued that early Christians appropriated for Jesus aspects of the role and position of Michael in pre-Christian Judaism.[5] But Lueken focused mainly on Michael and thus did not deal adequately with other indications of ancient Jewish interest in principal angels or with the other evidence concerning the divine agency tradition. Further, his work was flawed in method and results.[6]

In 1941 two studies appeared in which the relation of early Christology to Jewish angelology was a major concern. In *Christos Angelos*, J. Barbel dealt mainly with the patristic period of Christianity and the likening of Christ to an angel, or *the* angel of the Lord, in Justin Martyr and subsequent church fathers. His work is more valuable for the study of the christological controversies of later centuries, not of first-century Christianity.[7]

In the same year M. Werner presented his understanding of the development of Christian doctrine from the earliest church through the first several centuries.[8] As a disciple of Albert Schweitzer, Werner was convinced that the key development in Christianity was "the transformation of the eschatological Primitive Christianity into the Hellenistic mystery-religion of Early Catholicism."[9] For Werner, the Christology of the early church presented Jesus' resurrection as his transformation into a high-ranking angelic being. In sum, the original Christian interpretation of the exalted Jesus was through and through an "angelic christology."[10]

To his credit, Werner recognized that the reverence given to the exalted Christ began among Jewish Christians, far too early to be attributed to the oft-invoked direct influence of pagan cults via large numbers of converted Gentiles. He saw that the proper background was Jewish. In his handling of this Jewish background and the New Testament evidence, however, he made several major mistakes that rendered his presentation intriguing but also irritating.[11] Almost immediately (1942), he was taken to task by W. Michaelis,[12] who emphatically refuted Werner's characterization of earliest Christology.

Thereafter the investigation of the relevance of Jewish angelology for understanding the development of early Christian doctrine shifted to other questions. In 1956 G. Kretschmar argued that the early Christian trinitarian doctrine was influenced by Jewish speculations concerning principal angels, but he dealt mainly with developments in the second and third centuries.[13] Then in 1958 J. Daniélou portrayed "Jewish Christianity."[14] Daniélou attempted to illustrate those early Christian theological images and conceptions that seemed to reflect more the Jewish background than the Greek philosophical traditions so influential in what became mainstream Christian theology of the early centuries. Thus his chapter on "The Trinity and Angelology" (pp. 117–46) is a valuable survey of instances where "angelomorphic" language is used in ancient Christian texts, but he does not engage the question of the origins of the conception of the exalted Christ.[15]

Thus the major question in previous scholarship was whether early Christians understood the exalted Christ to be an angel, with Werner arguing yes but nearly all other scholars taking the opposite position. Further, satisfied that Christ was not thought of as an angel, at least in the tradition reflected in the New Testament, most scholars tended to conclude that Jewish angelology was not very important for understanding the origin and nature of earliest Christian views of the risen Christ. Daniélou was content with cataloguing evidence from the second century and later of how Christians sometimes employed angelomorphic language to describe Christ. But this angelomorphic language was regarded basically as an interesting historical curiosity from early Christian times, more reflective of the religious vocabulary of these Jewish Christians than of their actual view of Christ.

In his study of the origins of christological belief, J. D. G. Dunn devotes a mere ten pages to the relevance of Jewish angelology, and his discussion fully illustrates the positions summarized in the preceding paragraph.[16] Dunn repeatedly frames the question simply as whether the first Christians thought of Christ as an angel, answering firmly in the negative.[17] Following the example of Michaelis and others since him, Dunn emphasizes the contrast between Christ and angels in passages such as Hebrews 1—2 as proof that Jewish angelology was of little or no relevance for the origins of Christology. And again, Dunn allows Werner's thesis to control the whole discussion. Virtually the only question discussed is whether early Christians conceived of Christ as an angel. If they did not, then Jewish interest in angels is deemed of little importance.

I am urging the view that a proper investigation of the relevance of Jewish angelology for the origins of Christology demands that we frame the question differently and that we handle the evidence with greater sophistication. We need to ask, not merely whether the New Testament presents Christ as an angel, but whether Jewish angelology may have assisted early Jewish Christians in coming to terms theologically with the exalted Christ. It will not do to dismiss this question by pointing to New Testament passages in which Christ is contrasted with the angels (e.g., Hebrews 1—2; Col. 1:15-20; 1 Pet. 3:22). Such passages might in fact be taken as indirect evidence that early reflection on the exalted Christ was influenced by, and developed in opposition to, Jewish speculations concerning angels, perhaps especially certain chief angels and their status.

That Jewish speculations concerning chief angels may have been more important in the formation of early Christology than characteristically granted has been suggested by other scholars in recent years. In his study of the rabbinic condemnations of certain groups who held "two powers" heresies, A. F. Segal pointed to the importance of Jewish chief angel traditions and ventured this opinion:

> The relationships between these traditions of angelic mediation and Christianity are significance enough to call for a more complete study of the problem as background for Christology than has yet been attempted.[18]

Repeatedly in recent years, C. C. Rowland has drawn attention to the importance of Jewish chief angel traditions for early Christology. For example, in *The Open Heaven*, Rowland devotes a long section to Jewish interest in exalted angels and chides previous studies of early Christology for failing to give sufficient importance to this material.[19]

In his study of the roots of the gnostic demiurge in Jewish and Samaritan tradition, J. E. Fossum also shows connections between Jewish chief angel speculation and christological passages in early Christian writers.[20] While I hold reservations about some of their conclusions, I fully support the convictions of these scholars that more attention should be paid to speculation about principal angels in ancient Judaism in the investigation of the origins of Christology. Here I will attempt to address this need.[21]

PRINCIPAL ANGELS IN
ANCIENT JUDAISM

As previously indicated, I contend that interest in a principal angel is one important type of divine agency speculation in ancient Judaism. Here I intend to illustrate this interest by a consideration of various Jewish texts. The identification of this figure varies, as does the description of his duties. But what is common to all our references is the idea that there is a principal angel who has been placed by God in a position of unequaled power and honor, making the figure second only to God in rank. Indeed, in some texts this principal angel is described as participating in a unique way in the exercise of the authority and role of God (e.g., by bearing the divine name). We will show how ancient Jewish religion, with its characteristic monotheistic concern, was able to accommodate a second figure next to God, a chief angel, without any indication that this figure was necessarily a threat to the uniqueness of God.

Finally, we will address some major questions about the larger significance of these references to a principal angel. First, we will survey references to the principal angels in early Jewish texts that probably reflect the religious background of the first Christians.

As noted earlier, the idea of a principal angel with a unique relationship to God may have derived from the tradition of the "angel of the Lord" familiar especially in the Pentateuchal narratives (e.g., Gen. 16:7-14; 22:11-18; Exod. 14:19-20). It is certainly the case that the reference in Exod. 23:20-21 to a particular angel in whom the name of God dwelt was influential in later Jewish speculation. Since we are interested in the sort of principal angel figure featured in the later stages of ancient Jewish religion rather than in an earlier tradition, we emphasize texts that reflect later postexilic Judaism.

Principal Angels in Ezekiel
and Daniel

A case can be made that passages from Ezekiel and Daniel, especially Ezekiel, were influential upon later principal angel speculation.[22] Of particular importance are Ezek. 1:26-28; 8:2-4 and Dan. 7:9-14; 10:2-9.

In Ezek. 8:2-4, there is a figure whose appearance resembles the description given in Ezek. 1:26-28 of the "glory of the Lord." The figure is manlike in form, fiery in its lower half, its upper part gleaming like polished bronze. It is difficult to know whether we should understand the figure in 8:2–4 as God or as a messenger of God, an angel.[23] If the latter is correct, then the question remains whether the resemblance of this angelic being to the appearance of God in 1:26–28 means that this being participates somehow in the nature of God or only that we have what W. Zimmerli terms "a cliche-like description of a heavenly being" used here for an angel and in 1:26–28 for God.[24] If the figure in Ezek. 8:2–4 is an angel, we know next to nothing about his status and role other than that he acts here as a messenger.[25]

But if we cannot be sure about the exact nature of the being, there is reason to think that this passage, together with Ezek. 1:26–28, influenced the descriptions of heavenly beings in other ancient writings. One of the possible examples of this influence is the figure in Dan. 10:2–9.[26] Here also we have a vision of a heavenly figure of remarkable appearance—are we to take the figure as a particularly powerful angel or as an appearance of God? Note that the only direct correspondences between this figure and those of Ezek. 1:26–28 and 8:2–4 are that all are manlike in form and parts of their bodies gleam like bronze. Thus it is possible that Ezek. 1:26–28 and 8:2–4 provided some general resource for the writer of Daniel 10, but it does not seem that the latter writer was trying to make an exact comparison of his figure with the visions of Ezekiel.[27]

Certainly the detailed description in Dan. 10:2–9 gives the impression that this figure is of some importance; he has often been identified as Gabriel, who first appears in Dan. 8:15–26 (cf. also 9:21). Whoever or whatever the figure is, one reason for the detailed and impressive description of its appearance may be that the vision in 10:2–9 introduces the last revelation given to "Daniel," comprising chapters 10–12, which takes the reader up to the events of the very "end of days" (12:13). That is, the impressive appearance of the figure may have been intended to indicate the genuineness of the information the figure delivers. If, as seems likely, this figure is an angel, then we are apparently to be impressed with him, but we are given little information about his status in any heavenly hierarchy. Certainly, the description of the risen Christ in Rev. 1:12–20 resembles in some details the figure in Dan. 10:2–9.[28] But later Christian appropriation and adaptation of the language of Daniel 10 tells us little of how the writer of the latter passage intended the figure to be taken.

The situation improves, however, with the angel Michael. He is mentioned first in Dan. 10:13–21 as "one of the chief princes" (v. 13). He is singled out for his loyalty to the divine purpose (v. 21). Later, in 12:1, he is called "the great prince who has charge of your people [Israel]," and we are told that in the final time Michael will "arise," apparently meaning that he will play a leading role in the final salvation of the elect. Once again the information given is tantalizingly brief. Who are the other "great princes" alluded to in 10:13 and how many are there? What is Michael's comparative standing among them? Exactly what will Michael's assignment be when he arises in the last days? All these questions go without a direct answer in Daniel. We appear to have here a developing tradition of angel "princes," some of whom seem to be opposed to God (10:13-14, 21), and Michael is already connected with the destiny of Israel, but beyond this we cannot be sure.[29]

It is possible that the "one like a son of man" in Dan. 7:13-14 may also have been intended as a high angel, perhaps Michael, though this must be inferred and is a view not shared by all readers.[30] But whether this figure is to be taken as a heavenly being or as a figurative way of referring to the "saints of the most high" (cf. 7:27), in either case Dan. 7:9-14 presents us with the language of divine agency. We have here a description of a figure to whom is awarded "dominion and glory and kingdom, that all peoples, nations, and languages should serve him; his dominion is an everlasting dominion" (7:14). Further, note that this figure is to enjoy this status by the will of God. This means that the figure is pictured as ruling on God's behalf, functioning as God's vizier or chief agent. For my purposes, I will not discuss further the nature of the figure in Dan. 7:13-14.[31] I simply note that the description of this figure supplies us with evidence that ancient Jews of the time of Daniel were comfortable with picturing God as exalting some figure to the position of chief agent, with no threat to the uniqueness of God.

Thus in Ezekiel and Daniel we see indications of a developing interest in heavenly figures who are likened to God in varying ways. In Daniel especially there seems to be evidence of the divine agency idea, and Michael was possibly viewed as God's chief agent or vizier.

Michael in Other Texts

In other ancient texts that reflect the Jewish background of the first century, we see further interest in particular angels, who are given names and special functions. For example, Gabriel and Michael appear with other important angels in *1 Enoch* (e.g., 9:1; 10:1, 9; 40:9-10). There is also the endearing story of the angel Raphael, who describes himself as one of "the seven holy angels who present the prayers of the saints and enter into the presence of the glory of the Holy One" (*Tob.* 12:15). Then there are other references that single out a particular angel for special status above all others.

For example, Michael is featured in several references in what appears to be such a role. Thus in *2 Enoch*, Michael is often called the *archistratig* (Slavonic for "chief officer") of God (22:6; 33:10; 71:28; 72:5).[32] A similar title in Greek is given to Michael several times in recension A of the *Testament of Abraham* (e.g., 1:4; 2:2–12), in the Greek version of *3 Baruch* (11:6), and probably in *Joseph and Asenath* (14:4–7). E. P. Sanders is right to think that the term derives from the title given in the Greek Old Testament to the figure in Josh. 5:13–15 who announces himself as "the captain of God's [heavenly] army."[33]

In the War Scroll (*1QM*) of Qumran, the eschatological deliverance of the elect is to involve both the overthrow of the "kingdom of wickedness" and "eternal succour" for the redeemed "by the might of the princely Angel of the kingdom of Michael." At that time, God will "raise up the kingdom of Michael in the midst of the gods, and the realm of Israel in the midst of all flesh" (*1QM* 17:6–8).[34] This mention of Michael in connection with the eschatological deliverance is similar to the reference in Dan. 12:1–4 and should also be viewed in the light of *1QM* 13:10, where reference is made to "the Prince of Light," who is appointed by God to come to the aid of the elect in the last day and who may be taken as Michael.[35]

In all these texts, Michael is singled out from all other servants of God and given a unique status in the heavenly hierarchy. In short, the evidence shows that Michael speculation was widely known in ancient Judaism and exhibits the divine agency concept in which a particular servant of God is seen as exalted to a position next to God.[36] I suggest that terming Michael God's "commander in chief" and connecting the triumph of the elect with the exaltation of Michael are examples of this.

Other Chief Angel References

There are yet other texts that refer to a particular angelic being in terms that exhibit the divine agency concept. Many scholars think that Michael is the figure referred to in some of these texts. For me, the identity of the figures is here secondary to the role and status assigned to them.

We begin with a figure found in the Qumran texts, Melchizedek.[37] This figure appears explicitly in a fragmentary text known as *11Q Melchizedek*, where he functions as the leader and defender of the elect of the last days.[38] The elect are described as the "men of the lot of Melchizedek," and we are told that he will "restore them and proclaim liberty to them, relieving them [of the burden] of all their iniquities." This Melchizedek is to "exact the vengeance of El's [God's] judgments" and will protect and rescue the elect from "the hand of Belial" (2:4–25).[39] The parallel with the function of Michael in Dan. 12:1 and our other texts makes the widely held identification of Michael and Melchizedek a reasonable conclusion.

In the same passage, *11Q Melchizedek* (2:9–11) makes reference to Ps. 82:1–2, "God (*'elôhim*) has taken his place in the divine council; in the midst of the gods he holds judgment" (RSV), as a prediction of Melchizedek's eschatological activity. That is, in a passage where God is more often seen as the one referred to, the writer of *11Q Melchizedek* sees Melchizedek as the *'elôhim* who will arise. And Psalm 82 is only one of several passages to which the writer of *11Q Melchizedek* refers (e.g., Isa. 61:1–3; 49:8; Dan. 9:25) to give biblical support for what he says about the eschatological actions of this heavenly Melchizedek.

This text is further evidence that a heavenly figure referred to sometimes as Michael and other times as Melchizedek functioned in the thinking of the Qumran sect as God's chief agent or vizier. Further, this figure was so highly exalted and so closely identified with divine purposes that the community could see him referred to in quite exalted terms such as "Elohim" and in passages where one could more easily see God himself as the referent.[40] It may be that seeing Melchizedek as the one referred to in Ps. 82:1–2 arose from the identification of Melchizedek with Michael and reflects speculation on the meaning of Michael's name in Hebrew ("Who is like God [*El*]?"). Whatever the origin of such interpretation of the psalm, it is a remarkable development. Here it is sufficient to observe that the references to this Melchizedek in Qumran speculation are further support for the conclusion that the concept of divine agency involving a chief agent or vizier was a familiar part of ancient Jewish religious tradition.

Another example of principal angel interest in ancient Judaism may be detected in the *Apocalypse of Abraham.*[41] After stories of Abraham's conflict with his idolatrous father in Mesopotamia (chaps. 1—8), there follows a longer apocalyptic section, which describes God's self-revelation and his purposes (chaps. 9—32). After God speaks to Abraham from heaven (chap. 9), God commands a figure named Yahoel: "Through the mediation of my ineffable name, consecrate this man for me and strengthen him against his trembling" (10:3–4). This figure's name seems to be an allusion to, and a combination of, well-known Hebrew terms for God, *Yahweh* and *El.*[42] Further, the angel then describes himself as empowered by God's "ineffable name in me" to exercise impressive authority, including control over the "living creatures" who surround God's throne and also over "Leviathan" (10:8-17; and cf. 18:1-12). The angel concludes by saying that he is appointed by God to be "with you [Abraham] and with the generation which is predestined (to be born) from you" (10:17).

That he is indwelt by God's "name" seems to derive from Exod. 23:20-21, where God promises to send an angel to lead Israel to the place prepared for them, and warns the Israelites not to rebel against this angel, "for my name is in him." Given the enormous significance of the name of God in ancient Jewish tradition, the description of this Yahoel as indwelt by God's name suggests that this figure has been given exceptional status in God's hierarchy, perhaps superior to all but God himself.[43]

Note also the description of this Yahoel in 11:1-4: His body is like sapphire, his face like chrysolite, "and the hair of his head like snow." He wears some sort of headdress (a priestly turban?), "its look that of a rainbow," and he is attired in purple garments, with a golden staff in his right hand. Some of these details remind us of the visions recounted in Ezekiel (1:26-28) and Daniel (7:9; 10:5-6), although there is no exact duplication of any of the biblical visions. Rather than identifying Yahoel directly as any of the figures in these biblical passages, the writer may have intended to draw a more general comparison between Yahoel and the biblical figures.

Two details of the description of Yahoel are important: His hair is "like snow" and he holds a golden staff (or scepter) in his right hand. The first detail recalls the description of God in Dan. 7:9 and may be an attempt to portray graphically Yahoel's status as second in command to God, which he holds by virtue of being indwelt by God's name. The golden staff, a detail not drawn from any biblical vision, also seems to signify Yahoel's divinely appointed authority.[44]

The net effect of this description is to suggest that here we have yet another important example of divine agency speculation. If, as most scholars hold, the *Apocalypse of Abraham* reflects early Jewish tradition, then in Yahoel we have an additional principal angel seen by ancient Jews as God's vizier or chief agent.

There are still other examples of this divine agency conception. For example, in the *Apocalypse of Zephaniah* we encounter Eremiel (6:11-15), whose appearance is so glorious as to cause the seer to mistake him at first for God.[45] This angel's face shines "like the rays of the sun in its glory." He wears what looks like "a golden girdle . . . upon his breast" and his feet "were like bronze which is melted in a fire." These details probably describe an awesome being and evoke a general comparison with the biblical visions of heavenly beings. As to this angel's status and role in heaven, we are told only that he is "over the abyss and Hades." It is therefore not clear that the writer saw Eremiel as God's chief angel, but the description of the angel's appearance and its effect upon the seer certainly suggest a being of great heavenly status.

Another example appears in *Joseph and Asenath*, a document that probably originated among Greek-speaking Jews sometime between 100 B.C.E. and 150 C.E.[46] After recounting the meeting of Joseph and Asenath, the Egyptian girl he eventually marries (chaps. 1—9), we read of Asenath's repentance of her pagan religion (chaps. 10—13). Then a heavenly being appears who brings assurance of her acceptance before God (chaps. 14—17). This being is manlike in form, but his face is "like lightning and his eyes like sunshine," with hair "like a flame of fire." His hands and feet shoot forth sparks and are "like iron shining forth from a fire" (14:9-10). He describes himself as "the chief of the house of the Lord and commander of the whole host of the Most High" (14:8). Like Joseph, this angel wears a robe and crown and carries a "royal staff" (14:9); apparently he holds a position in heaven like that of the biblical Joseph in Egypt, "second only to the supreme ruler."[47]

When Asenath attempts to obtain the name of this angel "in order that I may praise and glorify you for ever" (15:11-12), he refuses to supply it. The angel does, however, indicate that his name is written in "the book of the Most High" and that it appears there "before all (the others)," because he is "chief of the house of the Most High." In the angel's refusal to cooperate with Asenath's desire to offer him cultic devotion, we probably have a reflection of the Jewish view that God alone is to receive such attention. But at the same time the treatment of the angel in this document is also another example of divine agency speculation in ancient Jewish monotheism. It may very well be that this figure is in fact Michael, as C. Burchard insists, but for our purposes the identity of the angel is less important than the status he holds.[48] Whatever the angel's name, his self-description makes it clear that he is the vizier or chief servant of God.

Summary. Various texts reflecting ancient Jewish tradition present a chief angel in the role of God's chief servant and describe this figure in remarkable ways. Perhaps most striking are the angel Yahoel, in whom the name of God dwells, and the heavenly Melchizedek who is identified as the Elohim of Psalm 82. This shows that ancient Judaism embraced the idea that God had a particular angel more exalted than all others, whose authority and status made him second only to God and who bore some measure of divine glory.

It is this sort of angel figure that is relevant for investigating the accommodation of the exalted Jesus in earliest Christianity. The principal angel figure in the texts mentioned here is not simply an angel. He functions in a way that sets him above all other angels. At least in some tests this figure seems to be something like God's vizier who acts for God and with full authority exercises the power of his name. That is, the principal angel figure in these texts holds a position next to God that resembles in interesting ways the status assigned to the risen Jesus in early Christian tradition. For me, then, the key question is not whether the exalted Jesus was seen by early Christians as an angel. Rather, the question is whether their understanding of the position given to him at his exaltation drew upon the sort of principal angel speculation described here. I propose the view that the principal angel speculation and other types of divine agency thinking I have surveyed provided the earliest Christians with a basic scheme for accommodating the resurrected Christ next to God without having to depart from their monotheistic tradition.

At the same time, it appears that early Christian devotion acquired a distinctive binitarian shape in comparison with known Jewish piety of the time. It also appears that the Christian inclusion of the exalted Jesus in their devotional life represented a distinctive mutation in ancient Jewish monotheistic tradition. Before turning to this matter, however, we must address the question of whether the interest in principal angels indicates that ancient Jewish religion had already experienced a significant mutation in its monotheistic tradition.

CHIEF ANGELS AND GOD

The texts already cited show that many ancient Jews were able to accommodate a principal angel who had close associations with God.[49] In view of the way this figure is described, we may wonder what was intended by the interest shown in such beings and whether this interest represented a significant change in the characteristic emphasis in ancient Judaism upon the uniqueness of God.

In my discussion (chap. 1) of claims that the worship of angels was a characteristic of ancient Judaism of the Greco-Roman period, I showed that such views are not well founded and that the evidence we have of ancient Jewish piety suggests strongly that it was monotheistic in nature, reserving worship for God alone. The notion that ancient Jewish piety experienced God as distant was discredited because pious Jews of the

Greco-Roman period thought of God as being concerned with them and as directly accessible to them through their prayers and devotion. Their interest in angels did not represent an erosion of monotheistic devotion. Instead, their interest in God's angelic retinue probably arose from a desire to portray God as powerful, capable, and in control of all things.

This Jewish attempt to think of and portray God's royal power was influenced by the available models of earthly royal power, the great imperial regimes of that time. Hence, God was described as effecting his will by means of a great body of heavenly servants, often portrayed as a highly organized hierarchy of various ranks, such as those of a great ruler. The intent was to give vivid expression to the conviction that God was the great ruler above all others and that nothing could legitimately avoid his dominion. Perhaps this is evidence that circumstances of the time seemed to challenge faith in God's care and control. But the interest in the angelic host was an attempt to counter such a challenge with a portrayal of God as the true king of all creation. The references to principal angels appear in texts that also show a lively commitment to monotheistic piety.

One example will suffice. Recall the texts in which Michael is featured—for example, *2 Enoch*, in which Michael is described as God's *archistratig* where the uniqueness of God remains unimperiled. We are told that the righteous are those "who walk without a defect before the face of the Lord, and *who worship him only*" (*2 Enoch* 9, emphasis mine).[50] At the summit of Enoch's ascent, he enters the tenth heaven and sees God himself "on his exceedingly high throne," far above all other powers, being worshiped ceaselessly by cherubim and seraphim (*2 Enoch* 20—21). This scene, in which worship is given to God alone, in all likelihood reflects the attitude and practice of the writer and his co-religionists. Note also 33:4-10, where God insists that he created all things, that nothing can oppose him, and that "there is no other God except myself." It is significant that Michael is described as God's chief servant here, but the commitment to the uniqueness of God is intact.

Similarly, in the *Apocalypse of Abraham* (10:4-17; 11:1- 3), there is no confusion of Yahoel with God. Instead, Yahoel prepares Abraham for God's self-manifestation, warning him of its powerful effect (16:1-4), and he leads Abraham in the worship of God when he does appear (17:1-21). Indeed, it is significant that upon God's appearance this mighty angel joins the ranks of other creatures and servants of God in offering worship to God, the only one who receives such devotion in the book. This description of Yahoel as indwelt by the divine name is a powerful indication of the status of this angel, especially in comparison with the rest of the heavenly retinue, but the text shows no indication that the divine name "in" Yahoel conferred upon him divinity in the sense of entitling him to cultic devotion.[51]

Moreover, in the *Apocalypse of Zephaniah* (6:11-15), "the great angel, Eremiel," of such mighty appearance as to cause the seer to mistake him at first for God, warns the seer, "Take heed. Don't worship me. I am not the Lord Almighty" (6:15). Here, when it comes to the praxis of Jewish piety, the distinction between God and any of his mighty angels is clear. Such a warning as that given by Eremiel might suggest that the writer was, for whatever reason, aware of the possible abuse of chief angel speculation. While clearly accepting chief angel tradition, the author opposed any idea that such beings should figure in the devotional life of the pious.

The evidence in *Joseph and Asenath* bears mentioning again. This figure is clearly an example of the principal angel tradition; his attire and appearance (14:9-10) with his self-descriptions (14:8; 15:12) present him as second only to God. Yet the refusal of the angel to give his name to Asenath, who wishes to "praise and glorify" him, means that this figure is not to be confused with God or given the cultic veneration due to God alone. Further, the document elsewhere makes a strong contrast between the Hebrews, who worship the one true God only, and the Egyptians with their devotions to many gods. This contrast is especially emphatic in the two soliloquies of Asenath (11:3-14, 16-18) and in her prayer of repentance (chaps. 12—13), in which she repeatedly registers her rejection of her previous worship of any god other than the Lord (11:4, 16-17; 12:5-9, 12-13; 13:11). Given this also, it is clear that *Joseph and Asenath* is further evidence of the accommodation of a principal angel second in status to God alone, together with a vital commitment to the uniqueness of God.

Note also that the Qumran texts combine strong interest in a heavenly chief agent together with a firm commitment to God alone as the proper object of cultic devotion (e.g., in the references to Michael and Melchizedek). It is perhaps even more striking, therefore, that the texts from the Qumran sect, which segregated itself from mainstream Jewish life, give no indication that any of God's angels were to receive worship, even principal angel figures such as Michael/Melchizedek.

S. F. Noll has demonstrated the prominent place of angels in the Qumran sect and the notion that God grants to the elect a close fellowship with his holy angels.[52] In this sense, the angels were the ideal to which the community aspired, and the principal angel, the leader of God's hosts, was therefore the heavenly leader of the Qumran sect as well. But there is no hint that the principal angel of these texts was ever an object of cultic devotion, receiving worship with God. To be sure, the Qumran sect seems to have been interested in the worship conducted by the heavenly beings, as the so-called Angel Liturgy texts show.[53] But this interest did not involve the inclusion of any figure except God himself as the object of worship in the liturgical practices of the group.

In short, the exalted descriptions of the principal angel figure go hand in hand with a distinction between him and God. This distinction is most evident when we look for the object of cultic devotion in the texts. Ancient Jews seem to have been surprisingly bold in the descriptive language used for the principal angel, sometimes suggestive of a deification of this being. But in the devotional life of these same ancient Jews this being was apparently not a second object of cultic devotion alongside God.

Chief Angels and the
Bifurcation of God

In some recent studies the ancient Jewish interest in the principal angel figure is taken as suggesting a kind of bifurcation of the divine or an embryonic binitarianism. There are, to be sure, significant variations in the way these studies represent the principal angel tradition, and binitarianism might not describe equally well the conclusions of them all. In varying ways, however, these studies focus on the principal angel tradition as indicating an important development in ancient Jewish monotheism. I agree that the tradition is important, but I want to register my differences of emphasis and disagreements with these studies concerning the nature and meaning of this tradition.

In chapter 1 I noted that Fossum argues for a connection between the gnostic doctrine of the demiurge and Jewish speculation about the role of angels as assistants to God in creation.[54] He appears to be correct in holding that Jewish speculation about God using angelic assistants in creation can be traced back to the pre-Christian period. Philo gives evidence of this (e.g., *Opf. Mun.* 72–75). Much more relevant to my agenda is Fossum's claim that a principal angel was often seen as the personification of the name (*Yahweh*) and glory of God.[55] As we noted earlier, the principal angel is sometimes described as being indwelt by the divine name (e.g., *Apoc. Abr.* 10:3–10). Further, one of the titles that Philo accords the Logos is "the name of God," and this figure is described as holding "the eldership among the angels, their ruler as it were" (*Conf. Ling.* 146). The Logos is thus presented in a role similar to the principal angel figures of other texts, which suggests that Philo may have drawn upon principal angel speculations in his reflections about the Logos.[56] The ancient descriptions of the principal angel are impressive. But what does this exalted language signify?

Fossum takes the indwelling of the divine name in the principal angel as meaning that this figure shared in "the divine nature," or the divine "mode of being,"[57] but he never defines clearly what he means. He also describes ancient Jews as seeking to express "the distinction and yet intimate association between God and the second power,"[58] but here too he does not elaborate beyond emphasizing that the principal angel was associated with God in the work of creation. If, however, by "divine nature" one means the creative, ruling, judging sovereignty of God, then it would be more precise to say that the principal angel, as God's chief agent or vizier, is made a major participant in the "authority" or "rule" of God, or in the exercise of God's power, indeed second only to God in some instances.

As we have noted, the principal angel, however majestic his status in comparison to all other servants of God, and however closely he is associated with the exercise of God's will, remains essentially distinct from God. When one looks at the honorific descriptions of the principal angel figures or the references to their visual appearance, similarities with God are clear and no doubt intentional. But when one investigates the relationship of principal angels and God in the realm of religious devotion, a different light is cast on the subject. That is, however much the principal angel acted as agent for God in creation, supervision of the world, and eschatological judgment, there seems to have been a reluctance to make this figure an object of cultic devotion. Although Fossum refers to the Jewish desire to maintain a distinction between God and the principal angel, his reference to the latter figure as sharing the "divine nature" seems to me to suggest a more ontological connection between God and his chief angel than the evidence of ancient Jewish devotion justifies.[59]

In C. C. Rowland's discussion of Jewish principal angel tradition, we have a view of the relationship between God and his chief agent that likewise seems to me to be open to question.[60] Beginning with the visions in Ezek. 1:26–28 and 8:2–4, and then in references to God's principal angel in later apocalyptic texts, Rowland sees a process in which the divine humanlike figure on the throne in Ezek. 1:26–28 becomes separated from the throne and functions as "the agent of the divine will."[61] He describes the early stages of this process as a "gradual splitting in the way the divine functions are described.''[62] Rowland sees Ezek. 8:2-4 as a crucial passage that reveals ''the separation of the form of God from the divine throne-chariot to act as quasi-angelic mediator,''[63] and he finds further evidence of this development in the heavenly being of Dan. 10:5-9, which represents ''the beginning of a hypostatic development.''[64] For Rowland, the mature form of this bifurcation of divinity may be seen in the *Apocalypse of Abraham.*[65]

In the light of my discussion of these passages, Rowland's intriguing suggestions require a few more comments. First, whatever the figure is in Ezek. 8:2-4, it is doubtful that this passage can support the momentous development Rowland describes. We are not told that this figure has separated from the throne mentioned in 1:26-28, nor are we shown an empty throne. As a matter of fact, in Ezek. 8:4 the seer says that he saw ''the glory of the God of Israel . . . like the vision that I saw in the plain,'' implying a scene identical to 1:26-28 and giving no indication of the sort of ''separation'' or ''splitting'' of God's *kābôd* (''glory'') from the throne such as Rowland alleges. Nor does Ezek. 10:4, where the divine glory rises from over the cherubim to go to another part of the temple, serve as evidence of the development that Rowland describes,[66] for in 10:18-19 the *kābôd* returns to the cherubim and is pictured thereafter in 11:22 in the same position.[67]

I also find serious problems with Rowland's intepretation of the Yahoel figure in the *Apocalypse of Abraham*[68] as well as with Fossum's.[69] Here I will respond to their views.

Recall that ''Yahoel'' is a name constructed from two Hebrew terms used for God himself, *Yahweh* and *El*, and seems intended as a reflection of his special status as the angel indwelt by God's ''ineffable name'' (10:3-10). The latter detail, a probable allusion to Exod. 23:20-21, clearly sets the angel apart as given special, likely surpassing, authority in the administration of God's rule. This unique status is further indicated in the angel's description of his duties in 10:8-17. Yahoel is thus a very important example of the principal angel tradition and an excellent illustration of the concept of divine agency.

But Fossum and Rowland argue that Yahoel should be seen as much more than God's chief agent. Fossum suggests that the angel's name means that the figure is ''a personification of the Divine Name.''[70] This, however, appears to exceed the warrants of the text. Yahoel is not said to be the divine name but is indwelt by it, which is intended merely to explain the medium of his special power and authority in the heavenly hierarchy.[71] The writer is not speculating about evolution in the deity; he is only explaining the basis for Yahoel's special privileges and capabilities.

Fossum also tries to make a case for Yahoel as the "divine Glory," that is, the personification of the divine figure mentioned in Ezek. 1:26-28, a view supported by Rowland as well.[72] The reasons offered for this view have to do with two things: the visual description of Yahoel in 11:1-4 and the description of the theophany in chaps. 17—19.

First we will deal with the description of Yahoel. There are indirect and direct allusions to visions of heavenly figures in Ezekiel and Daniel, but these should not be exaggerated. The only direct connections with biblical theophanies are the descriptions of Yahoel's hair as "like snow" (cf. the vision of the "ancient of days" [Dan. 7:9] whose hair was "like pure wool") and the reference to a rainbowlike head covering (see the rainbowlike effect in Ezek. 1:26-28). Careful comparison, however, will show that in other details the description of Yahoel in *Apocalypse of Abraham* 11 is only vaguely similar to the visions in Ezek. 1:26-28 and Dan. 7:9-10; 10:5-9. Indeed, as noted earlier, the probable familiarity of the writer with these biblical passages makes all the more interesting his failure to model the description of Yahoel more closely after the descriptions of God. The two direct similarities we notice in Yahoel's appearance show that the writer was capable of borrowing details when he wished, but even here the similarities with the biblical visions are not exact. That the writer did not appropriate more exactly the biblical imagery in his description of Yahoel is surely important and may well indicate that no full identification of Yahoel and God or his "glory" was intended.

Yahoel's white hair and his rainbowlike headdress may instead be intended to suggest a limited similarity between him and God, just enough to portray him as the divine vizier. Over against Rowland's suggestion that the description of Yahoel reflects the remnants of the idea that the divine *kābôd* became a personalized agent of God,[73] I suggest that we here have a creative attempt to portray the visual majesty accorded to the angel chosen by God as his chief agent.

As for the theophany scene in *Apocalypse of Abraham* 17—19, here again there is little justification for the idea that Yahoel represents some sort of separation of the divine figure from the throne. Both Rowland and Fossum make too much of the fact that in 18:1-5 there is no explicit description of a figure on the divine throne.[74] To take the absence of a description of a figure on the throne as "the lack of any figure on the throne" is simply a non sequitur.[75]

The throne is not said to be empty. Granted, the author does not portray God in human form, and instead describes the divine manifestation as fire (17:1; 18:1-4, 13-14; 19:1). But it must be noted that in 16:3-4 Yahoel tells Abraham that "the Eternal One" will come toward them, and continues, "You will not look at him himself." If the seer could not look directly upon God, how could he be expected to give a description of him? Note that the author does not engage in anthropomorphic description of God such as in Ezek. 1:26-28 (a reluctance shown also by the author of Revelation 4), but this is hardly evidence of an empty divine throne. The *Apocalypse of Abraham* gives no physical description of God beyond the traditional theophanic image of fire, but the author refers to a voice coming from the divine fire above the throne (17:1; 18:1-3; 19:1), suggesting that the throne is occupied, although no description is given of the one speaking.

Further reason to reject the notion that the *Apocalypse of Abraham* reflects a supposed separation of the divine figure from the throne is suggested in 19:1-5. Here the voice from the throne tells Abraham to note that "on no single expanse is there any other but the one whom you have searched for or who has loved you." After looking about, Abraham says, "I saw no one else there." This emphasis upon the singularity of the deity seems difficult to reconcile with the claim that the author saw Yahoel as a second divine being, perhaps the embodiment of the divine "glory" or the divine figure removed from the throne.

This investigation of recent claims about a bifurcation of the deity in pre-Christian Jewish tradition leads me to the conclusion that such a view is not clearly supported by the data.[76] The principal angel figure is not the reflection of some sort of splitting off of the glory of God or the divine occupant of the throne pictured in Ezek. 1:26-28. Rather, this figure is one major type of divine agency tradition, in which one of God's servants is portrayed as given a unique status in the administration of God's rule. In this chapter I have demonstrated that ancient Jews were comfortable with the idea that God had created or elevated a particular figure (e.g., a heavenly being) to act as his chief agent or vizier.

The pattern of ancient imperial regimes, which influenced the development of the divine agency tradition, required that the figure holding the position of God's vizier should be described in majestic terms. It also apparently seemed fitting that, in view of this figure's close relationship to God, he should be portrayed as somewhat visually similar to his master. Nevertheless the idea that God might appoint some figure to a unique participation in his rule does not seem to have led to the conclusion that this figure is truly "divine." This is apparent, as noted previously, when we investigate the characteristic devotional life of ancient Jews in the surviving evidence. Therefore we should avoid making too much out of the exalted descriptions of God's chief agent, even when he is referred to as being indwelt by the divine name.

SUMMARY

We have observed that interest in principal angels did not represent a weakening or significant modification of Jewish monotheistic faith and devotion. I have suggested that the references to a principal angel reflect one, perhaps the original, type of divine agency speculation. As with other types of divine agency speculation (see chaps. 2—3), interest in God's principal angel was characteristically accommodated by Jews with a lively commitment to the uniqueness of God.

Just as ancient Jews described God's supreme power and significance by employing the model of the imperial regimes of their time, so they no doubt found it appropriate to allow for the position of the grand vizier, the head of the imperial retinue, which is exactly the role of the principal angel. To be sure, there were already elements in the Israelite tradition that were useful in the development of this conception (e.g., the references to the angel indwelt by God's name [Exod. 23:20-21] and the "commander of the army of the Lord" [Josh. 5:13-15]). Thus, just as emphasis upon the heavenly hierarchy of angels was an attempt to portray the majesty of God and could be supported from Old Testament texts, the same was true of the interest in the principal angel.

But the chief angel was more than just an appropriate figure in the heavenly court with justification in earlier tradition. The religious meaning of the figure is indicated partly by the function he plays in various texts. Where the chief angel is Michael (e.g., *T. Abr.* 1:4-5; *Adam and Eve* 14:1-2), who is characteristically also the angel assigned to Israel, the point is that the greatest of God's heavenly servants is the one who has a special responsibility for Israel (cf. Dan. 12:1). In texts where the chief angel bears some other name, it still seems that this figure was intended as strong encouragement to the Jewish readers. Great power that he is, this angel characteristically delivers a revelation to some Old Testament worthy or guides him through the heavenly strata to a vision of the divine and, sometimes, to a heavenly exaltation. That is, God's chief servant, second only to God in heavenly authority, is ordered by God to act as the personal guide of a patriarchal figure, whose vision, ascent, and exaltation assure and prefigure the hope of the elect. The references to Melchizedek (probably another title for Michael) in the Qumran texts describe God's chief agent acting as personal representative of God in bringing eschatological salvation to the elect.

That God is pictured as employing a chief agent to deliver his message, to guide the seer, or to bring eschatological deliverance indicates a more sophisticated view of God's operations than would be conveyed if God were portrayed as doing all these jobs himself. But if it seemed more appropriate for God, as king above all kings, to employ his retinue in the execution of his will, nevertheless it is significant that the one who appears is none less than God's chief agent or vizier, the highest-ranking member of the heavenly hierarchy. This was in all likelihood intended to give greater weight to the message or vision conveyed. Further, since the elect were probably expected to see in the seer's experience an indication of their own significance (see chap. 3), that God assigned the highest-ranking member of the heavenly court to communicate with the seer would have communicated powerfully the special status of the elect.

Principal angel speculation was thus probably an important aspect of the religious thought of many ancient Jews. Segal has shown from rabbinic evidence of the second century C.E. and later that principal angel speculation came to be viewed with great suspicion, primarily because of the interest taken in this sort of figure by those whom the rabbis deemed "heretics" (*minim*), prominent among whom were Christians and Gnostics.[77] But Segal also notes that both within and outside rabbinic groups belief in a principal angel was not in itself a problematic issue. Rather, the question was whether the religious significance assigned to the figure in certain groups would have been seen by the rabbis as "compromising monotheism."[78] After surveying the roles characteristically assigned to the principal angel in literature reflecting the beliefs of Jewish sects of the first century C.E. and earlier, he concludes that it is difficult to show that these traditions were "heretical." That is, there is little indication that in pre-Christian Judaism principal angels "were considered independent enough to provide definite targets for the 'two powers' polemic" of the early rabbinic tradition.[79]

But the more fundamental idea that God has a "chief agent," whether principal angel, exalted patriarch, or some divine attribute described in personified language, was nevertheless an important development. In its various forms, this idea not only bore the religious meanings suggested in this chapter and in earlier ones but it also may have been influential in the development of other religious ideas within Gnosticism and Christianity.

Having now surveyed the three basic types of divine agency tradition in ancient Judaism, we are in a position to deal with the question of whether this tradition may have assisted the first Christians in their attempt to understand the exaltation of Jesus to heavenly authority next to God.

5

The Early Christian Mutation

In the preceding chapters we have been concerned with describing the sort of resources in the Jewish tradition that were available to help the first Christians accommodate conceptually the exaltation of Jesus next to God. Here we shall first examine early Christian evidence indicating that the exalted Jesus was understood along the lines of the Jewish divine agency tradition. Then we will attempt to characterize the nature of the distinctive mutation in this divine agency tradition and in the Jewish monotheistic devotion characteristic of early Christianity.

JESUS AS GOD'S CHIEF AGENT

As indicated in the Introduction, the connection of early christological thought to the Jewish background is a much studied matter. Usually, however, scholars have investigated the background of particular examples of early Christology or specific components of the body of christological doctrine found in the New Testament. For example, W. A. Meeks illumined the Jewish background of the use of Moses tradition in the Christology of the Gospel of John.[1] Or there is J. D. G. Dunn's discussion of the background of the early Christian doctrine of the preexistence of Christ.[2]

Our interest here, however, is the broader and more fundamental matter of the basic early Christian conviction that the crucified Jesus had been exalted to a position of heavenly glory. This basic conviction preceded and underlay all the titles given to Jesus in the early churches, all the christological emphases reflected in the various books of the New Testament, and all the doctrines such as the preexistence of Christ or his eschatological return (*parousia*). I contend that the formation of this initial and crucial premise of subsequent christological developments was assisted by the divine agency tradition of an exalted position next to God in heavenly glory. In order to recognize that we are dealing with a modification or mutation in the Jewish tradition, it is first necessary to discern the similarity and connection between the divine agency concept and early Christian presentations of the risen Jesus.

Although the impact of Jesus of Nazareth, the man, is not to be left out of consideration, it is commonly agreed that all Christian reflection on the person and work of Jesus flows from the belief in the resurrection of Jesus in the earliest Christian community. It is also generally accepted that the resurrection of Jesus was understood by the first Christians as involving two things: (1) the vindication of the one crucified as a messianic claimant;[3] and (2) his exaltation to a position of heavenly glory.

Acts 2:33-36. This passage contains a concise summary of the early Christian faith: it refers to Jesus' resurrection as his exaltation to God's "right hand" (v. 33, alluding to Ps. 110:1) and appeals to "the house of Israel" that "God has made him both Lord and Christ, this Jesus whom you crucified." The Book of Acts is usually dated from 65 to 85 C.E., but the emphasis upon God as active and Jesus as recipient of the divine action, plus the idea that the resurrection of Jesus marked his installation in a dignity and office not previously held, suggest strongly that we have here a reflection of Christian thought of yet earlier years. And this idea that the crucified Jesus has been exalted by God to high heavenly status is, I suggest, clear evidence that Jesus' resurrection was understood by means of Jewish divine agency tradition. The titles used here, "Lord and Christ," convey in this context specific christological claims, but fundamentally they amount to descriptions of the risen Jesus as God's chief agent who has been exalted to a position of superlative status, resembling the sort of status accorded to the chief agent figures in the Jewish tradition.

Later in this chapter (pp. 114-23) I shall offer suggestions about the factors that may have stimulated the faith we seek to understand here. But as I have already insisted, it would be naïve to think that Christian faith was produced simply by motifs of the Jewish (and/or pagan) tradition.[4] On the other hand, the religious mentality of the first Christians was undeniably shaped especially by the Jewish tradition. It was this mentality that provided the initial conceptual categories by which to interpret the religious experiences that provoked the earliest Christian convictions.

We have seen many variations in this divine agency tradition in the Jewish sources and it should not be surprising to find that there are Christian variations as well. We are not dealing with the simple borrowing of items but rather with basic conceptual categories of the ancient Jewish tradition put to the service of new religious experiences and somewhat innovative religious convictions.

Romans 1:1-4. Further evidence of the use of divine agency thinking is found in Rom. 1:1-4, where most scholars think we have an echo of pre-Pauline confessional language, probably taking us back to the earliest Christian communities of Palestine.[5] Specifically, in vv. 3-4, Jesus is described as "descended from David according to the flesh and designated Son of God in power according to the Spirit of holiness by his resurrection from the dead," phrasing that is easily seen as comprised of two parallel parts. The first part, referring to Jesus as of Davidic descent, is probably a reflection of the messianic claims made for him. The second part of the statement, however, presents the risen Jesus as having been installed or appointed (*horisthentos*) "Son of God" in divine power (*dynamis*). As M. Hengel observes, this phrase can only mean that the risen Jesus is here seen as having been "transformed" into a transcendent and heavenly state in which he "shares in the divine glory."[6]

As with Acts 2:36, so here also, Jesus' resurrection is seen as involving his exaltation to a heavenly position of central importance for the whole redemptive program of God. Thus Rom. 1:3-4 is another indication that the earliest christological conviction was that the risen Jesus had been made God's chief agent. Although in Jewish tradition "Son of God" can be linked with Israelite royal ideology (e.g., Ps. 2:7) and can describe the righteous individual (e.g., *Wis.* 2:18), here the title seems intended to convey the elevation of Jesus to a position of transcendent status and a uniquely close connection with God.

1 Thessalonians 1:9-10. The close connection of the exalted Christ with God is brought out in another Pauline reflection of the divine agency tradition (1 Thess. 1:9-10). Here we read of the conversion of the gentile recipients of the letter to serve the "living and true God" (echoing the polemical rhetoric of Judaism against pagan religion) and to await God's "Son from heaven. . . . Jesus who delivers us from the wrath to come." This last statement presents the risen Jesus in a role strikingly similar to the Melchizedek of *11Q Melchizedek*, who likewise functions as the divinely appointed deliverer of the elect, God's chief agent and vizier of

eschatological redemption. This similarity of roles, the clear influence of Jewish religious rhetoric, and the early date of 1 Thessalonians (ca. 50 C.E.) combine to make it likely that this text offers another glimpse of the early accommodation of the exalted Jesus alongside God.

1 Corinthians 15:20-28. The category of divine agency also underlies this passage. Here Paul describes the exalted Christ as appointed by God to rule until all enemies of the divine plan are put "under his feet" (vv. 25-26). The sweep of Christ's rule is portrayed in emphatic terms: "every rule and every authority and power" (v. 24), "all his enemies" (v. 25), "all things" (vv. 27-28). Nevertheless, Christ's rule is clearly presented as that of the divinely chosen chief agent. It is God who has put all things in subjection to Christ (v. 27). The climax of Christ's rule is the delivering over of the kingdom "to God the Father" (v. 24), when the Son will demonstrate his subjection to God the Father so that God is shown to be absolute (v. 28). As D. M. Hay notes, this passage does not depict "a sharing of government by two monarchs" but rather presents the exalted Christ "in such a way that one might call him a divine plenipotentiary holding absolute sway for a limited period."[7] This presentation of Christ's rule is evidently Paul's own composition. Thus the divine agency category is reflected both in the christological tradition that Paul inherited ultimately from the first circle of Palestinian Jewish Christians and in his own further reflection upon the significance of Christ.

Philippians 2:5-11.[8] This is commonly regarded as a hymn deriving from a Jewish-Christian setting.[9] Here, as with Rom. 1:3-4, in this document from the middle of the first century C.E. we have a "window" opening upon the faith and devotion of Jewish Christians from still earlier years.[10] Of the many interesting features of the passage, the description of the divine exaltation of Christ in vv. 9-11 is the most relevant for our inquiry. In apparent reference to Jesus' resurrection, we are told that God has "highly exalted" him and has bestowed upon him "the name which is above every name," with the intention that "every knee" in all spheres of creation is to bow and "every tongue confess that Jesus Christ is Lord, to the glory of God the Father."

This passage is particularly important for my argument precisely because it combines an amazing description of the exalted status of the risen Christ together with a clear commitment to the uniqueness of God. Consider the following observations. First, there is the unusual and intensified Greek verb form to describe God's exaltation of Christ (*huperypsōsen*, v. 9), which seems intended to set off this exalted figure from all others. Then, the heavenly Christ is described in terms that liken him to God. That Christ has a name "above every name" (v. 9) suggests that the divine name itself (*Yahweh*) is meant. And of course the acclamation, "Jesus Christ is Lord," gives him the title that was also a Greek translation of *Yahweh*.[11] Also, in vv. 10–11 the language of a classic monotheistic passage in the Old Testament (Isa. 45:23) is used to describe the eschatological acknowledgment to be given to Jesus.

At the same time, this stunning description of the exalted Christ is clearly not intended to make him a rival to God. Christ's unparalleled status has been given to him by God (v. 9), and the universal acclamation of Jesus in v. 11 is "to the glory of God the Father." That is, Christ holds his exalted heavenly status by the pleasure of God the Father, and the acclamation of Christ which is mandated by God is thus an affirmation of God's supremacy and sovereignty. To be sure, the status of the risen Christ is unsurpassed in any of the ancient Jewish references to God's chief agents. Further, if this passage was originally a hymn sung in early Jewish Christian gatherings, then it provides evidence that Christ was an object of cultic veneration, something unparalleled in the Jewish treatment of chief agents. Nevertheless, in view of the concern for the supremacy of God the Father, an indebtedness to the Jewish religious tradition, I suggest that the fundamental category by which Christ's status is interpreted here is the divine agency category.

1 Corinthians 8:1–6.[12] There are partial parallels to be drawn between the wording of this passage and the religiophilosophical discourse of the Greco-Roman environment, but the content reflects a Christian adaptation of fundamentally Jewish categories.[13] The distinctively Christian element consists of the insistence that it is the "one Lord, Jesus Christ, through whom are all things and through whom we exist" (v. 6). Both the claim that the crucified and risen Jesus is the universal agent and the acclamation of him as the "one Lord" to the exclusion of all others mean that the Christian adaptation here is a profound one, especially if the acclamation involves an allusion to, and modification of, the traditional Jewish confession of the uniqueness of the one God, the Shema.[14] Thus the adaptation builds upon the religious concepts of ancient Judaism.

The emphasis upon "one God" to the exclusion of all other "so-called gods" and the pejorative reference to other gods as "idols" (*eidōlon*) are clear marks of the Jewish religious tradition.[15] And it is widely recognized that the description of Christ's role here probably draws upon Jewish references to divine Wisdom.[16] All this supports the view that the conceptual accommodation of Christ here is a particular example of the influence of divine agency tradition. That "all things" are through Christ is intended to give him universal superiority, but at the same time he is the unique agent of the "one God." Alongside its Christian distinctives, this passage shows us the use of the divine agency category to grant Christ a position of enormous importance while still protecting the uniqueness of God.[17]

Because we are trying to understand better the initial conceptual accommodation of the exalted Jesus in earliest Christianity, I have concentrated on passages in the Pauline letters, with one brief glance at the Acts reports of the preaching of the first Christians, the Jerusalem church. Of the surviving literature of Christianity, Paul's writings are our earliest attestations of the beliefs and devotion of Christians; they even contain fragments of Christian tradition earlier than the time in which the letters were composed, ones that Paul receives and then passes on (e.g., 1 Cor. 11:23). If we seek to catch a glimpse of the formation of earliest Christian devotion, we can do no better than the evidence afforded in Paul's writings. Because I only want to show that earliest Christian reflection made use of the divine agency category, it is not necessary to survey all New Testament christological thought. The passages dealt with here should suffice to make clear the resemblances and the connections between the earliest available conceptions of the exalted Christ and the ancient Jewish category of the heavenly chief agent.

Readers familiar with the ancient world may wonder whether the concept of the exalted Christ is not simply derived from the Greco-Roman idea of the apotheosis of heroes. There is, of course, some similarity in that a human (e.g., some great man of the past or the Roman emperor at death) is elevated from earthly to heavenly and immortal status. I have no doubt that Gentiles especially, and perhaps Jews as well, would have noticed this. But there are several factors weighing against Jesus' exaltation as a direct adaptation of the idea of apotheosis. It is more likely that the concept of his exaltation is dependent on the Jewish divine agency category.[18]

First, remember that the conviction that Jesus had been exalted to heavenly status and power arose among pious Jews, people not easily disposed to accepting the idea of the deification of humans.[19]

Second, there is an important difference between the early Christian conception of the exaltation of Jesus and pagan notions of apotheosis. The former is firmly controlled by a monotheistic commitment inherited from the Jewish tradition. Jesus is not simply made a heavenly being, and although he receives a prominent place in the devotional life of the earliest Christians, he is not portrayed as another god with a cultus of his own. Rather, the following specifics make the probable connection with Jewish divine agency tradition apparent: (1) Jesus is exalted to a particular position, second only to the one God. (2) In this position, he acts by divinely granted authority and as God's principal agent in the execution of God's will. (3) He is directly associated with the one God and likened to him in certain ways (e.g., he is given the "name above every name"). That is, although the Christian appropriation of the Jewish divine agency category shows a significant mutation in this tradition and in monotheistic devotion, I insist that there are clear marks of the category being appropriated. The Christian conception of the exaltation of Christ shows a concern for the uniqueness and supremacy of the one God, just as we found in the Jewish evidence dealing with chief agents.

THE CHRISTIAN MUTATION

Now I turn to my second objective, namely, to demonstrate that earliest Christian devotion constituted a significant mutation or innovation in Jewish monotheistic tradition. By "mutation" I mean that earliest Christian devotion was a direct outgrowth from, and indeed a variety of, the ancient Jewish tradition. But at an early stage it exhibited a sudden and significant difference in character from Jewish devotion.[20]

First, one should note the most significant difference between earliest Christianity and other contemporary religious groups: the place of the exalted Jesus in the religious life, devotion, or piety of its adherents. I have shown that there are striking similarities between the titles given to Christ and those given to other divine agents in ancient Jewish tradition, and between the functions that Christ carries out and those connected with these other figures. In previous studies of early Christology, precisely the titles and functions assigned to Christ have been central. I suggest, however, that it is the religious practice of early Christianity that more clearly and significantly indicates an innovation—a mutation.

For my purposes, the terms "devotion," "piety," "religious practice," and "religious life" all overlap and all refer to the "actions which flow from and are determined by religious experience."[21] These actions include the inward sphere of feelings and thoughts, of course, but also involve outward and more observable religious practices, both those connected with corporate (cultic) worship and those not tied to this context.[22]

Second, the early Christian mutation in monotheistic devotion involves making the exalted Jesus an object of devotion. More specifically, Christ came to be included as an object of the devotional attention characteristically reserved for God in other examples of Jewish tradition. But this does not mean that Christ was a competitor for the devotional attention of the early Christian believers whose piety we seek to understand. Rather, they included Jesus in their religious devotion out of an apparent conviction that it was the will of the one God for them to do so and they saw their action as an affirmation of the sovereignty and glory of God.

Thus the third point to be emphasized is that this mutation in Jewish tradition may be seen as an unprecedented reshaping of monotheistic piety to include a second object of devotion alongside God, a figure seen in the position of God's chief agent, happening among a group that continued to consider itself firmly committed to "one God."

Fourth, and finally, this reshaping of Jewish monotheistic devotion began among Jewish Christians of the first few years after Jesus' execution and cannot be attributed simply to some later stage of the Christian movement and to the influx of converts from a pagan background. In short, we are dealing with a redefinition of Jewish monotheistic devotion by a group that has to be seen as a movement within Jewish tradition of the early first century C.E. The binitarian shape of early Christian devotion did not result from a clumsy crossbreeding of Jewish monotheism and pagan polytheism under the influence of gentile Christians too ill-informed about the Jewish heritage to preserve its character. Rather, in its crucial first stages, we have a significantly new but essentially internal development within the Jewish monotheistic tradition, a mutation within that species of religious devotion. Now we will examine the nature of this important development.

Six Features of the Mutation

We shall now examine six features of the religious devotion of early Christianity that indicate a significant mutation in the Jewish monotheistic tradition: (1) hymnic practices, (2) prayer and related practices, (3) use of the name of Christ, (4) the Lord's Supper, (5) confession of faith in Jesus, and (6) prophetic pronouncements of the risen Christ.[23] I will demonstrate that these features indicate that early Christian devotion may be characterized as strikingly binitarian and that this development can be traced back into the earliest years of the Christian movement.

No doubt, for some this last point will be a difficult possibility to entertain, for some scholars of Christian origins (e.g., W. Bousset and R. Bultmann) have insisted that cultic devotion simply could not have originated in the first stage of Christianity, the Primitive Palestinian Church as it is often called.[24] It is with such readers in mind that I point to other eminent figures (e.g., A. Deissmann and J. Weiss), who came to exactly opposite conclusions.[25] In short, my argument is not without precedent, but only a consideration of the evidence can determine whether it is correct.[26]

Early Christian Hymns

Here we turn to the place of Christ in early Christian devotion as indi- cated by hymnic practices. In Paul's list of activities in the early Christian worship gathering, the hymn is prominently mentioned (1 Cor. 14:26), although we are told little of the nature of this sort of composition. Other passages, such as Col. 3:16–17 and Eph. 5:18–20 likewise indicate that singing formed a familiar part of the worship of Christian groups. This singing may have included Old Testament psalms, especially those deemed to be prophecies of Christ (e.g., Psalm 110), but there were also fresh compositions celebrating his work.

There is a scholarly consensus that embedded within the New Testa- ment are examples of "Christ hymns"[27] which certainly include some from the first half of the first century C.E.: John 1:1–18; Col. 1:15–20; and Phil. 2:5–11 are widely accepted as major passages where early Chris- tian hymns concerning Christ have been incorporated. Various shorter passages are thought to exhibit fragments of hymns (e.g., Eph. 2:14–16; 5:14; 1 Tim. 3:16; 1 Pet. 3:18–22; Heb. 1:3).[28] In addition, the Book of Revelation contains hymns sung to God and Christ (Rev. 4:8, 11; 5:9–10; 15:3–4) and other passages that are hymnlike in form and function: Rev. 5:13–14 (a doxology); 7:15–17; 11:15; and the "Hallelujah" cries of 19:1–8. Although the author of Revelation attributes these passages to the figures seen in his visions, it is reasonable to assume that their general form and content may have been consonant with worship practices in the churches known to him and that such materials are valuable indications of the activities of these groups.

These New Testament passages have been examined by others mainly in the interest of determining their provenance, individual formal struc- ture, and christological teachings. I am concerned here with their partic- ular relevance as features of early Christian devotional life.

1. The hymnic passages in the New Testament are mainly devoted to celebrating the work and significance of Christ. If these earliest surviving fragments of Christian hymnody are representative, then it appears that

there was a decidedly binitarian shape to this aspect of the worshiping life of early Christian groups. That is, their hymnic celebrations of God's redemption seem to have been heavily concerned with glorifying Christ.[29]

2. These christological hymns exhibit the earliest observable stages of Christian reflection on the significance of Jesus and are probably the result of the fervent religious enthusiasm of the early Christian communities. Indeed, it is likely that such lyrical proclamations of Christian belief, arising from the religious experiences of the first generation of believers, set the pace for, and influenced the whole development of, christological thought.[30]

3. There are several good reasons to think that the practice of singing hymns in Christ's honor goes back to the earliest stratum of the Christian movement. First, the religious enthusiasm, involving eschatological joy and excitement arising from the conviction that Jesus had been exalted to heavenly glory, which generated such compositions seems to have characterized Christian groups from the very beginning.[31] Furthermore, several New Testament passages (e.g., Phil. 2:5-11) can be taken as glimpses of the worshiping life of Jewish Christian groups. This means that the hymnic celebration of Christ cannot be restricted to gentile churches.

Moreover, nothing indicates any awareness by Paul that the worship practices in his churches were essentially different from what was familiar among Jewish churches, including those in Palestine. If the worship of the risen Christ was an innovation of the gentile churches, and completely impossible and unacceptable among Palestinian Jewish Christians (as Bousset claimed), then where is the evidence of any criticism of the supposed innovation from the latter groups?[32] There is well-known evidence of differences between Paul and some in Jerusalem over other aspects of his gentile mission (e.g., circumcision of Gentiles), but there is no hint that the veneration of Christ reflected in the singing of hymns devoted to him was regarded as strange or suspicious.

In addition, the hymnic preoccupation with Christ which apparently began among Jewish-Christian groups does not seem to have a parallel in any other sect of Judaism known to us from antiquity. For example, the Qumran community, though interested in such divine agents as the heavenly Melchizedek, does not seem to have placed any such figure in a position of devotional prominence comparable to the place of the risen Jesus in the religious life of early Christians.[33]

Further, the New Testament displays both the hymnic celebration *of* Christ and indication of hymns sung *to* Christ. Ephesians 5:19 refers to "making melody *to the Lord (tō kyriō)* with all your heart," and the context makes it likely that Christ is intended.[34] Also relevant are passages in Revelation where the glorified Christ is the object of hymnic praise. In Rev. 5:8–10, the heavenly court falls down before "the Lamb" and sings to him of his worthiness to receive all heavenly honor and glory. And in Rev. 5:13–14 there is a doxology offered to him jointly with God "who sits upon the throne." Similarly, in Rev. 7:9–12 there is another scene of heavenly worship, this time offered by "a great multitude" of all peoples who direct their praise both to God and to the Lamb. These scenes of heavenly worship of Christ correspond to, and give justification for, the praise given to him on earth as in the doxology in Rev. 1:5–6.[35]

The Letter to the Ephesians is widely regarded as "deutero-Pauline" (written after Paul's death by admirers). The Book of Revelation is most commonly dated near the end of the first century. Thus we cannot be sure how much the passages cited reflect the hymnic practice of the very earliest Christian communities. It may be that these passages indicate an intensification of cultic devotion to Christ taking place in the latter half of the first century. On the other hand, both Ephesians and Revelation show the strong influence of the Jewish religious tradition, including the emphasis upon "one God" (e.g., Eph. 4:6), and also seem to be quite opposed to much innovation in Christian faith or practice. Thus the glimpses of hymnic devotion to Christ in these books may in fact preserve customs much earlier than the documents themselves.

In evaluating the evidence from Revelation, we should also note the concern about worship in this book where readers are warned against worshiping the beast and dragon (13:4–18; 14:9–12; 19:20–21), are cautioned to worship God alone (14:6–7), and where the seer is twice told that he is not to worship even the angel who shows him the visions (19:10; 22:8–9). In view of the strict concern about cultic experimentation reflected in the last two passages, one can reasonably assume that the sort of devotion given to "the Lamb" in his visions reflected long-standing devotional practices in the Christian groups with which the author was familiar. Given the author's rich familiarity with the Jewish apocalyptic tradition, it is likely that John either was a Jewish Christian or at least had received influences from some Jewish-Christian group. In either case, the author probably reflects attitudes and practices much earlier than the actual writing and familiar to at least some forms of Jewish Christianity.[36]

A perusal of the New Testament hymns to Christ will show variations in emphasis and in linguistic features, probably indicative of various situations in which the hymns were composed, and also certain similarities in content and intention. They all celebrate Christ as the supreme agent of God, whether in creation (e.g., Col. 1:15-17; Heb. 1:3; John 1:1-3), earthly obedience (Phil. 2:5-8) and redemptive suffering (Rev. 5:9-10), or eschatological triumph (Phil. 2:9-11; Col. 1:20). In short, and most important, they show that the devotional life of early Christianity involved the hymnic celebration of the risen Christ in the corporate worship setting. This is a clear indication of the binitarian shape of early Christian devotion, most likely from the earliest years of the movement.

Prayer to Christ

We now turn to the evidence concerning prayer customs and related matters.[37] First, note that in the New Testament, true to its Jewish religious matrix, early Christian prayer is characteristically directed to God "the Father." Paul's references—near the opening of his letters—to his prayers for his churches are illustrative (e.g., Rom. 1:8-10; 1 Cor. 1:4; 2 Cor. 1:3-4; Phil. 1:3-5; 1 Thess. 1:2-3; Philemon 4). Note also his appeal in Rom. 15:30-33 that his readers should join him in prayer to God for the success of his trip to Jerusalem.

Other references indicate that the heavenly Christ was also addressed directly in prayer. There is the well-known account of Stephen the martyr: in his last moments he cries out, "Lord Jesus, receive my spirit," and then, "Lord, do not hold this sin against them" (Acts 7:59-60). Less frequently noticed as possible evidence of prayer to Christ is Acts 1:24, where the assembled followers of Jesus implore the "Lord" (*kyrios*) to show them which of two candidates is to succeed Judas Iscariot as one of the apostles. Admittedly, it is difficult to be fully sure who is being addressed here, but in view of the contextual reference to "the Lord Jesus" (1:21) and the emphasis that the risen Christ has been made "Lord" (2:34-36), it is a good possibility that we are to take 1:24 as a prayer to the risen "Lord Jesus."[38]

Another important passage is 2 Cor. 12:2-10, where Paul says that he "besought the Lord" three times (v. 8) concerning a personal affliction ("a thorn...in the flesh, a messenger of Satan") which was given him (by God) to keep him humble in the face of his many revelations and visions. This too is almost certainly an example of (repeated!) prayerful petition of the exalted Christ. "The Lord" replies, "My grace is sufficient for you, for my power is made perfect in weakness"; and Paul's following comments—that he will therefore boast of his weaknesses so that "the power of Christ may rest upon me" and that "for the sake of Christ" he is then content in all his troubles (12:9b-10)—make it likely that the one addressed and the one who replied was Christ.

In other Pauline passages prayer to Christ seems to be reflected in prayer-like expressions such as "grace and peace" greetings common at the beginning of his letters and in the benedictions at their end. Examples of the former are Rom. 1:7; 1 Cor. 1:3; 2 Cor. 1:2; Gal. 1:3-4; Phil. 1:2; and Philemon 3, where there is the liturgical-sounding formula, "Grace to you and peace from God our [or "the"] Father and the [or "our"] Lord Jesus Christ."[39] Pauline benedictions usually invoke the "grace of the Lord Jesus Christ" upon his churches (e.g., Rom. 16:20b; 1 Cor. 16:23; Gal. 6:18; 1 Thess. 5:28; Philemon 25), but in 2 Cor. 13:14 this is expanded to include the invocation also of "the love of God and the fellowship of the Holy Spirit." That these expressions are to be taken as genuine prayers is confirmed by 1 Thess. 3:11-13, where in a similar form of expression "our God and Father himself and our Lord Jesus" are implored both to allow Paul to visit the Thessalonian church again and to bless the believers richly so that they are prepared for the return of Christ.

One should not try to avoid the force of these passages, as Bultmann did, by claiming that prayer directly to Christ was made only "outside of formal, liturgical worship...in the personal lives of individuals."[40] The distinction is facile for several reasons. First, it appears to demand the assumption that as early as Paul's ministry in the 50s there was such a thing as a "formal, liturgical worship" and that there was a conscious distinction between prayer permissible in such a setting and private prayer. This is, however, plainly anachronistic. Paul's treatment of problems in the gatherings of the Corinthian church (1 Corinthians 11—14), where he tries merely to require elementary rules of decorum and politeness (e.g., 14:23-33), reflects a liturgical procedure of great, even troublesome, flexibility.[41] There is some evidence of the use of traditional liturgical expressions but hardly the fixed pattern of worship that Bultmann appears to have assumed.

Second, the set formulaic phrasing in Paul's "grace and peace" letter greetings and in the benedictions with which he usually closed his letters suggests that the invocation of Christ reflected in these expressions was a much more familiar and public aspect of Paul's Christian devotion than is suggested by Bultmann's distinction between public and personal prayer practice. These expressions have a sonorous tone and could very well be adapted from cultic formulae in use in the churches. Moreover, to adapt an observation by A. W. Wainwright, Paul's incorporation of these formulaic invocations and the prayer in 1 Thess. 3:11-13 into epistles intended for public reading as part of the "liturgical" activities of his churches means that the sort of distinction made by Bultmann was not recognized by Paul and probably not by his churches.[42]

Nor was prayer to Jesus in the corporate gathering an innovation in Paul's churches. This is clear not only on the basis of arguments already advanced here but also because of a fascinating fragment of early Christian Aramaic-speaking worship, the much-discussed *maranatha* (1 Cor. 16:22).[43]

1. It is now commonly accepted that *maranatha* is preserved untranslated in Paul's Greek letter to Greek-speaking Christians at Corinth because it must have been familiar to his readers already. This in turn suggests that the expression was regarded as a sacred cultic formula, even among Paul's churches, and was therefore treasured and preserved. Another interesting Aramaic term preserved in Paul's letters is *abba* (Rom. 8:15–16; Gal. 4:6), "Father," used as a way of addressing God in prayer. It should be noted that both *abba* and *maranatha* are fragments of Aramaic prayers, *abba* addressed to God and *maranatha* addressed to Christ.

2. The expression should probably be vocalized as *marana-tha*, perhaps *maran-atha*, most likely meaning "Our Lord (or O Lord) come!" and it is thus a petition that looks primarily toward the eschatological revelation of the "Lord" and the salvation of the elect. This is supported by Rev. 22:20, where most scholars think we have a Greek translation of the phrase, which can be rendered in English as "Come, Lord Jesus!" and where the context is clearly dominated by eschatological expectation.

3. As indicated already, *maranatha* is no doubt an invocation whose origin and setting was in the worship gathering of Aramaic-speaking Christians, probably as part of their eucharistic practice. This conclusion is supported by Paul's allusion to the association of the hope for the return of Christ with the eucharistic meal in 1 Cor. 11:26, "You proclaim the Lord's death until he comes." Also, in the *Didache*, a Christian document written in Greek and usually dated in the second century C.E. but widely regarded as preserving tradition of a much earlier time, *maranatha* appears in the prescriptions for celebrating Eucharist (10:6).

4. *Maranatha* is an invocation of the risen Christ and thus indicates that such a custom was a regular feature of the worship of the first Christian communities, that is, among Jewish Christians of Palestine. The assertion, first made by Bousset and then retracted but again taken up by Bultmann, that in the original Palestinian Christian churches *maranatha*

may have been directed to God and not to Christ has nothing to support it and must be regarded as a stratagem of desperation.[44]

5. The appeal to the exalted Christ as *maran* ("our Lord") in the expression reveals the use of the Aramaic term *marêh* ("Lord") as a christological title. Like the Greek term *kyrios*, this title has a breadth of usage in the surviving Aramaic texts relevant to the period of earliest Christianity and does not automatically indicate that the one addressed by the term is seen as "divine." The term is used sometimes, however, as a title for God in Aramaic Jewish writings of the time, and so use of it as a title for Christ could connote a view of him as likened to God. Against some earlier claims, nothing requires us to think that the title was not capable of this connotation.[45] As a matter of fact, there are good reasons for concluding that the use of *marêh* for Christ did connote the conviction that he had been made to share in divine glory and transcendence and therefore was to be reverenced in terms and actions characteristically reserved for God.

Recall that there is no indication that the reverence given to Christ in Paul's churches represented a major innovation or that Palestinian Jewish Christians objected to it. This, plus the facts that Paul's adherence to Christian faith must be traced back to the first few years of the new movement and that he had long associations with such Palestinian Christians as Barnabas, makes it reasonable to conclude that the devotional reverence of Christ that he promoted derived in all likelihood from the very earliest stages of Christianity. Finally, Christ was apparently addressed regularly as *marêh* ("lord") precisely in the cultic setting, the worship gatherings of Aramaic-speaking Christians. Such a setting for the use of the title surely makes the term much more than a title of respect. Modern students of linguistics know that context is most determinative for the meaning of terms, and full context involves the situation in which terms are used.

Summary. The evidence indicates that the heavenly Christ was regularly invoked and appealed to in prayer and that this practice began among Jewish Christians in an Aramaic-speaking setting, probably the first stratum of the Christian movement. And, as is true of the dominant place of Christ in hymns of the early Christian groups, this regularized place of Christ in such prayer is without parallel in Jewish groups.[46] This is not the same as the Jewish belief in the intercessory role of angels. I have already shown (chaps. 1 and 4) that there is no indication that the intercessory angels were the objects of similar cultic devotion in the gatherings of Jewish groups. The practice of prayers addressed to the risen Christ in early Christian meetings is thus further reason to regard their devotional life as a noteworthy mutation in the religious practice of Jewish monotheism.

The Name of Christ

Various practices of the earliest Christians involved the use of the name of Christ and are additional evidence of a strikingly prominent place of the risen Christ in their devotional life.[47] Perhaps the most familiar practice involving the name of Christ is the Christian initiatory rite of baptism.[48]

The practice of baptism must go back to the beginnings of the church, as does the understanding of the rite as done "in the name" of Jesus.[49] L. Hartman's examination of the Semitic background of such expressions led him to conclude that "into the name" of something or someone "introduces a fundamental reference, reason, purpose or capacity of something or of an action."[50] Thus, to describe baptism as done "into the name of Jesus" meant that Jesus "was the fundamental reference for the rite of baptism, and the phrase would be able to carry a rather substantial content, provided by the context."[51] Since baptism signaled both initiation into the redeemed community and forgiveness of sins, baptizing "into the name" of Jesus suggests that Jesus is seen as the one who assures forgiveness and participation in the eschatological salvation hoped for by the first believers.[52]

Now to have made Jesus the exclusive agent of divine redemption, though significant, may not have been completely different from the hopes connected with the heavenly Melchizedek at Qumran. But there seems to be something more remarkable and unprecedented in the standardized use of the name of Jesus in the initiatory rite of the groups of Jewish Christians. I know of no comparable use of the name of any redeemer figure in other Jewish groups of the time. Such a use of Jesus' name put him at the center of the initiation process and in a cultic setting. Thus, baptism "into the name" of Jesus is another example of the Jewish-Christian modification of Jewish monotheism constituted by the prominence given to the risen Christ in their devotional and cultic life.[53]

Another matter in connection with the practice of baptism is that of the references to calling "upon the name" of Jesus the Lord (Acts 9:14, 21; 22:16; 1 Cor. 1:2; Rom. 10:13).[54] The phrase is apparently derived originally from Old Testament passages that refer to calling "upon the Lord" (*Yahweh*; e.g., Gen. 12:8; 13:4; 21:23; 26:25; Pss. 99:6; 105:1; Joel

2:32).[55] In Acts 22:16, baptism and calling upon Jesus' name are linked. Also, Rom. 10:9-13 may provide further evidence of this link. Here we are told that salvation comes by confessing that "Jesus is Lord" and by believing that God has raised him from death. Then Paul summarizes this thought with a quotation from Joel 2:32: "Every one who calls upon the name of the Lord will be saved." The fact that the act of "calling upon the Lord" is linked with the faith and confession that bring salvation may mean that all were involved in early Christian initiation. Similarly, the description of the Corinthian Christians as "washed," "sanctified," and "justified in the name of the Lord Jesus Christ" (1 Cor. 6:11) may allude to their baptism, and if so, it is additional evidence of the connection of "calling upon the name" with Christian initiation.

On the other hand, W. Kramer insisted that "calling upon the Lord" (Jesus) related initially to the acclamation of Christ in early Christian gatherings, perhaps in the form of such "confessions" as "Jesus is Lord" and from this "came to be applied to other characteristic activities of the Church such as baptism."[56] I am not persuaded that we are able to chart the development of the practice of calling upon Jesus' name with this precision, nor is it necessary here to do so. Kramer is correct in saying that "calling upon the Lord," whether done as part of baptisms or in other ways, took place in the worship of the church.[57] Thus the phrase refers to appeals to, and acclamations of, Christ as "Lord" as a regular part of the liturgical life of the early gatherings of Christians, further indication of the prominent place of the heavenly Christ in their corporate devotion. The description of Christians simply as those who "call on the name of our Lord Jesus Christ" (1 Cor. 1:2) may mean that the phrase had by that time already become a blanket description of the whole of Christian religious life, especially in the worship setting.[58] This verse alone is powerful evidence of the enormously prominent place of the risen Christ in Christian devotion of the first few decades.[59]

In 1 Cor. 5:1-5, we have another important reference to "the name of the Lord Jesus." Here Paul requires the Corinthians to assemble and "deliver to Satan" an unrepentant man guilty of a gross immorality "for the destruction of the flesh, that his spirit may be saved in the day of the Lord Jesus" (v. 5). It is difficult to be sure whether the phrase "in the name of the Lord Jesus" is to be connected with Paul's pronouncement of judgment in the matter (so the RSV translation), with the assembling of the church, or with the act of delivering the guilty man over to Satan. I depart from the RSV translation here and connect the phrase with the actions the church is to take. Since the assembling and the purpose for which the Christians were to assemble are clearly linked, it may be that the phrase applies to both. This seems to be confirmed by the phrase "with the power of the Lord Jesus" in v. 4, which describes the assembly and/or the action of delivering the man over to Satan. The "power" (*dynamis*) and the "name" of the Lord Jesus here seem to be closely associated. I suggest that "the name of the Lord Jesus" was to be used in pronouncing the man's judgment, as a way of invoking the power and presence of the heavenly Christ which makes the church disciplinary action fully effective in the spiritual sphere.

This use of "the name" is similar in some respects to the magical use of names of deities and angels in spells, curses, exorcisms and other healings that were widely practiced in the ancient world. Even more similar to such practices are the references to use of the name of Jesus in miracles such as are accounted in Acts 3:1-6. But the actions I have dealt with here are somewhat different.

First, unlike the magical use of various names the Christian invocation of the name of the Lord Jesus was a public, corporate act, part of "official" Christian devotion. Second, the Christian invocation of Jesus was not one element in the invocation of a string of deities. Unlike the magical texts, invocation of Jesus was made to the exclusion of all other figures, except of course God the Father. That is, the uses of the name of the Lord Jesus happened in a movement committed to the strict monotheistic tradition and thus represent a major modification of that tradition but a modification that did not involve a general openness to any and all divine figures, such as in the magical texts.

Finally, all the evidence suggests that "calling upon the name" of the risen Christ had its origin in the earliest Christian groups and must therefore be seen as an innovation in Jewish monotheistic practice by members of that tradition. The *maranatha* phrase is only one of several reasons for the conclusion that the acclamation and invocation of the heavenly Christ as Lord cannot be denied to this earliest stratum of Christianity.

The notion that earliest Christians only saw Christ as "Lord" in an eschatological sense, as the one who would bring future salvation, and that therefore they would not have related to him as Lord of the present and Lord of their gatherings surely must now be given a decent burial. W. Thüsing has shown that the present exalted status and significance of the risen Christ was in fact inseparably linked with the conviction that he was the coming Lord of the eschaton.[60] And D. Aune's valuable study shows that in the worship gatherings of ancient Jewish sects such as earliest

Christianity eschatological hopes were characteristically seen as "realized" and that the horizons of future and present merged.[61]

In short, in these references to the use of the name of the risen Lord, we have another glimpse of the nature of the distinctive devotional pattern of Christianity, a pattern that originated so early in the movement that it must be seen as a mutation in Jewish monotheism.

The Lord's Supper

The early Christians included sacred meals in their worship gatherings.[62] Only a few relatively uncontroversial matters concerning this practice are relevant to my investigation.

First, 1 Cor. 11:23–26 is proof that some sort of Christian sacred meal tradition goes back earlier than Paul's conversion to the Christian movement. It is well known that the terms translated "received" (*paralambanō*) and "delivered" (*paradidōmi*) in v. 23 refer to the passing on of fixed tradition and that equivalent Hebrew terms were used to describe the handing on of Jewish traditions.[63] Whatever variations there were in sacred wording used at such meals (cf., e.g., Mark 14:22–25 and Luke 22:14–20 with this passage) and whatever variations there were in other aspects of the way the meal was held, this passage indicates that a sacred meal was held with a regularity in the gatherings of early Christians during the first years of the Christian movement.

This means that we must attribute some such practice even to Jewish-Christian groups of the first decade. Further, the sort of ceremony described here by Paul as derived from earlier Christians apparently had as its purposes the setting forth of Christ's redemptive death and the expectation of his eschatological victory (esp. v. 26).[64] This means that this glimpse, among the earliest we have, of the corporate gatherings of Jewish Christians shows us another example of the prominent place of the risen Christ in their devotional practice. It is significant that Paul calls the meal "the Lord's supper" (*kyriakon deipnon*, v. 20). We cannot say with full assurance that some form of "Lord's supper" was always a part of Christian worship gatherings in the earliest decades, but some such Christ-centered meal was in all likelihood a familiar and normal aspect of corporate Christian religious life.

Once again we have indication of the reshaping of monotheistic devotion involved in early Christianity and another example of a devotional innovation for which we do not have a parallel in Jewish groups of the time. Common meals, yes, as at Qumran. But meals devoted expressly to celebrating and perhaps communing with God's heavenly "chief agent" are not found in the records of ancient Jewish devotion.

Confessing Jesus

Another important indication of early Christian devotion is the practice of "confessing" (*homologeō*) Jesus. The verb is used both in Paul (Rom. 10:9) and in other New Testament writings (e.g., Matt. 10:32; John 9:22; 1 John 4:2-3, 15), indicating that it was a widely shared part of early Christian vocabulary. These passages suggest that the term applied both to owning up to one's faith before others who did not share it (e.g., Matt. 10:32) and to affirming one's faith in gatherings of believers (e.g., Rom. 10:9). There may also be traces of such actions in passages that do not use the technical term "confess." Thus most scholars think that Rom. 1:3-4 offers a glimpse of a "pre-Pauline" confession in which Jesus is acclaimed as "seed of David" (Messiah) and "Son of God." And passages in Acts that picture the preaching of the early Christians may likewise reflect early confessional practice (Acts 2:38; 5:42; 9:22; 10:36). The exact wording of the confessions shows some variation in these passages, specifically with regard to the title by which Jesus is acclaimed: "Lord" (Rom. 10:9), "Son of God" (Rom. 1:3-4; 1 John 4:15), and "Christ" (e.g., Acts 9:22).

We have observed that many scholars focus on one or more of these christological titles, but for our purposes the more relevant matter is the *action* of "confessing" or acclaiming Jesus as a regular aspect of the religious devotion of early Christians.[65] To cite only our earliest references to such a practice, Paul in Rom. 10:9-13 makes confessing "Jesus is Lord" the verbal mark of Christian faith, in a context which as we have already noted seems to refer to Christian initiation. Confession of the same claim in the worship setting is reflected in 1 Cor. 12:1-3, where Paul makes it an indication of the work of the Holy Spirit.[66] And in Phil. 2:9-11, where we have the conclusion of the early hymn that Paul is believed to have quoted, all spheres of creation are pictured in a scene of eschatological triumph making the same sort of acclamation that characterized early Christian groups.

In reference to the *maranatha* phrase, we have found reason to conclude that the invocation and acclamation of the risen Christ, including the use of the Aramaic term for "Lord," can be traced back to the Aramaic churches—a striking innovation in Jewish religious practice. It is undisputed that the early Jewish Christians acclaimed, and proclaimed, Jesus as "the Messiah" (Christ), and there is evidence of the use of other honorific terms, such as "servant" (*pais*, Acts 4:27, 30). In varying ways, these titles all present the risen Christ, even in the earliest forms of Christian faith, as the divinely chosen one through whom the eschatological hope of salvation is to be realized and with whom now one must come to terms. All this means that it is most probable that already in these earliest years "confessing" Jesus was an established aspect of Christian devotion. It served to distinguish Christians from other examples of religious practice. This distinction consisted not only in claiming an exalted and exclusive status for the crucified Jesus but also in "confessing" God's chief agent, indicating that he held a regular and prominent place in their devotional life.

In contrast, the Qumran sect also apparently believed that they were the elect and that the rest of Israel had gone astray following wicked leaders. They too referred to a heavenly figure (Michael/Melchizedek) whom they expected would be God's agent of redemption in the eschaton. But nothing in their surviving writings suggests that they identified themselves to others as those who "confessed" Melchizedek or that they made acclamation of such a figure a requirement of membership or a regular part of their worship gatherings. The Qumran sect celebrated the liturgy offered by angels in heaven and perhaps sang of the future victory to be won under the leadership of the heavenly Melchizedek, but this does not make angels an object of cultic veneration in the way the risen Christ was in early Christian groups. Thus it is not enough to say that the early Christians gave Christ a more prominent place in their religious life simply because he was a specific figure while other Jewish groups awaited a Messiah or other figure whose identity they did not yet know. The Qumran community were sure that they knew their eschatological redeemer, Michael/Melchizedek, but this did not lead to a binitarian type of religious devotion such as we seem to have in early Christianity.

In contrast with the Qumran group, we have an interesting illustration of the novelty involved in the early Christian confession of the risen Jesus and yet another example of the distinctive shape of their religious life.

Prophecy and the Risen Jesus

Finally, one additional feature of early Christian devotion must be considered: prophecy uttered as the words of the heavenly Christ.[67] Revelation 1:17—3:22 is an undeniable instance of an early Christian prophet, John, giving the words of Christ in the first-person form. There has been debate over whether this form of Christian oracle was exceptional or typical.[68] Elsewhere in the New Testament we have prophecy attributed to the

Holy Spirit (e.g., Acts 11:27; 21:10-11), but Aune seems correct in insisting that the author of Revelation could have hoped to have his book accepted as authentic only if "his modes of speech were such that they would be recognized as characteristically prophetic."[69]

If this is correct reasoning, then we must assume that prophetic address presented as coming from the risen Lord was one acceptable form of prophetic address and was probably a relatively common feature of early Christian gatherings. And this, I suggest, is significant for early Christian religious devotion. If a person was able to command the attention and acceptance of early Christian groups and be regarded as a true prophet by convincing them that he or she spoke the words of the risen Christ, this means that these groups gave to the words of this Lord the same sort of authority as they accorded to the prophetic address of God himself or of his "Spirit." Note that we are referring to Jewish Christians, probably in Palestine, as the groups among whom such Christian prophetic practices began. Thus we have groups, nourished by the Jewish monotheistic commitment and its traditional concern about false prophecy (e.g., Deuteronomy 13), which make no functional distinction between prophetic directions from God or from his chief agent, the exalted Jesus, and grant room for prophetic words of the latter figure as a formal part of their devotional life. Once again there does not seem to have been such an equivalent practice among other Jewish groups.

Conclusion. I submit that the foregoing devotional innovations support my contentions *(a)* that early Christian devotion can be accurately described as binitarian in shape, with a prominent place being given to the risen Christ alongside God, and *(b)* that this binitarian shape is distinctive in the broad and diverse Jewish monotheistic tradition that was the immediate background of the first Christians, among whom these devotional practices had their beginnings.

CAUSES OF THE
CHRISTIAN MUTATION

Just as languages undergo change and development, often including the disappearance of some dialects and the emergence of others, so religious traditions change and develop, and sometimes new variations within religious traditions appear. In the case of such a development as the binitarian nature of early Christian religious devotion, it is natural and correct to look for some of the seeds in the mother tradition, Jewish monotheism of the Greco-Roman period. I hope to have shown that the ancient Jewish tradition included the concept of divine agency, evidenced by the speculation and interest in chief agent figures given the chief position next to God himself, and that this widespread acceptance of a chief agent position in heaven provided the early Christians with important conceptual resources for accommodating the exalted Christ.

But the Jewish divine agency tradition, however much one might think of it as the seed of some form of binitarianism, was not in itself sufficient cause of the true binitarian devotion that suddenly and pervasively developed in the early Christian groups. Here I wish to outline what I think we can reasonably posit as the factors that produced the Christian mutation in Jewish monotheistic devotion. I suggest that these factors are all aspects of the religious experiences of earliest Christianity and that the new development in religious devotion we have been examining was the result of religious experiences and their aftermath. The result was that the early Christians had an altered standpoint from which to reinterpret many elements of their Jewish tradition, including the limits of monotheism.[70]

The Ministry of Jesus

In chronological order, the first factor that must be considered is the ministry of Jesus himself and its likely effect upon his immediate followers. Given the effort expended by so many in the attempt to recover with some precision the nature of his message and the specific claims, if any, that he may have made for himself, it is disappointing to find that there is so little confidence shared in the ability to be precise about these matters.[71]

It is commonly granted that Jesus exercised a kind of prophetic authority with regard to his followers and his message and that this prophetic activity made his own person and significance unavoidably prominent. Mark 8:38, for instance, reflects this prominence, making the hearers' response and loyalty to Jesus determinative for participation in eschatological salvation. Indeed, one might say that the central issue in the ministry of Jesus was the legitimacy of his prophetic authority, for he seems to have rested all that he did upon the firm conviction that he had been sent by God. By the reckoning of most scholars, Jesus' ministry brought on a conflict with various authorities, obviously the Roman governor who crucified him and most probably certain Jewish leaders, such as the priestly leaders. That is, for his followers, Jesus' ministry provoked a crisis that had to do with his validity as one sent by God. Indeed, given the apparent significance he attached to his mission, we could restate this crisis as precisely the question of whether he was the one now sent by God, for Jesus seems to have made response to his ministry the key factor in preparing for eschatological judgment.

In short, by the end of his ministry, Jesus had generated among his followers the conviction that he held an honored place in the plan of God, as the eschatological spokesman of the final divine word. But a further crisis occurred for the followers of Jesus—their master was crucified. Thus both the firm authority with which Jesus conducted himself and the rejection and humiliation he suffered in death combined to make the question of his person the central matter for his followers.

If, as some think, Jesus distinguished between himself and the future "Son of man" figure who would conduct the eschatological judgment and who would actually bring redemption to the elect,[72] then for Jesus' followers there would also have been another, unidentified future figure of supposedly common expectation to reckon with. But whether Jesus' followers expected another, distinct figure to act as eschatological judge, who might therefore be thought of as God's "chief agent," the burning question for them was Jesus' own legitimacy as representative for God. So the earliest form of Christian faith that meets us after the crucifixion is one that presents the risen Jesus as the chief agent above all others and the one to be sent again by God to bring eschatological redemption. I submit that this conviction could not easily have arisen, in view of Jesus' crucifixion, without something new and powerful in effect having happened to Jesus' followers. But, in turn, the exalted position of the crucified Jesus in the faith of the first Christians cannot be understood adequately without the prior effect upon them of his own ministry and its crisis concerning his personal validity as spokesman for God.

Thus a key factor that must be taken into account in understanding the rise of early Christian devotion to Jesus is the pre-Easter ministry of Jesus and its effect upon his followers. In all subsequent religious experiences of the post-Easter period, the early Christians of the first decades remained sure that they were having further experiences of, and fuller insight into the present and future significance of, the same one who had taught and led his first followers in Galilee—the one who had suffered crucifixion under the charge of claiming to be a king (Mark 15:26). This firm conviction of continuity between the man Jesus and the exalted heavenly figure of the post-Easter faith and visions can only mean that in his own lifetime Jesus had made a powerful and lasting impression.

Easter and Afterward

Whatever is thought today of the accounts of the empty tomb and the first appearances of the risen Christ to his followers, one thing can be stated with full confidence. Shortly after Jesus' execution, at least some of his followers became convinced that he had been delivered by God from the hold of death.[73] But not only this, they were also quite sure that Jesus had been exalted to heavenly glory and chosen as God's chief agent of eschatological salvation, probably involving his exaltation over all other authorities in God's hierarchy.

This of course is remarkable enough, though not perhaps entirely beyond the imagination. The unexpected development is the early emergence of the risen Jesus at the center of religious devotion, next to God, in the early Christian groups. That is, this particular "chief agent" of this particular Jewish sect quickly became the object of the sort of religious devotion normally reserved for God alone. This in turn suggests that the early religious experiences of the Jewish-Christian groups involved factors that would have led to this development. Their experiences of the risen and exalted Jesus included visions of him sharing the glory of God and participating so directly and fully in God's glory and majesty that their early devotional practices were the only appropriate responses. In short, early Christians underwent actual experiences which they perceived as communicating the resurrection and exaltation of Jesus.

The postresurrection appearances recounted in the New Testament Gospels are disappointingly quiet about the details of what the disciples saw. They recognized the figure as the same Jesus they had followed, but we are told little more. Yet perhaps there are glimpses of the nature and importance of such experiences in these narratives. For example, Luke 24:25-27, 36-49 makes such experiences of the risen Christ the basis for the new ability to see that the Old Testament predicts the sufferings and exaltation of Jesus and the message of forgiveness to be preached in his name. In the light of our interest here in chief agent figures to whom God has committed the leading place in the exercise of his rule, it is noteworthy that the well-known ending of Matthew (28:16-20) has the risen Christ inform his disciples, "All authority in heaven and on earth has been given to me." These passages reflect the redactional work of the Evangelists but may also preserve for us the creative effect of the early postresurrection encounters of Jesus' followers with the exalted Christ, creative effects that included a new hermeneutical standpoint from which to reinterpret the Old Testament and a heightened sense of the place of the risen Jesus in the divine plan.

We have another important reference to a vision of the risen Christ in the famous account of Stephen's death in Acts 7:55-56: the martyr is pictured as seeing the heavens open to reveal "the glory of God, and Jesus standing at the right hand of God." Whatever the value of the account as a report of the death of Stephen, it is in all likelihood an accurate reflection of the sort of visionary experiences that were formative of earliest Christian belief and devotion.[74] This sort of experience is formally different from the more familiar resurrection appearances narrated in the Gospels (and in Acts 1:1-11) in that Christ is seen in heaven rather than on earth. But it is clear that the early Christians thought of Jesus both as victorious over death and as elevated to transcendent honor and authority before God. I suggest that visions of Jesus in heavenly exaltation were the major impetus for the latter conviction.

The earliest references to encounters with the risen Christ come in Paul's letters. Although the details of what Paul himself experienced are sparse, nevertheless a few suggestions are possible.[75] First, Paul insists that what he saw was Jesus (1 Cor. 9:1; 15:8), and thus we must begin by understanding Paul's Damascus road experience (and, no doubt, subsequent "visions and revelations of the Lord," 2 Cor. 12:1) as involving a vision of the risen and exalted Christ himself. Second, in what is probably another reference to the same initial, visionary experience (Gal. 1:12, 15-16), Paul uses the term "revelation" (*apokalypsis*, 1:12) to define it and says that it consisted in God "revealing" (*apokalyptō*, v. 16) "his Son" to (or in, *en emoi*) Paul. This suggests that he may have understood his experience by means of the apocalyptic tradition with its references to visions of heaven and heavenly beings. It also indicates that something about the vision itself apparently communicated Christ's honorific status as God's Son.[76] In the light of Paul's initial opposition to the Christian message, whatever convinced him to take an entirely different view of Jesus would have to have been something potent and transformative.[77]

This brings us to a few other passages that can be taken as more specific hints of what it was that Paul saw. In Phil. 3:20-21, Paul refers to Christ's "glorious body" or, alternatively, his "body of glory" (*sōmati tēs doxēs autou*) as the pattern for the resurrected and changed bodies of the elect in the future. It seems reasonable to conclude that this description of Christ's resurrection body was based on Paul's own vision of it and that Paul therefore "saw" the crucified Jesus in a body radiant with the bright glory of God.[78]

This conclusion is confirmed in 2 Cor. 3:4—4:6, where Paul appears to draw upon his own revelatory experience to describe the illumination accorded to believers in the gospel. In this passage,[79] Paul contrasts the fading glory reflected in Moses' face (3:7-9) with the lasting and superior glory (3:10-11) connected with the gospel. At the end of the passage (4:4-6), an apparent allusion to his own first experience of the risen Christ, Paul refers to seeing "the light of the gospel of the glory of Christ, who is the likeness of God" (4:4) and says that God "has shone in our hearts to give the light of the knowledge of the glory of God in the face of Christ" (4:6). These verses are autobiographical glimpses and suggest that Paul's conversion vision involved a sight of Christ glorious in appearance, bearing the bright glory of God in unique fullness. Paul's reference to Jesus as "the Lord of glory" in 1 Cor. 2:8 likewise probably draws upon his own visionary experience. As S. Kim has concluded,

> So the risen Christ must have appeared to Paul accompanied by the radiance of light which was perceived by him as the divine glory.[80]

Probably the latest vision of the exalted Jesus in the New Testament is given in Rev. 1:12—3:22. This differs from all the other passages considered in the detail with which the writer describes what he saw (1:12-16). It has often been noted that this description of the glorious Christ seems to draw upon the visions of Ezekiel and Daniel for its imagery, and the general similarity is clear.[81] Another difference between this vision and the others is the lengthy verbatim speech attributed to Christ by the seer. This passage raises several questions.

First, for some there is the question of whether the experience narrated in this passage is a real one or purely a literary device of the writer. Whether this particular experience really happened or not, the fact that the writer relays it as the basis for sending his prophetic book to the churches addressed in Revelation 2—3 indicates that such visionary experiences were an accepted part of the Christian tradition of the recipients. That is, this vision of Christ is evidence that such experiences were a known feature of the religious life of early Christians. The writer could hope to have his visionary account accredited only if visions of the heavenly Christ were not strange in the religious tradition of his first readers. Therefore we may use his vision narrative as indication of the nature of some of these experiences.

Second, the commonly accepted date of Revelation, near the end of the first century C.E., raises the question of how well the vision reflects earlier Christian visionary experiences. There is good reason to take Revelation as building upon and reflecting a conservative Christian tradition that takes us back in time prior to the probable date of its composition. I contend that the vision scene here is a reliable indication of the sort of experiences that early Christian religious life included, especially in worship gatherings, where visions and prophetic addresses of the risen Lord would most likely have happened.[82]

I now wish to make some observations about the actual vision and words of the heavenly Jesus given here. The visual description of Christ in Rev. 1:12-16 resembles the descriptions of visions of chief angels (see chap. 4) and portrays Christ in majestic and awesome images. In Rev. 1:13, he may be associated or identified with the "one like a son of man" in Dan. 7:13 to whom is given all authority in the divine plan. Other features, such as his white hair (1:14; cf. Dan. 7:9) and his mighty voice (1:15; cf. Ezek. 1:24), however, are allusions to visions of God and connote Jesus' participation in divine glory.

The words of Christ, too, are significant. He identifies himself with the crucified Jesus (1:18) but also makes powerful claims for himself. The striking assertion that he is "the first and the last" echoes Old Testament passages that refer to God himself (e.g., Isa. 44:6; 48:12). And the claim to hold "the keys of Death and Hades" also seems to indicate a direct participation in the power of God. Then there are the addresses to the churches (2:1—3:22), where Christ himself passes judgment upon the conduct of his followers, ordering repentance or giving commendation, again exercising the divine prerogative.

These observations are sufficient to show the dramatic way that Christ is communicated in the vision. Although we should allow for a variety in the types of visionary experiences in the early decades of the church, this scene is probably representative of some such experiences. The vision of Christ in Revelation may be dependent upon a long tradition of such experiences as well as upon several decades of christological reflection in Christian circles. I suggest however that in the earliest stages of the Christian movement such experiences were not the simple products of prior christological convictions but were often the generative cause of christological convictions. That is, Rev. 1:12—3:22 may illustrate the sort of powerful, indeed overwhelming (1:17), visionary-prophetic experience that produced the firm conviction that Jesus had been made to share so fully in divine prerogatives and heavenly glory that he was to be included in the devotional life of the elect and given the sort of veneration in their groups previously appropriate only for God.

Visions of the exalted Jesus and prophetic words from him may not, by any means, exhaust the range of early religious experiences that provoked and shaped the christological convictions of the first Christians. But the sort of visions we have dealt with here were surely among the most powerful in effect, both upon recipients and upon those to whom the experiences were related. If such experiences happened in the context of corporate worship, something that is most likely in many cases,[83] then the effect of them upon other believers present would have been more immediate and more powerful.

In short, one of the most likely causes of the new mutation in Jewish monotheistic tradition that early Christian binitarian devotion represents was this sort of religious experience. Rather than trying to account for such a development as the veneration of Jesus by resort to vague suggestions of ideational borrowing from the cafeteria of heroes and demigods of the Greco-Roman world, scholars should pay more attention to this sort of religious experience of the first Christians. It is more likely that the initial and main reason that this particular chief agent (Jesus) came to share in the religious devotion of this particular Jewish group (the earliest Christians) is that they had visions and other experiences that communicated the risen and exalted Christ and that presented him in such unprecedented and superlative divine glory that they felt compelled to respond devotionally as they did.

One final aspect of their experiences merits attention. These experiences of the exalted Christ which generated such firm convictions about his heavenly status also undoubtedly communicated the conviction that it had been God's pleasure to install Jesus in such glory. We remember that early Christian devotion to Jesus was not a cultus of its own. Jesus is praised and acclaimed as their Lord "to the glory of God the Father" (Phil. 2:9–11). Devotion to Jesus did not involve confusing him with God or making Jesus a second god. The Christian enlargement of monotheistic devotional practice to include the exalted Christ seems to have been motivated by the belief that to have done otherwise would have been to disobey the one God whom they sought to obey.

This allows us to be more precise about one probable aspect of the experiences in question. In all likelihood they involved not just seeing Jesus in heavenly glory but also visions of him in connection with God or some symbol of God such as the divine throne in such a fashion that God's pleasure in Christ's status was communicated along with the understanding that Christ's position did not threaten the uniqueness of God. The account of Stephen's vision of Jesus "standing at the right hand of God" (Acts 7:55–56), though dependent on Ps. 110:1a, may reflect just the sort of experience we are to imagine. Or there is John's heavenly vision in Revelation 5, where Christ as the Lamb appears before the "one seated on the throne" and is hailed as the uniquely worthy one to execute God's eschatological plan of judgment and redemption (Rev. 5:5–12). Such experiences as these were in all likelihood among the stimuli that shaped the new faith in its earliest years. Initial visions and other such experiences were reinforced in subsequent years by similar experiences that seem to have formed a regular part of Christian worship gatherings in the first century especially (1 Cor. 14:26).

This explanation of the Christian mutation, as based on religious experiences that had creative effects upon the interpretation of the inherited tradition, is not usually offered in much scholarly writing on Christian origins. But such an explanation, I suggest, not only accords with the information we have about the nature of early Christian groups but also helps to account for the sudden and rapid development of christological beliefs and Christ-oriented devotional practices within the first decades of the Christian movement. The movement took several more centuries to come to terms intellectually and philosophically with its basic convictions and its devotional practices in framing a doctrine of God and Christ as reflected in the Nicene Creed.[84] But the fundamental Christian conviction concerning the heavenly significance of Jesus seems to have appeared without any such traceable process of long ideational development.[85] Such a sudden and rapid development of religious beliefs is not without parallel in history, and where they have happened, religious experiences of a powerful leader figure or of a core group or groups have been very important as causes. The modern Pentecostal movement, with its distinctive doctrine concerning the significance of tongue-speaking (glossolalia) is only one more recent example of the creative impact of potent religious experiences in shaping doctrines and in generating new religious movements.[86]

Opposition to the New Movement

The final factor deserving of consideration is the probable effect of opposition to the new movement, especially from the "mother tradition," the Jewish religious tradition of the time. The Jewish concern for the uniqueness of God probably led many pious Jews to regard with suspicion aspects of the Jewish-Christian devotion to Jesus. This in turn would have required these early Christians, who saw themselves as sharing the same monotheistic commitment, either to soften their emphasis upon the heavenly glory of Jesus or to justify more fully and firmly their conviction about his significance. It is safe to say that some Jewish Christians took one course of action and some took the other.

Among those who felt compelled to take the latter course of action, such as Paul the Apostle, there is clear evidence of a defense of Jesus' status that included reinterpretation of traditional scripture texts (such as Psalms 8 and 110) and the appropriation for Jesus of traditional titles ("Lord") and prerogatives most characteristically associated with God.[87] Basically such Jewish Christians seem to have felt required to formulate a view of Christ that justified the devotion to him to which their religious experiences drove them. They also maintained firmly the overarching superiority and uniqueness of the one God and their traditional religious orientation to him. This, I suggest, is essentially the view of Christ and essentially the devotional intention that is indicated in Paul's letters and characteristically reflected throughout the rest of the New Testament. That is, this form of monotheistic devotion resulted initially not from the supposed influence of pagan spirituality and was not simply an imitation of the honor given to various cult deities of the Greco-Roman environment. Primarily and initially, this binitarian devotion arose from the combination of the force of the religious experiences of early Christians and the monotheistic "constraints" of the Jewish "mother tradition."[88] Ironically, opposition and criticism from other pious Jews probably played a significant role in the early Christian reflection upon the exalted Jesus and may have been a key factor in helping to shape a form of religious devotion that is best described as a mutation in Jewish monotheism. The earliest Christians needed to see and show themselves faithful to one God. They also needed to find whatever justification they could within their inherited tradition for the striking and innovative attention they felt compelled to give to the risen Jesus. They did not always succeed in convincing other Jews of the legitimacy of their views and practices, but the need to try to do so or to have defenses against Jewish critics is one important factor to reckon with in understanding the early development of Christian devotion.[89]

SUMMARY

The argument of this chapter can be summarized as follows.

1. At the earliest stages, Christian experience of and reflection upon the risen Jesus were probably influenced by and drew upon the divine agency category. Jesus was experienced and understood as exalted to the position of God's chief agent. The divine agency tradition was important

in providing the resources for accommodating a heavenly figure second only to God in authority and glory. More important initially than the Jewish interest in any one chief agent figure was the basic idea that God might have some such figure in this sort of role in the exercise of his creative and/or saving plan.

2. Rapidly and at an early date, Christian experience of and reflection upon Jesus produced what must be regarded as a mutation in the treatment of such chief agent figures and in Jewish monotheistic devotion. This innovation was first manifested in the devotional life of early Christian groups, in which the risen Christ came to share in some of the devotional and cultic attention normally reserved for God: the early Christian mutation in Jewish monotheism was a religious devotion with a certain binitarian shape. The earliest and key innovation in Christianity was not the use of certain honorific titles or other christological rhetoric. Rather, it was the nature of the religious praxis of early and influential groups.[90]

3. This innovation in religious devotion can, with high probability, be traced back to the earliest stages of Christianity, including the Aramaic-speaking churches. Devotional developments, as well as doctrinal developments, were not uniform in nature or pace, but among at least some groups of the earliest Jewish Christians the sort of distinctive development we have discussed here seems to have been accepted. Thus the binitarian devotion of early Christianity was an innovation initiated by Jewish Christians loyal to their ancestral concern for the uniqueness of God.[91]

4. Prominent among the causes of this mutation in Jewish monotheism were powerful religious experiences of the early believers in which Jesus was experienced as exalted to heavenly glory and legitimated by God himself as an object of their devotion.

Conclusions

The specific results of this study have been stated at several points and thus I will conclude by offering a few reflections on the study of Christian origins that arise from the results of this work.

First, chronological indications should be observed carefully. Of course, it is difficult to be precise in chronological matters connected with Christian origins, such as the exact date of many New Testament writings. But where the evidence permits us to be relatively precise, as is the case, for example, with the undisputed letters of Paul, we should treat this evidence seriously. All along, the evidence in the Pauline letters pointed to an origin of the cultic veneration of Jesus in the earliest years of the Christian movement and among Christians from an undeniably Jewish background, including Aramaic-speaking believers. Some earlier history of religions researchers apparently found it difficult to reconcile this with their notions of what could be expected of Jewish Christians. Thus they attributed the origin of the cultic veneration of the risen Christ to a later stage of the Christian movement and invoked the influence of pagan cults as the cause. This is a sad example of a supposedly rigorous historical enterprise, though not the only case of a triumph of preconceptions over evidence. But if we respect fully the chronological indications, then we must recognize that the development of early Christian religion did not take place in a slow process that can easily be charted in linear stages but rather seems to have blossomed quite quickly. This is not to say that it defies historical analysis; I hope that the present investigation rather affirms such work. I only wish to emphasize that this historical analysis must be more carefully controlled by the constraints of the data than has sometimes been the case.

Second, just as modern linguists know that word meaning and reference can be determined only in specific contexts and can vary so considerably that it is dangerous to generalize, so students of ancient religions such as postexilic Judaism and early Christianity must be more careful to see that conclusions about the meaning of phenomena pertaining to these religions are governed by the evidence concerning the practice of the religions. If this principle is observed, the widely repeated idea that postexilic Judaism represented an eroded or weakened form of a supposedly pure monotheism of earlier times should be laid to rest. Here again we have a notion based on assumptions controlling the evidence rather than the other way around. Such a view reflects both a romanticized conceit about preexilic Israelite religion and also an insensitive analysis of the evidence of the postexilic period.

Scholars have assumed quite confidently that the ancient Jewish interest in angels and personified divine attributes could have developed only as a result of some sort of existential estrangement from the God of the Old Testament, without bothering to inquire what the evidence of actual Jewish religious practice of the period indicated. Ancient Jews do not seem to have seen angels and the other figures as taking the place of their God. We should be careful about making claims to the contrary without convincing evidence, and such evidence must have to do with the actual religious life of the people concerned. A list of the honorific things said about supposedly intermediary beings is hardly sufficient indication of the way these figures actually functioned in the faith and piety of ancient Jews. We must not only be governed by the evidence, the evidence must be appropriate to the question. In the study of ancient Judaism and early Christianity, the evidence concerning the actual religious life of the ancient adherents must be given more careful consideration, for I am not persuaded that we have yet fully escaped the trap of focusing too narrowly on doctrinal and intellectual developments and neglecting the other aspects of these important religious movements.

Third, especially in the study of new religious movements and the development of religious innovations, such as earliest Christianity, greater attention should be given to the creative role of the religious experiences of founders and founding groups. No doubt, specialists in Christian origins and related areas of ancient religion can learn something from modern studies of new religious movements in forming hypotheses about the processes that such movements often undergo in their development and growth.[1] I can claim no great expertise in the sociological or psychological study of religions, but I do not think that full expertise in these subjects is required for the sort of awareness of the importance of religious experience I call for here.[2] History, both ancient and more recent, affords us many examples of new religious movements often arising as an innovative reinterpretation of an established religious tradition, an innovation flowing from an altered hermeneutical perspective provided by potent religious experiences of influential members and/or groups in the new movement.[3]

Some such process seems to have been involved in the origin of religious movements as diverse in time and place as Buddhism, the Qumran sect, Sikhism, and modern Pentecostalism, to name but a few. By all indications, earliest Christianity is another important and obviously influential example. The historical-critical pursuit of parallels and precedents for this or that feature of early Christian faith, the favorite enterprise of much historical investigation of Christian origins, must be supplemented by an informed appreciation of the generative power of religious experience.

In early Christianity, the reinterpretation of the established religious tradition (i.e., ancient Judaism of the Greco-Roman period) included a significant and apparently novel reinterpretation of the limits of the practice of exclusivist monotheistic devotion. If the present investigation is correct, this innovation manifested itself quickly in the devotional practice of Christians of the earliest years of the movement. It also involved, probably from the first, a reflective reexamination of their understanding of God's purposes. Initially Christians concentrated on Old Testament passages, evidenced by the often remarkable cases of Old Testament texts that originally referred to *Yahweh* being applied to Christ. A prime example is the appropriation of Isa. 45:23 in Phil. 2:9–11.

The reflective process continued in the subsequent centuries of Christianity and, of course, received further impulses from such sources as Greek philosophy, leading to the classic formulations of Christian faith associated with Nicaea and Chalcedon and the developed doctrine of the Trinity.[4] It would be simplistic and naïve to collapse the distinctions between these later stages of Christian reflection and the foundational stage we have been examining in this book. But it would also be simplistic to ignore the fact that the intricate and often heated doctrinal discussion leading to these later formulations was set in motion quite early in the Christian movement by the appropriation of the divine agency category of ancient Judaism and was fueled in large part by the devotional practice of Christians which took shape so early. The major effort at theological reflection exhibited in the christological controversies of the first several centuries was demanded precisely because of the traditionally monotheistic commitment of most Christians, inherited from Judaism, and because of the binitarian devotional tradition whose roots we have examined. This binitarian devotional pattern, together with the theological reflection it embodied and promoted, was originally generated by the sort of religious experiences that provide the basis for a reinterpretation of a "parent" religious tradition.

That is, behind the debates of councils and the framing of creeds, there were the binitarian devotional practices of generations of Christians who reverenced the exalted Christ along with God in ways that amounted to a mutation in monotheism. The christological rhetoric of the New Testament and of the later christological controversies and creeds reflects the attempt to explain and defend intellectually a development that began in human terms in profound religious experiences and in corporate worship. Whoever would seek to understand truly the fervent christological discussion of ancient or modern times must first appreciate the religious life that preceded and underlay the ancient development and that continues to inspire sacrificial commitment and intense intellectual effort to this very day.

Notes

Introduction

1. Although much has been made of a so-called monotheism supposedly popular among pagans of the Greco-Roman world, this needs to be distinguished from the sort of monotheism of Judaism and Christianity. To be sure, there is evidence of the concept of a chief god under whom the many classes of lesser divinities were arranged, but this is hardly the same as the exclusive monotheism of Jews and Christians. The latter two groups regarded the many pagan deities either as demonic (e.g., 1 Cor. 10:14-21) or as sheer illusion, while the other religious groups of the day regarded them as all worthy to receive worship and as all validly divine. Note the discussion by R. McMullen, *Paganism in the Roman Empire* (New Haven: Yale Univ. Press, 1981), 83-94. He offers the term "megalodemonia" to describe the pagan idea of a chief god (p. 88). J. Teixidor (*The Pagan God: Popular Religion in the Graeco-Roman Near East* [Princeton: Princeton Univ. Press, 1977], 13-17) refers to pagan monotheism but acknowledges that what he is describing is not the same thing as the exclusive devotion to one god characteristic of ancient Judaism (p. 17). This being the case, I suggest that in the interests of historical accuracy and clear communication the term "monotheism" should be used only to describe devotion to one god and the rejection of the pantheon of deities such as were reverenced throughout the Greco-Roman world.

Teixidor's reference to a "trend toward monotheism" (p. 17) is also a curious turn of phrase, implying that Greco-Roman paganism was developing a genuinely monotheistic theology in the proper sense of the term and would have reached this kind of faith on its own, without the influence of Judaism or Christianity. There is, however, scarce indication that Roman paganism underwent any such substantial development (cf. McMullen, *Paganism*, 62-73, 92-93), and it is useless to speculate about what might have happened had Judaism and Christianity not appeared. Teixidor himself admits that what he refers to as pagan monotheism was not the result of profound religious experience but rather was a reflection in the religious sphere of the political unity of the Near East brought about by

Persian and Greek influence (p. 15). See also M. P. Nilsson, *Geschichte der griechische Religion, Vol. 2: Die hellenistische und römische Zeit,* 2d ed. (Munich: C. H. Beck, 1961), 569–78. Nilsson referred to a "tendency" (*Neigung*) and the "urge" (*Drang*) toward monotheism but likewise acknowledged that he was really only pointing either to an arrangement of lesser gods under a high god or to a bare philosophical principle; cf. idem, "The High God and the Mediator," *HTR* 56 (1963): 101–20; and H. Kleinknecht, *TDNT,* 3:71–79. On early Christian and pagan ideas about deity, see now R. M. Grant, *Gods and the One God* (Philadelphia: Westminster Press, 1986).

   2. The context deals with the reverence given to pagan deities (1 Cor. 8:1–13), and the terms "gods" (*theoi*) and "lords" (*kyrioi*) of v. 5 are the labels for these. Consequently, Paul's use of the term "Lord" as a title for Jesus here must be taken as signifying that this term for pagan divinities belongs to Christ. See H. Conzelmann, *1 Corinthians,* Hermeneia (Philadelphia: Fortress Press, 1975), 139–45; C. K. Barrett, *A Commentary on the First Epistle to the Corinthians* (New York: Harper & Row, 1968), 187–94; and R. A. Horsley, "The Background of the Confessional Formula in 1 Kor. 8:6," *ZNW* 69 (1978): 130–34. Also, if 1 Cor. 8:6 alludes to the Jewish confession, the Shema, which in its Greek form used both *theos* and *kyrios* as titles for Yahweh, we have further reason for seeing the *kyrios* term here used for Christ as connoting divine honor.

   3. For an investigation of the ancient Jewish criticism of "two powers" heretics, see A. F. Segal, *Two Powers in Heaven,* SJLA 25 (Leiden: E. J. Brill, 1978).

   4. See the study of Paul's conversion experience and its theological effects by S. Kim, *The Origin of Paul's Gospel* (Tübingen: J. C. B. Mohr [Paul Siebeck], 1981; Grand Rapids: Wm. B. Eerdmans, 1982); and my review in *JBL* 103 (1984): 122–23. For an investigation of Paul's persecution of Jewish Christians, see A. J. Hultgren, "Paul's Pre-Christian Persecutions of the Church: Their Purpose, Locale, and Nature," *JBL* 95 (1976): 97–111. E. P. Sanders (*Paul, the Law, and the Jewish People* [Philadelphia: Fortress Press, 1983]) argues on the basis of Gal. 5:11; 6:12; 2 Cor. 11:23; and 1 Thess. 2:16 that the major cause behind the persecution of Paul, and Paul's own persecution of Jewish Christians earlier, was the admission of Gentiles to Christian groups without requiring them to be circumcised (190–92), but the following points are worth noting. First, although it is correct that Paul connected the persecution he experienced with his gentile mission (e.g., 1 Thess. 2:16), he also described the basis of his position on circumcision as his view of Jesus and his crucifixion (e.g., Gal. 6:12 refers to being "persecuted for the cross of Christ"). Note also Phil. 3:2–21, where Paul contrasts his previous religious life with his subsequent stance, which is distinguished essentially by devotion to Christ in the most intense terms (vv. 3, 7–10, 14, 20–21). Second, I am not sure that the Jewish Christians in Jerusalem, against whom Paul's persecutions apparently began (Gal. 1:23), can be credited with a gentile mission. Acts 6:11–14 mentions only that Stephen's message blasphemed "Moses and God" and challenged the temple and (therefore?) the Mosaic laws. Whatever the message of these Jewish Christians, it was probably also based on a high estimate of the status of the exalted Jesus. See M. Hengel, *Between Jesus and*

Paul (Philadelphia: Fortress Press; London: SCM Press, 1983), 71; W. Horbury, "The Benediction of the *Minim* and Early Jewish-Christian Controversy," *JTS* 33 (1982): 19–61; and G. N. Stanton, "Aspects of Early Christian-Jewish Polemic and Apologetic," *NTS* 31 (1985): 377–92.

5. I use the term "veneration" without any technical significance, such as is given to the term in scholastic distinctions between the proper reverence accorded to the saints, the Virgin Mary, and God. I use the term broadly to refer to the religious reverence accorded to beings regarded as divine (see chap. 5).

6. In addition to the works by McMullen, Teixidor, and Grant (n. 1), practically any discussion of ancient Greco-Roman religion will indicate the wide range of deities and heroes reverenced. For more specialized studies, note D. E. Aune, "The Problem of the Genre of the Gospels: A Critique of C. H. Talbert's What Is a Gospel?" *Gospel Perspectives 2*, ed. R. T. France and D. Wenham (Sheffield: JSOT Press, 1981), 9–60, and the literature cited there.

7. The classic presentation of this position is by W. Bousset, *Kyrios Christos* (Göttingen: Vandenhoeck & Ruprecht, 1913, 1921); the English translation is cited here (Nashville: Abingdon Press, 1970). We may cite, e.g., the following statement by Bousset: "This placing of Jesus in the center of the cultus of a believing community, this particular doubling of the object of veneration in worship, is conceivable only in an environment in which Old Testament monotheism no longer ruled unconditionally and with absolute security" (p. 147). On the relevance of the criticisms of Bousset's judgments, see, e.g., M. Casey, "Chronology and the Development of Pauline Christology," in *Paul and Paulinism: Essays in Honour of C. K. Barrett*, ed. M. D. Hooker and S. G. Wilson (London: SPCK, 1982), 124–34. Casey echoes Bousset's emphasis upon the supposed influence of gentile converts in producing the view of Jesus as divine (esp. pp. 130–33). On other aspects of Bousset's work, see L. W. Hurtado, "New Testament Christology: A Critique of Bousset's Influence," *TS* 40 (1979): 306–17.

8. I have borrowed "comfortable" from an essay by S. Sandmel ("Palestinian and Hellenistic Judaism and Christianity: The Question of the Comfortable Theory," *HUCA* 50 [1979]: 137–48) in which Sandmel had the courage to admit his own preferences and how they affected his critical judgments.

9. On the chronological data and their importance for the origins of Christology, I am indebted to M. Hengel, "Christology and New Testament Chronology: A Problem in the History of Earliest Christianity," in *Between Jesus and Paul*, 30–47.

10. One should still consult the discussion of the theological relationship of Paul to the Jerusalem church by J. Munck, *Paul and the Salvation of Mankind* (Atlanta: John Knox Press; London: SCM Press, 1959). More recently, there is the careful and persuasive treatment of Paul and the Jerusalem church by B. Holmberg, *Paul and Power: The Structure of Authority in the Primitive Church as Reflected in the Pauline Epistles* (Philadelphia: Fortress Press, 1980), 9–56. See also A. M. Hunter, *Paul and His Predecessors*, 2d ed. (London: SCM Press, 1961).

11. See my treatment of these passages in chap. 5. Bousset's shifting attempts to counter the importance of the "Maranatha" phrase only show his own unwill-

ingness to countenance the possibility that the cultic invocation of Jesus may have had its origins in a Palestinian Jewish-Christian setting. Neither the assertion that the "Lord" invoked was not Jesus but God, nor his other, more desperate assertion that the phrase resulted from translating into Aramaic an invocation originally framed in Greek in some bilingual Diaspora city is held today, even by his contemporary followers (*Kyrios Christos*, 129). The more recent attempt to minimize the significance of the phrase by claims that the Aramaic term for "lord" (*marêh*), which lies at the heart of the "Maranatha" phrase, could not have connoted divinity and that the phrase cannot therefore reflect a genuine cultic veneration of Jesus is now rendered even less convincing than before by recent discoveries of the use of *marêh* as a divine title in certain Aramaic texts from Qumran (against, e.g., S. Schulz, "Maranatha und Kyrios Jesus," *ZNW* 53 [1962]: 125–44). See now J. A. Fitzmyer, "The Semitic Background of the New Testament *Kyrios*-Title," in *A Wandering Aramean: Collected Aramaic Essays*, SBLMS 25 (Missoula, Mont.: Scholars Press, 1979), 115–42; idem, "New Testament Kyrios and Maranatha and Their Aramaic Background," in *To Advance the Gospel: New Testament Studies* (New York: Crossroad, 1981), 218–35; and Hengel, *Between Jesus and Paul*, 162–63 n. 43.

12. R. Deichgräber, *Gotteshymnus und Christushymnus in der frühen Christenheit* (Göttingen: Vandenhoeck & Ruprecht, 1967); Hengel, *Between Jesus and Paul*, 78–96; R. P. Martin, "Some Reflections on New Testament Hymns," in *Christ the Lord: Studies in Christology Presented to Donald Guthrie*, ed. H. H. Rowdon (Leicester: Inter-Varsity Press, 1982), 37–49.

13. See L. Hartman, "Baptism 'Into the Name of Jesus' and Early Christology: Some Tentative Considerations," *ST* 28 (1974): 21–48.

14. A. W. Wainwright (*The Trinity in the New Testament* [London: SPCK, 1962], 93–104) discussed briefly the worship of Jesus in the New Testament. See further chap. 5 of this book. On the scene in Revelation 4—5, see L. W. Hurtado, "Revelation 4—5 in the Light of Jewish Apocalyptic Analogies," *JSNT* 25 (1985): 105–24.

15. Bousset's attempt to limit Paul's acquaintance with the beliefs of the Jerusalem church to "a most meager kind" (*Kyrios Christos*, 119) is not convincing, even in its modified form. It rests almost entirely upon Paul's statement, in a highly defensive account of the origin of his apostleship (Gal. 1:11—2:21), that his first trip to Jerusalem after his conversion was a fifteen-day visit with Cephas (Peter, Gal. 1:18). Bousset withdrew his earlier assertion that Paul's persecution of Jewish Christians did not include Palestinian churches (ibid., 119 n. 2) but failed to accord the significance it deserved to the likelihood that Paul therefore would have had some familiarity with the beliefs of Palestinian Jewish Christians even before his own conversion. Further, he never took account of Paul's long associations with other Jewish Christians from a Palestinian church background, such as Barnabas and Silas, in estimating Paul's opportunities to familiarize himself with the beliefs of the Palestinian Primitive Community.

16. There has been a complicated discussion about the definition of the term "Jewish Christianity." By "Jewish Christians," I mean Christians of Jewish

racial and religious background. For a discussion of important issues and literature, see M. Simon, "Reflexions sur le Judéo-Christianisme," in *Christianity,
Judaism and Other Greco-Roman Cults: Studies for Morton Smith at Sixty: Part
Two*, ed. J. Neusner (Leiden: E. J. Brill, 1975), 53-76; A. F. J. Klijn and G. J.
Reinink, *Patristic Evidence for Jewish-Christian Sects* (Leiden: E. J. Brill, 1973);
and F. Manns, *Bibliographie du Judéo-Christianisme* (Jerusalem: Franciscan Pub.,
1979).

17. See again Grant, *Gods and the One God*; and A. D. Nock, *Early Gentile
Christianity and Its Hellenistic Background* (New York: Harper & Row, 1964).

18. J. D. G. Dunn, *Christology in the Making: A New Testament Inquiry Into the
Origins of the Doctrine of the Incarnation* (Philadelphia: Westminster Press, 1980).
Cf. C. R. Holladay, "New Testament Christology: A Consideration of Dunn's
Christology in the Making," *Semeia* 30 (1984): 64-82; and Dunn's response in the
same issue (97-104), "Some Clarifications on Issues of Method: A Reply to Hol-
laday and Segal."

19. For a similar emphasis upon the Jewish background of early Christianity,
see such recent studies as C. C. Rowland, *Christian Origins* (London: SPCK,
1985); and A. F. Segal, *Rebecca's Children: Judaism and Christianity in the Roman
World* (Cambridge: Harvard Univ. Press, 1986).

20. H. J. Schoeps, e.g., had to resort to an unconvincing attempt to describe
Paul as insufficiently familiar with, or appreciative of, his Jewish background in
order to explain how he could have embraced the Christian faith, in *Paul: The
Theology of the Apostle in the Light of Jewish Religious History* (Philadelphia: West-
minster Press; London: Lutterworth Press, 1961). Cf. W. D. Davies, *Paul and
Rabbinic Judaism*, 4th ed. (Philadelphia: Fortress Press, 1980 [1948]); E. P.
Sanders, *Paul and Palestinian Judaism* (Philadelphia: Fortress Press; London:
SCM Press, 1977); idem, *Paul, the Law, and the Jewish People*.

21. See the criticisms of rigid simplifications of ancient Judaism and Christianity by I. H. Marshall, "Palestinian and Hellenistic Christianity: Some Critical Comments," *NTS* 19 (1972/73): 271-87.

22. On the languages used in first-century Palestine, see Fitzmyer, *A Wandering Aramean*, 29-56. Cf. S. Lieberman, *Greek in Jewish Palestine* (New York:
Jewish Theological Seminary, 1962).

23. M. Hengel, *Judaism and Hellenism*, 2 vols. (Philadelphia: Fortress Press;
London: SCM Press, 1974). Cf. also D. Flusser, "Paganism in Palestine," in *The
Jewish People in the First Century, Volume Two*, ed. S. Safrai and M. Stern (Phila-
delphia: Fortress Press, 1976), 1065-1100; J. F. Strange, "Archaeology and the
Religion of Judaism in Palestine," *ANRW* 19/1:646-85; E. M. Meyers, "The
Cultural Setting of Galilee," *ANRW* 19/1:686-702. On oversimplifications about
Diaspora Judaism, see A. T. Kraabel, "Paganism and Judaism: The Sardis Evi-
dence," in *Paganisme, Judaisme, Christianisme: Influences et affrontements dans le
monde antique, Mélanges offerts à Marcel Simon*, ed. A. Benoit, M. Philonenko,
and C. Vogel (Paris: E. de Boccard, 1978), 13-33; idem, "The Roman Diaspora:
Six Questionable Assumptions," *JJS* 22 (1982); 445-64. J. J. Collins, *Between
Athens and Jerusalem: Jewish Identity in the Hellenistic Diaspora* (New York: Cross-

road, 1983) is an introduction to relevant primary texts; cf. the review by M. Goodman in *JJS* 35 (1984): 214–17.

24. There is, e.g., Barnabas, an early member of the Jerusalem church but a native of Cyprus, Acts 4:36. The "Hellenists" of Acts 6:1 are probably such Jews from the Diaspora who returned to Palestine, and we read of Jews living in Jerusalem from a variety of locations in Acts 6:8–9. See the convincing discussion by Hengel, *Between Jesus and Paul*, 1–29.

25. See the handy summary description of various Jewish religious groups by M. Simon, *Jewish Sects in the Time of Jesus* (Philadelphia: Fortress Press, 1967).

26. This point has been argued most vigorously by J. E. Fossum, *The Name of God and the Angel of the Lord: The Origins of the Idea of Intermediation in Gnosticism*, WUNT 1/36 (Tübingen: J. C. B. Mohr [Paul Siebeck], 1985). See also Segal, *Two Powers in Heaven*, 217–19, 266–67. In spite of differences of opinion on certain matters, I agree with the general drift of these studies, that Jewish monotheism was much more complex and diverse than has sometimes been recognized.

27. Note Segal's statement on the importance of principal angels (*Two Powers in Heaven*, 205): "The relationships between these traditions of angelic mediation and Christianity are significant enough to call for a more complete study of the problem as background for christology than has yet been attempted."

28. Here I try to describe and underline *both* the indebtedness of early Christian reflection on the exalted Jesus to ancient Jewish interest in "divine agents" *and* the apparently distinctive features of early Christian devotion. I do not wish to be taken as emphasizing either at the expense of the other.

29. L. W. Hurtado, "The Study of New Testament Christology: Notes for the Agenda," in *Society of Biblical Literature 1981 Seminar Papers*, ed. K. H. Richards (Missoula, Mont.: Scholars Press, 1981), 185–97; idem, "New Testament Christology: Retrospect and Prospect," *Semeia* 30 (1984): 15–27.

30. Prominent figures included W. Heitmüller, O. Pfleiderer, R. Reitzenstein, W. Wrede, and W. Bousset. See the critical discussion of this school by H. C. Kee, *Miracle in the Early Christian World* (New Haven: Yale Univ. Press, 1983), 1–41. For an introduction to these scholars and their work as it relates to Christian origins, see W. G. Kümmel, *The New Testament: The History of the Investigation of Its Problems* (Nashville: Abingdon Press, 1972), 206–324.

31. The attempt to find a pre-Christian redeemer myth in the Mandean materials has been decisively refuted by C. Colpe, *Die religionsgeschichtliche Schule. Darstellung und Kritik ihres Bildes vom gnostischen Erlösermythus* (Göttingen: Vandenhoeck & Ruprecht, 1961). Cf. also H. M. Schenke, *Der Gott "Mensch" in der Gnosis* (Göttingen: Vandenhoeck & Ruprecht, 1962); E. Yamauchi, *Pre-Christian Gnosticism: A Survey of Proposed Evidences* (Grand Rapids: Wm. B. Eerdmans, 1973); idem, *Gnostic Ethics and Mandean Origins*, HTS 24 (Cambridge: Harvard Univ. Press, 1970); K. Rudolf, "Der Mandäismus in der neueren Gnosisforschung," in *Gnosis. Festschrift für Hans Jonas*, ed. B. Aland (Göttingen: Vandenhoeck & Ruprecht, 1978), 244–77. See R. Reitzenstein's attempt to locate the source of many features of early Christianity in the ancient

mystery religions in *Hellenistic Mystery-Religions: Their Basic Ideas and Significance* (Pittsburgh: Pickwick Press, 1978). Cf. criticisms of such views by B. M. Metzger, "Methodology in the Study of the Mystery Religions and Early Christianity," in *Historical and Literary Studies: Pagan, Jewish, and Christian* (Grand Rapids: Wm. B. Eerdmans, 1968), 1–24; and D. H. Wiens, "Mystery Concepts in Primitive Christianity and in Its Environment," *ANRW* 2. 23/2:1248–84. Cf. also A. J. M. Wedderburn, "Paul and the Hellenistic Mystery Cults: On Posing the Right Questions," in *La Soteriologia del Culti Orientali nell' Impeiro Romano*, ed. U. Bianchi and M. J. Vermasseren (Leiden: E. J. Brill, 1982), 817–33.

32. See, e.g., the introduction to modern linguistics by J. Lyons, *Language and Linguistics: An Introduction* (Cambridge: Cambridge Univ. Press, 1981). He discusses the "etymological fallacy" on p. 55. On the dangers of pressing "parallels," see S. Sandmel, "Parallelomania," *JBL* 81 (1962): 1–13; and A. Deissmann, *Light from the Ancient East* (Grand Rapids: Baker Book House, 1965 [1922]), 265.

33. E. P. Sanders, *Paul and Palestinian Judaism*, esp. 12–18.

34. See, e.g., W. Bousset, *The Faith of a Modern Protestant* (London: T. Fisher Unwin, 1909), for the views of one prominent member of the group. His discussion of Christian faith affirms Jesus only as an example of piety, and he describes the development of Christology as "the confused mass of speculations concerning the Triune God" and as "the abstractions and sophistries of speculation" (p. 46).

35. Indeed, this attitude is not always so subtly expressed. Bousset (*Kyrios Christos*, 151) refers to the "doubtful aspects" of the veneration of Jesus and "the burdening and complicating of the simple belief in God through the introduction of the cultic worship of the Kyrios Christos." Yet, he continues, "one will have to concede that it came about with an inner necessity," for the "environment," the worship of various cult deities, demanded it, and the "Hellenistic Christian communities" had to compete by introducing a new cult deity of their own. His comments beg the question of the historical basis for judging the veneration of Jesus as "burdening" and "complicating" the "simple belief in God," and the answer is that there is no historical basis but only the clearly implicit theological preferences of Bousset by which to account for his somewhat strange remarks. Bousset's notion about the supposed influence of pagan cults as the source of the veneration of Jesus is not only simplistic but also rendered implausible by the chronological evidence described earlier.

36. For discussion of these later developments, see, e.g., A. Grillmeier, *Christ in Christian Tradition*, 2d ed. (London: A. R. Mowbray, 1975).

37. See now B. Lindars, *Jesus Son of Man: A Fresh Examination of the Son of Man Sayings in the Gospels in the Light of Recent Research* (London: SPCK, 1983; Grand Rapids: Wm. B. Eerdmans, 1984), esp. "The Myth of the Son of Man," 1–16; and M. Casey, *Son of Man: Interpretation and Influence of Daniel 7* (London: SPCK, 1979).

38. The literature on these matters is simply too vast to list more than a few major works: F. Hahn, *The Titles of Jesus in Christology* (New York: World Pub-

lishing Co., 1969); W. Kramer, *Christ, Lord, Son of God*, SBT 50 (London: SCM Press, 1966); and M. Hengel, *The Son of God: The Origin of Christology and the History of Jewish-Hellenistic Religion* (Philadelphia: Fortress Press; London: SCM Press, 1976).

39. Now see J. D. G. Dunn, *Christology in the Making*. Cf. I. H. Marshall, "Incarnational Christology in the New Testament," in *Christ the Lord*, ed. Rowdon, 1-16.

40. The question is dealt with in more limited fashion in J. Ernst, *Anfänge der Christologie*, SBS 57 (Stuttgart: Katholisches Bibelwerk, 1972); W. Thüsing, *Erhöhungsvorstellung und Parusieerwartung in der ältesten nachösterlichen Christologie*, SBS 42 (Stuttgart: Katholisches Bibelwerk, 1970); idem, *Per Christum in Deum* (Münster: Aschendorff, 1965); H. R. Balz, *Methodische Probleme der neutestamentlichen Christologie*, WMANT 25 (Neukirchen-Vluyn: Neukirchener Verlag, 1967).

41. See R. G. Hamerton-Kelly, "The Idea of Pre-Existence in Early Judaism: A Study in the Background of New Testament Theology" (diss., Union Theological Seminary, New York, 1966); idem, *Pre-Existence, Wisdom and the Son of Man* (Cambridge: Cambridge Univ. Press, 1973); and G. Schimanowski, *Weisheit und Messias: Die jüdischen voraussetzungen der urchristlichen Präexistenzchristologie*, WUNT 2/17 (Tübingen: J. C. B. Mohr [Paul Siebeck], 1985).

42. See, e.g., N. A. Dahl, "Christ, Creation and the Church," in *The Background of the New Testament and Its Eschatology: Studies in Honour of C. H. Dodd*, ed. W. D. Davies and D. Daube (Cambridge: Cambridge Univ. Press, 1954), 422-43.

43. To be sure, Paul's relativizing of the law of Moses was also a very significant modification of the Jewish piety he had inherited. But see n. 4 above.

Chapter 1
Divine Agency in Ancient Jewish Monotheism

1. G. F. Moore ("Christian Writers on Judaism," *HTR* 14 [1921]: 227-54) showed that the claim of a "distant God" in ancient Judaism is an essentially modern, Protestant assertion and that there are good reasons for seeing it as less an objective description of ancient Jewish piety than a theologically motivated polemic.

2. Segal, *Two Powers in Heaven*, 244-59; Fossum, *The Name of God*.

3. Segal, *Two Powers in Heaven*.

4. See chap. 2 on "hypostases" where I argue that the term "hypostasis" is not particularly helpful in understanding what these figures represent. I am inclined to think that "personification of divine attributes" more accurately describes them. Even though I do not think that ancient Jewish writers intended them to be taken as real beings in themselves or as something in between real beings and divine emanations, nonetheless the description of them employs the language and seems to reflect the concept of divine agency.

5. See now P. J. Kobelski, *Melchizedek and Melchireša'*, CBQMS 10 (Washington, D.C.: Catholic Biblical Association, 1981).

6. In *Wisdom of Solomon* 10–11, "Wisdom" is connected with major events in sacred history, but no eschatological role is ascribed either here or elsewhere.

7. Note the description of the angel's appearance in *Apoc. Abr.* 11:1-3, which is probably intended to resemble loosely the descriptions of OT theophanies and angelophanies such as Ezek. 1:26-28. Cf. the reference to 'Ashtart-Shem-Ba'1 in the Eshmun'azar inscription, *ANET*, 662, where the goddess Ashtart is closely linked with the name of Baal.

8. Of course, in other texts, such as the Samaritan documents discussed by W. A. Meeks, *The Prophet-King: Moses Traditions and the Johannine Christology*, NovTSup 14 (Leiden: E. J. Brill, 1967), 216-57, Moses is associated with eschatological hopes. This association may be much earlier than the sources (fourth century C.E. and later). See M. F. Collins, "The Hidden Vessels in Samaritan Traditions," *JSJ* 3 (1972): 97-116. My point is that the specific nature of the role assigned to divine agents such as Moses varies significantly across the spectrum of ancient evidence.

9. I do not mean to claim that interest in such figures was a new development of this period. It is likely that divine agency was in fact a conception of much older origin in Jewish religious tradition. This question, however, is not pursued here.

10. See D. M. Hay, *Glory at the Right Hand: Psalm 110 in Early Christianity* (Nashville: Abingdon Press, 1973).

11. W. Bousset, *Die Religion des Judentums im späthellenistischen Zeitalter*, 3d ed., ed. H. Gressmann (Tübingen: J. C. B. Mohr [Paul Siebeck], 1926); hereafter cited as *Die Religion*.

12. See the evaluation by E. P. Sanders in *Paul and Palestinian Judaism*, esp. 55-56; idem, *Jesus and Judaism* (Philadelphia: Fortress Press; London: SCM Press, 1985), 24-26, 360 n. 12; and Moore, "Christian Writers on Judaism," 241-48.

13. The relevant section of Bousset's *Die Religion* is entitled "Der Monotheismus und die den Monotheismus beschränkenden Unterströmmungen," 302-57.

14. Ibid., 319-31.

15. So, e.g., ibid., 319, 329-31.

16. Ibid., 329. But see Moore, "Christian Writers on Judaism," esp. 227-53.

17. Ibid., 357. Here Bousset places the origin of the view of the risen Jesus as a heavenly, preexistent being very early ("Indeed, we may almost say, in the theology of the primitive community"). He states that this development is not understandable without the preparation for it in Judaism—the interest in *Mittelwesen*. This seems to be a somewhat different emphasis from that found in his *Kyrios Christos* (pp. 119-52). There he repeatedly asserts the importance of "Hellenistic" (gentile) Christian communities as the setting for the origin of the view of Jesus as the exalted *Kyrios* and minimizes the possible influence of Jewish factors such as angelology (p. 148). One notices, however, that in *Die Religion* he stopped short of according to the "primitive community" the view of Jesus as a heavenly

being and regarded the erosion of Jewish monotheism as likely to have progressed more fully "in the little supervised circles of Diaspora Judaism" (p. 330). So, in referring to the influence of a weakened Jewish monotheism upon early Christianity, he may have meant Diaspora Judaism, with which his "Gentile Christian Primitive Communities" would have come into contact. (But cf. pp. 355–57: "We should not think the Palestinian rabbis to have been conventional and dogmatically correct. Many of them, contemporaries of Paul, were mystics and ecstatics.") Still, it appears to me that the emphases of the two books do not quite agree: *Kyrios Christos* asserts the influence of pagan cults in the formation of early Christology and *Die Religion* points to the sort of Jewish religious thought described here. For a critique of Bousset's general view of the development of earliest Christianity and especially his emphasis upon the "pre-Pauline Hellenistic community," see Hengel, "Christology and New Testament Chronology," in *Between Jesus and Paul*, 30–47.

18. Bousset, *Die Religion*, 329.
19. Ibid., 329–30, "From this sort of religious expression to the cultus of angels is not a very far distance" (p. 330).
20. Ibid., 330.
21. Ibid., 331. Accusations of Jewish worship of angels appear in citations of the *Kerygma Petrou* in Clement of Alexandria (*Strom.* 6.5.39–41) and Origen (*Comm. Joh.* 13.17). A related criticism of Jews is offered by Celsus in Origen *Contra Celsum* 1.26 and 5.6. For an introduction to the *Kerygma Petrou*, see E. Hennecke and W. Schneemelcher, *New Testament Apocrypha* (Philadelphia: Westminster Press; London: SCM Press, 1965), 2:94–102. Bousset also saw *4 Ezra* 6:1–6 as directed against the Jewish reverence of angels, but I fail to find anything in this passage to demand such a view. It is much more likely that the text simply reflects the sort of polemic against other deities that was a familiar part of Jewish tradition (e.g., Isa. 41:28; 43:10–13; 44:2, 6, 24; 45:5–8, 12, 18, 21).
22. Bousset, *Die Religion*, 321.
23. P. Schäfer, *Rivalität zwischen Engeln und Menschen. Untersuchungen zur rabbinischen Engelvorstellung* (Berlin and New York: Walter de Gruyter, 1975), 9. Although the bulk of Schäfer's work deals with rabbinic materials, he offers an overview of the Jewish apocryphal/pseudepigraphical literature and the Qumran materials (pp. 9–40). See also H. B. Kuhn, "The Angelology of the Non-Canonical Jewish Apocalypses," *JBL* 67 (1948): 217–32.
24. S. F. Noll, "Angelology in the Qumran Texts" (Ph.D. diss., Manchester, 1979), 180.
25. Cf. H. Bietenhard, *Die himmlische Welt im Urchristentum und Spätjudentum*, WUNT 2 (Tübingen: J. C. B. Mohr [Paul Siebeck], 1951), 101–42.
26. So also H. B. Kuhn, "Angelology," esp. 219, 224, 230–32.
27. To be sure, particular examples of these "servants" are described in exalted terms, especially the principal angel figures. My thesis is that the exalted role given to these various figures did not represent a displacement of God in Jewish religious thought and instead formed part of an attempt to magnify God and his power on behalf of the elect.

28. Bietenhard, *Die himmlische Welt*, 103. Similarly, Kuhn's survey of the role of angels in the postexilic Jewish apocalyptic literature led him to conclude that "there is no orderly pattern in the writings of this period which would definitely indicate that there existed any definite metaphysical scheme or doctrine of divine transcendence which necessitated the placing of angels as mediators of the hiatus between God and man" (p. 230).

29. H. J. Wicks, *The Doctrine of God in the Jewish Apocryphal and Apocalyptic Literature* (New York: Ktav, 1971 [1915]). Wicks also states that, with the possible exception of a few isolated passages, the facts show that the authors of postexilic Jewish literature conceived God to be "nigh at hand and not far off" (pp. 125–26). G. W. E. Nickelsburg and M. E. Stone (*Faith and Piety in Early Judaism* [Philadelphia: Fortress Press, 1983]) offer an introduction to ancient Jewish literature and ideas but do not give detailed attention to prayers and other devotional practices.

30. J. H. Charlesworth, ed., *The Old Testament Pseudepigrapha*, 2 vols. (Garden City, N.Y.: Doubleday & Co., 1983, 1985), hereafter cited as *OTP*; and H. F. D. Sparks, ed., *The Apocryphal Old Testament* (Oxford: Clarendon Press, 1984), hereafter cited as *AOT*.

31. On Bousset's "disdain" for ancient Judaism, see E. P. Sanders, *Jesus and Judaism*, 24–26; and Moore, "Christian Writers on Judaism," 252–54.

32. See, e.g., N. B. Johnson, *Prayer in the Apocrypha and Pseudepigrapha: A Study of the Jewish Concept of God*, SBLMS 2 (Philadelphia: Society of Biblical Literature, 1948). Johnson's work shows how much the view I am rejecting here is simply an uncritical assumption. He asserts that the belief in angelic agents reflected in the postexilic Jewish literature must mean that God was seen as removed from the world (p. 65), even though his own investigation refuted his assumption, as shown by the following statement a few pages later in the same work: "Although a belief in angels should logically [!] suggest that God is remote from our world, the Jew evidently felt no compulsion to abandon faith in God's immanence" (p. 69). I am simply mystified by the "logic" involved in the first part of his sentence.

33. On the study of ancient Jewish piety as background for early Christianity, see J. H. Charlesworth, "A Prolegomenon to a New Study of the Jewish Background of the Hymns and Prayers in the New Testament," *JJS* 33 (1982): 265–85. See also J. N. Lightstone, *The Commerce of the Sacred: Mediation of the Divine among Jews in the Graeco-Roman Diaspora* (Chico, Calif.: Scholars Press, 1984), for occasionally controversial analysis of less well-known aspects of ancient Jewish life.

34. See also the discussion by M. Simon, "Remarques sur l'angélolatrie juive au début de l'ère chrétienne," in *Académie des inscriptions et belles-lettres, comptes rendus des séances de l'année 1971*, 120–35.

35. See the often-cited work by W. Lueken, *Michael. Eine Darstellung und Vergleichung der jüdischen und der morgenländisch-christlichen Tradition vom Erzengel Michael* (Göttingen: Vandenhoeck & Ruprecht, 1898), 2–12. The following discussion will show that Lueken seriously misunderstood matters.

36. See E. R. Goodenough, *Jewish Symbols in the Greco-Roman Period: Volume 2, The Archaeological Evidence from the Diaspora* (New York: Pantheon Books, 1953), 153–207, 229, 232. Goodenough shows that the names of angels, especially the four most widely known archangels—Michael, Ouriel, Raphael, and Gabriel—appear in charms, sometimes alongside the names of pagan deities, but the question remains unsettled as to whether these are charms used by Jews borrowing the names of pagan deities or by pagans borrowing the names of archangels from Jewish tradition, Goodenough's insistence on the former theory notwithstanding. For a review of Goodenough's work, see A. D. Nock, *Essays on Religion and the Ancient World* (Cambridge: Harvard Univ. Press, 1972), 2:791–820, 877–918.

37. See the discussion of rabbinic references in Schäfer, *Rivalität*, 67–72.

38. See n. 21 above.

39. As Stier observed, "An occasional appeal (*Bitte*) directed to angels is, however, not really prayer (*Beten*) to angels." So F. Stier, *Gott und sein Engel im alten Testament* (Münster: Aschendorffschen, 1934), 147 n. 64.

40. Contra Lueken, *Michael*, 11 n. 2.

41. Goodenough, *Jewish Symbols*, 2:145–46.

42. A. Deissmann, *Light from the Ancient East* (London: Hodder & Stoughton, 1927), 414–18. He gives the inscription with translation. Note that in the thirteen volumes of Goodenough's *Jewish Symbols* this inscription was put forth as his best evidence of Jewish prayer to angels. Note also Simon, "Remarques," 123–24.

43. Note this same caution in A. L. Williams, "The Cult of Angels at Colossae," *JTS* 10 (1909): 423. See the recent discussion of the *Testaments of the Twelve Patriarchs* in *OTP*, 1:775–81; and in J. H. Charlesworth, *The Pseudepigrapha and Modern Research with a Supplement* (Chico, Calif.: Scholars Press, 1981), 211–20.

44. That is, the writer may show a familiarity with the sort of idea reflected in *11Q Melchizedek*, where an apparently angelic being named Melchizedek (and perhaps to be identified with Michael) is to come to the rescue of the elect in the last days. See Kobelski, *Melchizedek*, 139. A similar notion is found in Dan. 12:1 and *T. Mos.* 10:2–3.

45. Note the variation in Greek manuscripts in this verse: instead of "intercedes for you" (*paraitoumenō*), there is the variant "accompanies you" (*parepomenō*), the latter reading perhaps being an allusion to Exod. 23:20–21. For Greek variants and supporting witnesses, see M. de Jonge, *The Testaments of the Twelve Patriarchs: A Critical Edition of the Greek Text* (Leiden: E. J. Brill, 1978), 109.

46. So, e.g., Williams, "The Cult of Angels at Colossae," 423.

47. We see the use of the term "angel" as a title for the preincarnate Christ in Justin Martyr (e.g., *Dial.* 56:4, 10; 61:1ff.). On Justin's view of the preexistence of Christ, see D. C. Trakatellis, *The Pre-Existence of Christ in the Writings of Justin Martyr*, HTRDR 6 (Missoula, Mont.: Scholars Press, 1976).

48. Note Josephus *Antiquities* 8.2.5. He refers to Solomon's composition of incantations for healing illnesses and for exorcisms. For more complete informa-

tion on the ancient Jewish tradition of Solomon as possessor of such powers, see the discussion by D. C. Duling *OTP*, 1:935–59.

49. Thus also Williams, "The Cult of Angels at Colossae," 424–25. Note also L. H. Schiffman, "Merkavah Speculation at Qumran: The 4Q *Serekh Shirot Olat ha-Shabbat*," in *Mystics, Philosophers, and Politicians: Essays in Jewish Intellectual History in Honor of Alexander Altmann*, ed. J. Reinharz and D. Swetschinski (Durham, N.C.: Duke Univ. Press, 1982), 17–47. He suggests that the proliferation of angelic names in esoteric speculation about heaven happened no earlier than the revolt of 66–73 C.E. (p. 46).

50. Simon, "Remarques," 124–25. He seems to refer with greater confidence to the worship of angels in "Jewish or Judaizing" sectarian circles in Phrygia in the early Christian centuries (p. 132). He appears to base his assertion on an incorrect interpretation of Col. 2:16–19 (cf. Simon, "Remarques," 126–28).

51. See the *Mekilta* on Exod. 20:4, 20; and note also Targum *Pseudo-Jonathan* on Exod. 20:20. These and the other rabbinic references described in this paragraph are discussed in Schäfer, *Rivalität*, 67–74; and in Lueken, *Michael*, 6–7.

52. Schäfer, *Rivalität*, 67, 68, 70, 72, 74.

53. Ibid., 74. This also seems to be the drift of the remarks by Schiffman, "Merkavah Speculation at Qumran," 46.

54. Segal, *Two Powers in Heaven*, 73. The identification of the heretic as a Christian is supported also by R. T. Herford, *Christianity in Talmud and Midrash* (London: Williams and Norgate, 1903), 285–86, and by E. E. Urbach, *The Sages: Their Concepts and Beliefs* (Jerusalem: Magnes Press, 1979), 139. The heretic's position seems to reflect the attempts of Christians to justify their worship of Jesus by trying to find texts showing a second divine figure in the OT, as is shown also in Justin Martyr's *Dialogue with Trypho*.

55. Segal, *Two Powers in Heaven*, 70–71.

56. See Williams, "The Cult of Angels at Colossae," 413–14.

57. E.g., the RSV translation of Col. 2:18 seems to reflect this understanding of the phenomenon in question: "insisting on self-abasement and worship of angels." In an otherwise solid essay, Simon takes the phrase as clear evidence of an angel cult in the area of Colossae ("Remarques," 127–28). Such an interpretation of the passage must be the basis for Hengel's reference to a "pre-Christian angel cult under Jewish influence, e.g., in Phrygia"; see Hengel, *The Son of God*, 85 n. 146.

58. F. O. Francis, "Humility and Angelic Worship in Col. 2:18," *ST* 16 (1962): 109–34; reprinted in *Conflict at Colossae: A Problem in the Interpretation of Early Christianity Illustrated by Selected Modern Studies*, ed. F. O. Francis and W. A. Meeks, rev. ed. (Missoula, Mont.: Scholars Press, 1975), 163–95. Francis shows a familiarity with the early Jewish evidence concerning the interest in angels and their participation in the heavenly liturgy. His interpretation of Col. 2:18 is accepted by W. Carr, *Angels and Principalities: The Background, Meaning and Development of the Pauline Phrase hai archai kai hai exousiai* (Cambridge: Cambridge Univ. Press, 1981), 69–71. See also C. A. Evans, "The Colossian

Mystics," *Bib* 63 (1982): 188-205; and R. Yates, " 'The Worship of Angels' (Col. 2:18)," *ExpTim* 97 (1985): 12-15. One of the earliest examples of interest in the heavenly liturgy of angels is the Angel Liturgy from Qumran, on which see Schiffman, "Merkavah Speculation at Qumran"; and now C. Newsom, *Songs of the Sabbath Sacrifice: A Critical Edition*, HSS 27 (Atlanta: Scholars Press, 1985). A readily available translation and brief discussion appears in G. Vermes, *The Dead Sea Scrolls in English*, 2d ed. (Baltimore: Penguin Books, 1975), 210-12.

59. E. Schweizer (*Der Brief an die Kolosser* [Zürich: Benziger Verlag, 1976], 122-24) insists that worship of angels is what is meant, but I find his case unconvincing.

60. In the treatment of these passages I am indebted to the discussions by Williams, "The Cult of Angels at Colossae," 426-28, and Simon, "Remarques," 125-32.

61. Origen, *Contra Celsum* 5:6 (cf. 1:26).

62. The quotation in Origen does not mention archangels and has a few other minor variations in wording which do not affect the sense of the statement.

63. The statement translated here is in the Syriac recension, and I have used the translation given in Williams, "The Cult of Angels at Colossae," 426.

64. See Simon, "Remarques," 126-32. Cf. Lueken (*Michael*, 5), who regarded the *Kerygma Petrou* passage as "a direct witness for angel worship among the Jews."

65. Simon, "Remarques," 126.

66. Note that I do not flatly identify the law of Moses with these inferior powers, and I do not think that Paul did so either. I understand Paul's concern in both passages to be the question of whether Gentiles needed to observe these ritual practices in order to be full members of the elect in Christ. I agree that in theory he had no objection to Jewish Christians continuing to observe the law of Moses *so long as it did not interefere with their ability to accept gentile converts as full members of the church*. But it seems evident that from early on these passages were interpreted by Christians as a criticism of Judaism as such and that Paul's original concern with his gentile mission was overlooked in Christian theological interpretation of his thought until recent years. On Paul's view of the law of Moses and related matters, see now E. P. Sanders, *Paul, the Law, and the Jewish People*; and H. Räisänen, *Paul and the Law* (Tübingen: J. C. B. Mohr [Paul Siebeck]; Philadelphia: Fortress Press, 1983).

67. Study of ancient magical texts indicates, however, that Jewish influence should not be exaggerated; M. Smith, "The Jewish Elements in the Magical Papyri," in *Society of Biblical Literature 1986 Seminar Papers*, ed. K. H. Richards (Atlanta: Scholars Press, 1986), 455-62.

68. See Bousset, *Die Religion*, 342-57, for his treatment of "Die Hypostasen-Vorstellung."

69. G. F. Moore, "Intermediaries in Jewish Theology," *HTR* 15 (1922): 41-85.

70. H. L. Strack and P. Billerbeck, *Kommentar zum Neuen Testament aus Tal-*

mud und Midrasch (Munich: C. H. Beck, 1922–28), 2:302–33.

71. Bousset, *Die Religion*, 342 n. 1.

72. Ibid., 342, 343. In addition to personified Wisdom, Bousset included in this hypostasis category the divine glory (*doxa/kābôd, shekinah*), the "word of God" (*logos, memra*), the Spirit of God, and the Name of God (pp. 342–50). He also had a special section on Philo, whom he regarded as presenting the greatest elaboration of hypostases in ancient Judaism (pp. 351–54). The disdainful tone of the latter quotation is all too characteristic of Bousset's attitude toward ancient Judaism.

73. On *memra*, see R. Hayward, *Divine Name and Presence: The Memra* (Totowa, N.J.: Allanheld, Osmun & Co., 1981). Whether or not Hayward's own definition of the precise meaning of the term is accepted, he has at least clearly shown that *memra* cannot properly be understood as a "hypostasis." On *shekinah*, see A. M. Goldberg, *Untersuchungen über die Vorstellung von der Schekinah in der frühen rabbinischen Literatur* (Berlin: Walter de Gruyter, 1969); and E. E. Urbach, "The Shekina—The Presence of God in the World," in *The Sages*, 1:37–65.

74. G. Pfeifer, *Ursprung und Wesen der Hypostasenvorstellungen im Judentum* (Stuttgart: Calwer Verlag, 1967), 102–3. Pfeifer points out that of 106 writings and authors he surveyed, 69 contain no trace of hypostasis concepts. In the rest, what some (including Pfeifer) term hypostases appear casually, bearing no great importance.

75. Ibid., 66. S. Olyan is conducting a major research project on hypostatization in West Semitic religions. He informs me that evidence of such developments goes back at least to the Bronze Age and that there was apparently an increase in the tendency to hypostatize aspects of gods from the middle of the first millennium B.C.E. onward. He agrees, however, that true hypostatization involves the figure receiving cultic veneration such as sacrifice. This is important to note, for I emphasize the lack of cultic veneration of personified divine attributes in postexilic Judaism as an indication that these figures are not the same thing as the "hypostatized" figures in other contemporary religions.

76. The definition appears in W. O. E. Oesterley and G. H. Box, *The Religion and Worship of the Synagogue*, 2d ed. (London: Isaac Pitman & Sons, 1911), 195. It is accepted by H. Ringgren, *Word and Wisdom: Studies in the Hypostatization of Divine Qualities and Functions in the Ancient Near East* (Lund: Hakan Oholsson, 1947), 8. This seems to be the definition to which Bousset also subscribed in *Die Religion*, 342. Cf. Pfeifer's discussion of attempts to define "hypostasis" in *Ursprung und Wesen der Hypostasenvorstellungen*, 14–16. Olyan has described hypostatization as a process whereby an abstract quality/characteristic, title or epithet of a deity, or some item of the cultus of a deity (temple, altar, etc.) becomes treated as a new deity, receiving cultic devotions, or a process whereby the names of two or more deities are combined to form a new deity independent of the original deities.

77. See also R. Marcus, "On Biblical Hypostases of Wisdom," *HUCA* 23 (1950–51): 157–71; and A. Gibson, *Biblical Semantic Logic* (Oxford: Basil Blackwell, 1981), 92–96. See also chap. 2 of this book.

78. See, e.g., C. C. Rowland, *The Open Heaven: A Study of Apocalyptic in Judaism and Early Christianity* (New York: Crossroad; London: SPCK, 1982), 94–113.

79. Fossum, *The Name of God*. Fossum elaborates and defends views put forth earlier by his mentor, G. Quispel, "Gnosticism and the New Testament," in *The Bible and Modern Scholarship*, ed. J. P. Hyatt (Nashville: Abingdon Press, 1965), 252–71; idem, "The Origins of the Gnostic Demiurge," in *Kyriakon. Festschrift Johannes Quasten*, ed. P. Granfield and J. A. Jungman (Münster: Aschendorff, 1970), 1:271–76.

80. Fossum, *The Name of God*, v.

81. R. Bauckham, "The Worship of Jesus in Apocalyptic Christianity," *NTS* 27 (1980–81): 322.

82. Fossum argues that Simon Magus may have been thought of as a divine being and may have had a role in the cultus of his followers in his own lifetime. (See chap. 3 where I treat Simon and give a critique of Fossum's view.)

83. The curious Elephantine colony, whose temple ceased to function in the early fourth century B.C.E., may have preserved for a time something of the comparatively greater syncretism of preexilic Israelite religion, so frequently denounced in the OT prophets. See E. G. Kraeling, *IDB*, 2:83–85; idem, "New Light on the Elephantine Colony," *BA* 15/3 (1952): 50–67; A. Vincent, *La religion des Judéo-araméens d'Eléphantine* (Paris: Librairie orientaliste Paul Geuthner, 1937); and M. H. Silverman, *Religious Values in the Jewish Proper Names at Elephantine*, AOAT 217 (Neukirchen-Vluyn: Neukirchener Verlag, 1985). One preexilic Israelite religion and its Canaanite background, see, e.g., J. Day, "Asherah in the Hebrew Bible and Northwest Semitic Literature," *JBL* 105 (1986): 385–408; J. A. Emerton, "New Light on Israelite Religion: The Implications of the Inscriptions from Kuntillet 'Ajrud," *ZAW* 94 (1982): 2–20; and S. Olyan, *Asherah and the Cult of Yahweh in Israel*, SBLMS (Atlanta: Scholars Press, forthcoming).

84. See Hengel, *Judaism and Hellenism*, 1:267–309, for discussion of the "Hellenist reform party" and other attempts at assimilation.

85. "Little is known about the origin and development of traditions and beliefs within Samaritanism as a sect independent from Judaism between the late first century B.C.E. and the fourth century C.E." So M. F. Collins, "The Hidden Vessels in Samaritan Traditions," *JSJ* 3 (1972): 99. On Samaritan studies, see the surveys by J. Macdonald, "The Discovery of Samaritan Religions," *Religion* 2 (1972): 141–53; R. Pummer, "The Present State of Samaritan Studies II," *JSS* 22 (1977): 27–47; and the following works: J. Bowman, *The Samaritan Problem: Studies in the Relationships of Samaritanism, Judaism and Early Christianity* (Pittsburgh: Pickwick Press, 1975); H. G. Kippenberg, *Gerizim und Synagoge. Traditionsgeschichtliche Untersuchungen zur samaritanischen Religion der aramäischen Periode* (Berlin: Walter de Gruyter, 1971); R. J. Coggins, *Samaritans and Jews: The Origins of Samaritanism Reconsidered* (Oxford: Basil Blackwell, 1975); and S. J. Isser, *The Dositheans: A Samaritan Sect in Late Antiquity* (Leiden: E. J. Brill, 1976).

Chapter 2
Personified Divine Attributes as Divine Agents

1. See U. Wilckens, *Weisheit und Torheit*, BHT 26 (Tübingen: J. C. B. Mohr [Paul Siebeck], 1959); H. Hegermann, *Die Vorstellung vom Schöpfungsmittler im hellenistischen Judentum und Urchristentum*, TU 82 (Berlin: Akademie-Verlag, 1961); H. -F. Weiss, *Untersuchungen zur Kosmologie des hellenistischen und palästinischen Judentums*, TU 97 (Berlin: Akademie-Verlag, 1966); B. L. Mack, *Logos und Sophia. Untersuchungen zur Weisheitstheologie im hellenistischen Judentum* (Göttingen: Vandenhoeck & Ruprecht, 1973); Hamerton-Kelly, *Pre-Existence, Wisdom and the Son of Man*; B. A. Pearson, "Hellenistic-Jewish Wisdom Speculation and Paul," in *Aspects of Wisdom in Judaism and Early Christianity*, ed. R. L. Wilken (Notre Dame: Univ. of Notre Dame Press, 1975), 43–66.

2. See, e.g., Dunn, *Christology in the Making*, 163–250.

3. On Paul's use of wisdom speculation, see Pearson, "Hellenistic-Jewish Wisdom Speculation and Paul." For a summary of the evidence concerning the background of the Johannine prologue, see E. J. Epp, "Wisdom, Torah, Word: The Johannine Prologue and the Purpose of the Fourth Gospel," in *Current Issues in Biblical and Patristic Interpretation: Studies in Honor of M. C. Tenney*, ed. G. F. Hawthorne (Grand Rapids: Wm. B. Eerdmans, 1975), 128–46.

4. E.g., Bousset, *Die Religion*, 357; and chap. 1 of this book.

5. For a discussion of ancient Jewish Wisdom tradition, see G. von Rad, *Wisdom in Israel* (Nashville: Abingdon Press; London: SCM Press, 1972); J. L. Crenshaw, *Old Testament Wisdom: An Introduction* (Atlanta: John Knox Press, 1981); Ringgren, *Word and Wisdom*; and J. Marböck, *Weisheit im Wandel. Untersuchungen zur Weisheitstheologie bei Ben Sira* (Bonn: Peter Hanstein, 1971).

6. I assent to this interpretation of *'amôn* rather than "nursling," "little child," or the like. So, e.g., Ringgren, *Word and Wisdom*, 102–3.

7. On Wisdom's identification with Torah, see J. T. Sanders, *Ben Sira and Demotic Wisdom*, SBLMS 28 (Chico, Calif.: Scholars Press, 1983), 16–17, 24–26.

8. See the discussion of alternative figures in Ringgren, *Word and Wisdom*, 128–49; and E. Schüssler Fiorenza, "Wisdom Mythology and the Christological Hymns of the New Testament," in *Aspects of Wisdom in Judaism and Early Christianity*, ed. R. L. Wilken, 17–41.

9. See Schüssler Fiorenza's discussion of "reflective mythology," ibid.

10. See, e.g., Urbach, *The Sages*, 1:198–201.

11. The classic studies are E. R. Goodenough, *By Light, Light* (New Haven: Yale Univ. Press, 1935); and H. A. Wolfson, *Philo: Foundation of Religious Philosophy in Judaism, Christianity and Islam*, 2 vols. (Cambridge: Harvard Univ. Press, 1947). The best starting point for the beginner is S. Sandmel, *Philo of Alexandria: An Introduction* (New York: Oxford Univ. Press, 1979). See also the articles by Sandmel, E. Hilgert, and P. Borgen in *ANRW* 2. 21/1, which include bibliographies and surveys of research. On Philo's Logos doctrine and its relation to Jewish Wisdom speculation, see Mack, *Logos und Sophia*. See also Dunn, *Christology in the Making*, 220–30; and L. K. K. Dey, *The Intermediary World and Patterns of*

Perfection in Philo and Hebrews, SBLDS 25 (Missoula, Mont.: Scholars Press, 1975).

12. The creative and royal powers are given special prominence in Philo, who likens them to the cherubim over the mercy seat in the tabernacle and expounds the two Greek terms for God in the LXX (*theos* and *kyrios*) as representing these two attributes (e.g., *Quaest. Exod.* 2.62; *Vit. Mos.* 2.99; *Quaest. Gen.* 2.51; 4.2; *Cherub.* 27). See the discussion of Philo's view of these two attributes in connection with rabbinic traditions by Segal, *Two Powers in Heaven*, 159-81, and 38-56, 85-89, 98-108. He shows how such language may have been exploited by gnostic groups to justify the notion that there was more than one god in heaven. See also Urbach, *The Sages*, 1:448-61, for a discussion of the two *middoth* ("attributes") of God—"justice" and "mercy"—in rabbinic literature. There these personifications appear in stories (*haggadah*) designed to make a point about the character of God usually to emphasize that his mercy is dominant. See also N. A. Dahl and A. F. Segal, "Philo and the Rabbis on the Names of God," *JSJ* 9 (1978): 1-28.

13. Cf. *Quaest. Exod.* 2.68, where Philo portrays the ranking of the Logos and the other chief divine attributes by using imagery from the tabernacle.

14. The personification of divine attributes/activities includes God's glory (*kābôd*), name, voice, word, arm, face, power or powers, justice, truth, righteousness, mercy, and law; see Pfeifer, *Ursprung und Wesen der Hypostasenvorstellungen im Judentum*. For discussions of the *shekinah*, a rabbinic way of speaking of God in encounter with the world, see Goldberg, *Untersuchungen über die Vorstellung von der Scheikinah*; and Urbach, *The Sages*, 1:37-65. From earlier discussions, see Moore, "Intermediaries in Jewish Theology." Moore argues that the hypostases are only phenomena of ancient Jewish religious language. See also Marcus, "On Biblical Hypostases of Wisdom."

15. See above, pp. 35-39.

16. For a discussion of the hypostasis question from the standpoint of modern linguistics, see Gibson, *Biblical Semantic Logic*, 92-96.

17. E.g., Ringgren, *Word and Wisdom*; Bousset, *Die Religion*; and Fossum, *The Name of God*.

18. Dunn, *Christology in the Making*, 163-76, 213-30. I am not persuaded by his exegesis of important New Testament texts in support of his conception of the origin and meaning of the early Christian doctrine of the preexistence of Christ.

19. Schüssler Fiorenza, "Wisdom Mythology," esp. 26-33.

20. Marcus, "On Biblical Hypostases of Wisdom," esp. 167-71. He borrows the term "constancy fallacy" to describe the error he warns against.

21. Fossum, *The Name of God*, 345-46. Note that *2 Enoch* 30:8 says that God commanded his wisdom to create man, but in 30:11-12 we read that man was created to be great and glorious "and to have my wisdom," which suggests that wisdom is a divine attribute that can be shared. Fossum shows the continuing influence of Ringgren, *Word and Wisdom*. Ringgren's interpretation of personified divine attributes in ancient Judaism as hypostases was designed to support his argument that "the hypostatization of divine functions has played a considerable part in the origin and growth of polytheism" (p. 193), against the evolutionistic

theory of a development from *mana* on through polytheism to monotheism. I suspect that this polemic controlled too much his interpretation of the ancient Jewish texts and forced upon the personification of divine attributes in Judaism a meaning and significance derived more from his theory about the development of polytheism than from the texts themselves or from the religious life of ancient Jews. He noted that the personification of divine attributes in ancient Judaism did not result in their becoming deities (p. 192) but failed to recognize that this fact really calls into question his whole understanding of what the Jewish personification of divine attributes represented. Cf. Marcus, "On Biblical Hypostases of Wisdom."

22. On the religious significance of the divine name in ancient Judaism, see, e.g., Urbach, *The Sages*, 1:124–34; and Bietenhard, *TDNT*, 5:252–70. Old Testament texts (e.g., Deut. 16:1) that refer to God's name as dwelling in the temple seem to reflect an attempt to refer to God as both truly present there but also not fully "contained" by the temple. God's name is not really a distinct entity, because no separate sacrificial cultus was directed to it but only to Yahweh himself, at least in post-exilic time.

23. This important distinction is discussed in Gibson, *Biblical Semantic Logic*, 92–96.

24. For a brief introduction to *Joseph and Asenath* and bibliography, see Charlesworth, *The Pseudepigrapha and Modern Research*, 137–40. My quotations are from *AOT*, 465–504.

25. See H. -F. Weiss, *Untersuchungen zur Kosmologie*, esp. 318–31. Regarding the Logos, Weiss wrote, "For Philo the Logos did not represent an absolutely self-existent being, but merely an aspect of the concept of God" (p. 320). And as for the personified attributes of ancient Judaism collectively, I find Weiss's description quite apt: "In Philo, as also in rabbinic Judaism, Wisdom, Torah and the Logos are only the sides of God turned toward the world and men respectively. That is, they represent his acts of revelation as they come to expression in the creation (and in redemption)" (p. 330). Goodenough (*By Light, Light*) also noted that Philo resisted the pagan tendency to hypostatize divine attributes (p. 45) and that Philo's talk of the "powers" was only a human way of thinking of God (pp. 45–46). In my judgment, Pfeifer (*Ursprung und Wesen der Hypostasenvorstellungen im Judentum*) was mistaken in thinking that Philo's discussion of divine "powers" involved an exclusion of God from direct action in the world and amounted to a prominent hypostasis conception (p. 103). Pfeifer failed to understand that Philo was concerned to affirm that God does act upon the world and that God is far greater than these acts reveal.

26. Note the same point in Dunn, *Christology in the Making*, 170.

27. Hengel (*Judaism and Hellenism*, 1:153–56) assents to Bousset's view that postexilic Judaism was characterized by many hypostases, but he also grants that such figures had no role in the religious devotion of Jews and had their place purely in reflection (ibid., 1:155, agreeing with Pfeifer, *Ursprung*, 16).

28. Goodenough, *By Light, Light*, 38–39. Note, e.g., Philo *Conf. Ling.* 168–75; *Leg. Alleg.* 3.115; *Spec. Leg.* 4.92, 123, 168; 3.111; *Quaest. Gen.* 2.75.

29. Despite the familiarity with Greek language and thought, shown in *Wisdom of Solomon*, the book retains a strong emphasis upon Jewish traditions. Note, e.g., the description of the righteous man, who reproaches the ungodly "for sins against the law" (2:12), whose "manner of life is unlike that of others," whose "ways are strange," and who regards the ways of the ungodly as "unclean" (2:15-16), surely references to the perception of the observant Jew from the viewpoint of the unobservant and the Gentile. Although the explicit language of resurrection is not used, such eschatological hope is surely reflected in passages like 3:1-8, which refers to a time of divine "visitation" when the righteous will "govern the nations and rule over peoples."

30. E.g., Philo *Fug.* 101, "chiefest of all Beings intellectually perceived"; *Opf. Mun.* 24-25. "The world discerned only by the intellect is nothing else than the Word of God. . . . The world described by the mind, would be the very Word of God."

Chapter 3
Exalted Patriarchs as Divine Agents

1. D. S. Russell, *The Old Testament Pseudepigrapha* (Philadelphia: Fortress Press, 1987), is an introductory discussion of this matter.

2. Opinions vary as to whether Christians were unique in ascribing such heavenly glory to a contemporary and, if this was a unique step, then what the significance of it was. See, e.g., Segal, *Two Powers in Heaven*, 218, and n. 97 (also pp. 65-69 of this chapter).

3. See J. C. VanderKam, *Enoch and the Growth of an Apocalyptic Tradition*, CBQMS 16 (Washington, D.C.: Catholic Biblical Association, 1984), who deals mainly with the early stages of the Enoch tradition. See also P. Grelot, "La légende d'Henoch dans les apocryphes et dans la bible," *Recherches de science religieuse* 46 (1958): 5-26, 181-210, esp. 199-210, where he discusses the religious significance of Enoch in ancient Judaism.

4. So, e.g., Charlesworth, *The Pseudepigrapha and Modern Research*, 143; and J. C. VanderKam, *Textual and Historical Studies in the Book of Jubilees*, HSM 14 (Missoula, Mont.: Scholars Press, 1977). The quotations are from *AOT*, 10-139.

5. Another hint of a body of Enoch lore is found in *Sir.* 44:16, where the Greek version calls Enoch "an example of repentance (*hypodeigma metanoias*) to all generations." The Hebrew text of *Sirach* at this point calls him "a sign of knowledge (*'ôt da'at*) for all succeeding generations." See Grelot, "La légende d'Henoch," 181-83. Cf. also *Wis.* 4:10-15, which is probably an allusion to, and elaboration of, Gen. 5:24.

6. Note the reference in *T. Zeb.* 3:4 to the "law of Enoch." This is striking, since one expects to see the name of Moses associated with divine law.

7. Note that *T. Abr.* 13:21-27 (as in *AOT*; cf. 11:6ff. in *OTP*) explicitly restricts Enoch's activity in the last judgment to that of recorder of human deeds, insisting that "it is the Lord who sentences." This seems to be a (deliberate?) contrast with his role in *1 Enoch* where he is designated the "Son of man" (71:14), who is said

to carry out eschatological judgment (e.g., 49:4; 55:4; 69:27).

8. Scholars tend to agree about the date of the earliest layer of material more than about the latest (*1 Enoch* 37—71), known as the Parables or Similitudes. But there is an emerging consensus in dating these chapters in the late first century C.E. In addition to the literature listed in Charlesworth, *The Pseudepigrapha and Modern Research*, 98-103, see also D. W. Suter, *Tradition and Composition in the Parables of Enoch*, SBLDS 47 (Missoula, Mont.: Scholars Press, 1979); and M. Black, *The Book of Enoch or 1 Enoch: A New English Translation* (Leiden: E. J. Brill, 1985). Other recent English translations and introductory discussions appear in *OTP*, 1:5-89 and in *AOT*, 196-319.

9. See, e.g., Charlesworth, *The Pseudepigrapha and Modern Research*, 103-6; *OTP*, 1:91-221; *AOT*, 321-62.

10. On the growth of the tradition, see Grelot, "La légende d'Henoch"; and VanderKam, *Enoch and the Growth of an Apocalyptic Tradition*.

11. Because the title "Son of man" appears frequently in the Gospels as a self-designation of Jesus, there is a vast body of scholarship on the background and possible meaning(s) of the term. See, e.g., M. Casey, *Son of Man*; Lindars, *Jesus Son of Man*; and C. Colpe, *TDNT*, 8:400-77. As used here in *1 Enoch* 37-71, see Black, *The Book of Enoch*, 188-89, 206-7.

12. In *1 Enoch* 51:3 the manuscripts vary between "his throne" and "my throne" (i.e., God's). In 62:2 all manuscripts agree in reading "the Lord of Spirits sat upon the throne of his glory," but it is often insisted that the context demands that it is the "Elect One" who sits upon the throne. See, e.g., Black, *The Book of Enoch*, 235.

13. In this passage the title "Chosen One" does not appear, but 46:2 says, "The Lord of spirits has chosen him." Thus he is clearly the same figure elsewhere referred to as the "Chosen One." The influence of Dan. 7:9-14 can be seen in the description of God with hair white like wool (46:1; cf. Dan. 7:9b) and perhaps most notably in the description of the second figure as "that Son of man" (46:2; cf. Dan. 7:13). It is worth noting that the first reference to the Chosen One as "Son of man" is in this passage, where the influence of Dan. 7:13-14 is apparent.

14. For comments on this passage, see Black, *The Book of Enoch*, 206-9; and L. Hartman, *Prophecy Interpreted* (Lund: C. W. K. Gleerup, 1966), 118-26.

15. Some have insisted that the manlike figure of Dan. 7:13-14 was intended by the writer as only a symbol of the "saints of the most high": so M. D. Hooker, *The Son of Man in Mark* (London: SPCK, 1967). Others take the figure to be a genuine heavenly being: so Rowland, *The Open Heaven*.

16. Note that in 71:15, Enoch is linked with the eschatological hope ("the world which is to come") and is promised everlasting enjoyment of God's favor ("You will have it [peace] for ever and for ever and ever"). He is also told that the elect will "walk according to your [Enoch's] way" and will be joined with him in eschatological blessing forever (71:16). The older English translation of *1 Enoch* in R. H. Charles, *Apocrypha and Pseudepigrapha of the Old Testament*, 2 vols.

(Oxford: Clarendon Press, 1913), obscures this identification of the "Son of man" with Enoch, emending without manuscript support or good reason the statement "You are the Son of man" (71:14) to read "This is the Son of man."

17. See, e.g., J. H. Charlesworth, "The SNTS Pseudepigrapha Seminars at Tübingen and Paris on the Books of Enoch," *NTS* 25 (1979): 315-23; and M. A. Knibb, "The Date of the Parables of Enoch: A Critical Review," *NTS* 25 (1979): 345-59; and C. L. Mearns, "Dating the Similitudes of Enoch," *NTS* 25 (1979): 360-69.

18. See P. S. Alexander, "The Historical Setting of the Hebrew Book of Enoch," *JJS* 28 (1977): 156-80; and his introduction to his translation of *3 Enoch* in *OTP*, 1:223-53.

19. On Metatron, see H. Odeberg, *3 Enoch* (Cambridge: Cambridge Univ. Press, 1928; reprinted with prolegomenon by J. C. Greenfield, New York: Ktav, 1973), 79-146; G. Scholem, *Jewish Gnosticism, Merkabah Mysticism and Talmudic Tradition*, 2d ed. (New York: Jewish Theological Seminary, 1965), 42-55; S. Lieberman, "Metatron, the Meaning of His Name and His Functions," appendix in I. Gruenwald, *Apocalyptic and Merkabah Mysticism* (Leiden: E. J. Brill, 1980), 235-41; and Alexander's discussion and references in *OTP*, 1:243-44. All the evidence suggests that "Metatron" is a comparatively late variation in chief angel speculation, though the idea of a chief angel/agent is probably much earlier.

20. So Knibb's translation in *AOT*. Black (*The Book of Enoch*, 251) translates the first part of the statement more freely, "My whole body became weak from fear," and he cites a similar expression in 60:3.

21. I follow the division numbering and translation by F. I. Andersen in *OTP*, 1:91-221.

22. Although there are some serious flaws in the discussion by M. Casey, "Chronology and the Development of Pauline Christology," I agree with his emphasis upon the "dynamic creative process" in ancient Judaism that produced many variations in the way "intermediary" figures were elaborated, their functions and status often increasing under changing religious conditions (see, e.g., ibid., 128).

23. W. A. Meeks, "The Divine Agent and His Counterfeit in Philo and the Fourth Gospel," in *Aspects of Religious Propaganda in Judaism and Early Christianity*, ed. E. Schüssler Fiorenza, 43-67, esp. 45.

24. See esp. Meeks, *The Prophet-King*; idem, "Moses as God and King," in *Religions in Antiquity: Essays in Memory of Erwin Ramsdell Goodenough*, ed. J. Neusner (Leiden: E. J. Brill, 1968), 354-71. Moses was also dealt with in pagan sources; see J. G. Gager, *Moses in Greco-Roman Paganism*, SBLMS 16 (Missoula, Mont.: Scholars Press, 1972).

25. See, e.g., L. Rost, *Judaism Outside the Hebrew Canon* (Nashville: Abingdon Press, 1976).

26. This translates the Greek *hōmoiōsen auton doxē hagiōn*. For "holy ones" denoting angelic beings, see, e.g., Sir. 42:17; Deut. 33:3; Job 5:1; *1 Enoch* 1:9; 9:3; *Ascen. Isa.* 6:8; 10:6. Cf. Philo's description of Abraham (*Sac.* 5) as made "equal to the angels" (*isos angelois gegonos*).

27. R. Smend (*Die Weisheit des Jesus Sirach. Hebräisch und Deutsch* [Berlin: G. Reimer, 1906]) restores the Hebrew phrase here as [*we yikanehôh be*]'*elôhim* and renders the phrase "Er gab ihn den Ehrennamen eines Gottes." W. O. E. Oesterley (*The Wisdom of Jesus the Son of Sirach or Ecclesiasticus* [Cambridge: Cambridge Univ. Press, 1912], 204) accepted Smend's restoration and translated it, "And he be-titled him with (the name of) God." In his translation of *Sirach*, Oesterley later rendered the phrase, "He made him glorious as God" (*The Wisdom of Ben-Sira* [London: SPCK, 1916]). F. Vattioni (*Ecclesiastico: Testo ebraico con apparto critico e versioni greca, latina e siriaca* [Naples: Istituto Orientale di Napoli, 1968]) offers the Hebrew as *we* [*yikanehoh iš*]'*elôhim*, which may be translated, "And he titled him, though a man, 'god.'"

28. M. R. James, trans., *The Biblical Antiquities of Philo* (New York: Ktav, 1971 [1917]). There is further evidence of early speculation about Moses' Mt. Sinai ascent: e.g., *Jubilees* claims to be an angelic revelation given to Moses on this occasion (see the Prologue and 1:27). For discussion of rabbinic traditions about the Sinai ascent, see D. J. Halperin, *The Merkabah in Rabbinic Literature* (New Haven, Conn.: American Oriental Society, 1982), 128-33; and Meeks, *The Prophet-King*, 205-9.

29. Charlesworth, *The Pseudepigrapha and Modern Research*, 110-11; Meeks, *The Prophet-King*, 147-50; C. R. Holladay, "The Portrait of Moses in Ezekiel the Tragedian," in *Society of Biblical Literature 1976 Seminar Papers* (Missoula, Mont.: Scholars Press, 1976), 447-52; P. W. van der Horst, "Moses' Throne Vision in Ezekiel the Dramatist," *JJS* 34 (1983): 21-9; H. Jacobson, "Mysticism and Apocalyptic in Ezekiel's Exagoge," *ICS* 6 (1981): 272-93; idem, *The Exagoge of Ezekiel* (Cambridge: Cambridge Univ. Press, 1983); and the review essay by P. W. van der Horst, "Some Notes on the *Exagoge* of Ezekiel," *Mnemosyne* 37 (1984): 354-75. The surviving portion was preserved by the church father Eusebius, *Praeparatio Evangelica* (9.28.2-4; 29.5-16), who was quoting from the work of the ancient historian Alexander Polyhistor, *Peri Ioudaion*. The Greek text is published in A.-M. Denis, *Fragmenta Pseudepigraphorum quae supersunt Graeca* (Leiden: E. J. Brill, 1970), 207-16; B. Snell, *Tragicorum Graecorum Fragmenta I* (Göttingen: Vandenhoeck & Ruprecht, 1971), 288-301; and in Jacobson, *The Exagoge of Ezekiel*, 50-67 (Greek with translation on facing papers). Hereafter I cite Jacobson's line numbers.

30. Moses is given the symbols of rule, the throne, scepter, and crown (lines 74-75), and beholds "the whole earth" and everything beneath and above it (lines 77-78); and the interpretation says that he will both lead and have prophetic knowledge (lines 85-89).

31. Meeks, *The Prophet-King*, 148-49; van der Horst, "Moses' Throne Vision," 25. A similar view was taken by Goodenough, *By Light, Light*.

32. Jacobson, "Mysticism and Apocalyptic in Ezekiel's Exagoge," esp. 272-78.

33. Holladay, "The Portrait of Moses in Ezekiel the Tragedian." Holladay sees the play as a piece of Jewish propaganda directed to a pagan audience (p. 448). Meeks (*The Prophet-King*, 149) sees it as "wholesome entertainment" intended

for a Jewish audience. Jacobson (*The Exagogè of Ezekiel*, 18) and van der Horst ("Some Notes on the Exagoge of Ezekiel," 358, 366) see the intended audience as composed of Jews and pagans, with the latter "the most important part" (ibid., 366).

34. See also Jacobson's critique of Holladay ("Mysticism and Apocalyptic in Ezekiel's Exagoge," 287–89) and his discussion (*The Exagoge of Ezekiel*, 89–97) where he shows how the author has probably drawn upon both Jewish and Greek traditions in the dream scene.

35. Meeks, *The Prophet-King*. Holladay's attempt to distinguish this passage from other Jewish texts in which the divine throne is mentioned does not, I think, succeed. There are variations, to be sure, but also fundamental similarities.

36. Jacobson ("Mysticism and Apocalyptic in Ezekiel's Exagoge," 279) sees the figure as "a surrogate for the Deity Himself" and thinks that Ezekiel deliberately intended to reject traditions according Moses direct contact with God.

37. Jacobson (*The Exagoge of Ezekiel*, 90–92) quite correctly points to passages such as Pss. 110:1–2; 147:4; Isa. 40:26; Dan. 7:13–14; and *1 Enoch* 25:3 as reflections of the background of the imagery for the author and for Jewish audiences.

38. Cf. Pseudo-Philo *Bib. Ant.* 18:5 where Abraham is raised "above the firmament" and is shown "all the orderings of the stars." The behavior of the stars in the *Exagōgē*, however, may suggest that here they are to be taken as living beings, probably angels.

39. See Jacobson (*The Exagoge of Ezekiel*, 201 n. 14) for references to later Samaritan and rabbinic texts in which Moses is connected with a throne, although these texts seem to picture the throne as earthly. Cf. also Matt. 23:2.

40. I do not think that Jacobson's view is persuasive. He makes too much of the distinctive features of the vision and interpretation in the *Exagōgē*, which may have arisen under the influence of the literary traditions Jacobson himself cites (*The Exagoge of Ezekiel*, 95–97). On the other hand, van der Horst's claim ("Moses' Throne Vision," 25) that the vision scene "certainly implies a deification of Moses" seems to me an exaggeration. The seating of Moses on the throne need imply nothing more than the appointment of Moses as ruler (perhaps cosmic ruler) on God's behalf.

41. See also Goodenough, *By Light, Light*, 199–234; Meeks, *The Prophet-King*, 100–30; idem, "Moses as God and King"; idem, "The Divine Agent and His Counterfeit"; C. R. Holladay, *Theios Aner in Hellenistic Judaism*, SBLDS 40 (Missoula, Mont.: Scholars Press, 1977), 103–98; R. Williamson, "Philo and New Testament Christology," in *Studia Biblica 1978: III*, ed. E. A. Livingstone (Sheffield: JSOT Press, 1980), 439–45; B. L. Mack, "Imitatio Mosis," *Studia Philonica* 1 (1972): 27–55. Cf. also W. Richardson, "The Philonic Patriarchs as *Nomos Empsuchos*," in *Studia Patristica I*, ed. K. Aland and F. L. Cross (Berlin: Akademie-Verlag, 1957), 515–25.

42. I cite the LCL twelve-volume edition of Philo, ed. and trans. F. H. Colson, G. H. Whitaker, and R. Marcus (Cambridge: Harvard Univ. Press, 1929–53).

43. See esp. the treatment of Philo's references to Exod. 7:1 by Holladay, *Theios Aner in Hellenistic Judaism*, 108–55.

44. The Hebrew text of *Sir.* 45:2 indicates that the likening of Moses to a "god," alluding to Exod. 7:1, preceded Philo and was familiar in Palestine as well as Alexandria.

45. Thus, e.g., Meeks's description of Philo's view of Moses as "intermediary *par excellence* between the divine and the human" ("The Divine Agent and His Counterfeit," 47) must be understood in the sense that Moses' endowment with knowledge of God and with the qualities of God's character set him above other humans, even other godly examples, but only so that he may serve as the pattern for the religious aspirations of others (cf. ibid., 53–54; and idem, "Moses as God and King," 355).

46. Thus my position differs from that of Goodenough (*By Light, Light,* 199–234). He understood Philo as espousing a view of Moses as "a divine savior" (p. 220). He described Philo as thoroughly captive to the ancient "popular tendency to deify great figures and heroes" (p. 224), and in tension with his monotheistic tradition. I suggest that Philo represents an ethicizing and philosophical adaptation of the glorification of Moses and furnishes only indirect evidence of a conception of Moses as God's exalted chief agent and the heavenly vizier. Cf. also Holladay, *Theios Aner in Hellenistic Judaism,* 103–98.

47. Philo: *Vit. Mos.* 1.158; *Prob.* 42–44; *Somn.* 2.187–89; *Mut.* 19, 125–29; *Sac.* 8–9; *Leg. Alleg.* 1.40–41; *Migr. Abr.* 84; *Det.* 160–62; and the Greek fragment in *Quaest. Exod.* 2.6.

48. Holladay, *Theios Aner in Hellenistic Judaism,* 108–55. He discusses all the Philonic passages (n. 47) carefully and persuasively.

49. See Holladay's concluding comments to his discussion of Philo's references to Exod. 7:1, ibid., 154–55. See also Meeks, "The Divine Agent and His Counterfeit." He also points to Philo's interaction with these Hellenistic king traditions (esp. pp. 48–54).

50. Goodenough, *By Light, Light,* 223–34.

51. Cf. Holladay, *Theios Aner in Hellenistic Judaism,* 155–98.

52. Goodenough, *By Light, Light,* 226.

53. Meeks, "Moses as God and King," 354–65; idem, "The Divine Agent and His Counterfeit," 45–49. Goodenough himself had earlier shown in Philo the influence of Hellenistic ideals of kingship (*By Light, Light,* 181–87); idem, "The Political Philosophy of Hellenistic Kingship," in *Yale Classical Studies,* ed. A. H. Harmon (New Haven: Yale Univ. Press, 1928), 1:55–102.

54. Meeks, "The Divine Agent and His Counterfeit," 49–54. For major examples of Philo's polemic, see *Flaccus* and *The Embassy to Gaius.*

55. See the many references to Moses in vol. 10 of the LCL edition of Philo (pp. 378–90). Meeks has also shown that Moses was highly revered in a wide array of ancient Jewish and Samaritan sources (*The Prophet-King,* 100–257). Although much of this material is not pre-Philonic, and although we cannot easily assume that all that was said of Moses in these later sources goes back to the pre-Philonic period, nevertheless the prominence of Moses in them is probably evidence that the general tradition of Moses as God's appointed agent is quite old.

56. Note the prominence of such figures as Adam and Abraham in Philo. See

the index of names in vol. 10 of the LCL edition of Philo (pp. 271–80, 280–86). See, e.g., the representation of Adam as God's "viceroy" (*hyparchōn*) deemed "worthy of second place" in Philo *Opf. Mun.* 148.

57. The document is quoted in Origen *Comm. Joh.* 2.31 and in *Philocalia* 22.15. The Greek text is printed in Denis, *Fragmenta Pseudepigraphorum*, 61–62. See the discussion by J. Z. Smith, "The Prayer of Joseph," in *Religions in Antiquity*, ed. Neusner, 253–94, and the secondary literature he cites. Smith also introduces and translates the text in *OTP*, 2:699–714.

58. J. Z. Smith ("The Prayer of Joseph," 254) notes that the work is described by Nicephorus in his *Stichometry* as a document of 1,100 *stichoi*.

59. The statement about the descent is placed on the lips of Uriel. Taking the statement as a reference to Jacob requires seeing it as an indirect quotation rather than a direct quotation. But if the latter is preferred, then the statement might be a claim by Uriel to be this descending angel. See J. Z. Smith's discussion, "The Prayer of Joseph," 257.

60. Ibid., 281–92.

61. Ibid., 259–71.

62. Note that *1 Enoch* 51:4–5 appears to promise that all the elect will "become angels in heaven," suggesting that the description of certain patriarchs as angels was part of a larger conception of the reward of the righteous as inheriting angelic nature. Cf. also Mark 12:24/Matt. 22:30/Luke 20:36, which may be a modified reflection of the same idea.

63. Meeks, "Moses as God and King," 365–71; idem, "The Divine Agent and His Counterfeit," esp. 49–54; Grelot, "La légende d'Henoch," 191–210.

64. Cf. J. J. Collins, "The Heavenly Representative: The 'Son of Man' in the Similitudes of Enoch," in *Ideal Figures in Ancient Judaism: Profiles and Paradigms*, ed. J. J. Collins and G. W. E. Nickelsburg (Chico, Calif.: Scholars Press, 1980), 111–34; and Grelot, "La légende d'Henoch," 207–10.

65. Goodenough, *By Light, Light*, 263.

66. Ibid., 233. Goodenough likens the address to Moses here with the prayers of "Christian mystics" directed to Christ.

67. See, e.g., the review of *By Light, Light* by A. D. Nock in *Gnomon* 13 (1937): 156–65; reprinted in Nock, *Essays on Religion and the Ancient World*, 1:459–68. Cf. E. R. Goodenough, "Literal Mystery in Hellenistic Judaism," in *Quantulacumque: Studies Presented to Kirsopp Lake*, ed. R. P. Casey (London: Christophers, 1937), 227–41. Meeks says that "we cannot exclude the possibility" of some sort of Philonic mysticism, but on the whole he seems to find Goodenough's theory less than demonstrable ("The Divine Agent and His Counterfeit," 53). Goodenough's *Jewish Symbols* was intended to give final proof of a widespread ancient Jewish mystery religion, but see M. Smith, "Goodenough's *Jewish Symbols* in Retrospect," *JBL* 86 (1967): 53–68.

68. So, e.g., Williamson, "Philo and New Testament Christology," 442; M. Casey, "Chronology and the Development of Pauline Christology," 127, 130; van der Horst, "Moses' Throne Vision," 26 n. 40. Van der Horst seems to press Philo's talk of the "divinity" of Moses somewhat woodenly. He shows no knowl-

edge of the study by Holladay, *Theios Aner in Hellenistic Judaism*, which cogently "unpacks" Philo's rhetoric.

69. See, e.g., *Spec. Leg.* 1.13–31, which emphatically rejects any object of worship except God.

70. See Meeks, *The Prophet-King*, 125 n. 3: "The 'prayer' addressed to Moses as Hierophant (*Somn.* 1.164f.) is quite possibly rhetorical, though admittedly the language is strong."

71. Isser, *The Dositheans*; idem, "Dositheus, Jesus and a Moses Aretalogy," in *Christianity, Judaism and Other Greco-Roman Cults: Studies for Morton Smith at Sixty, Part Four*, ed. J. Neusner (Leiden: E. J. Brill, 1975), 167–89.

72. See the review of research by W. A. Meeks, "Simon Magus in Recent Research," *RelSRev* 3 (1977): 137–42; and Pummer, "The Present State of Samaritan Studies II," esp. 27–35. Cf. K. Rudolf, "Simon—Magus oder Gnosticus?" *TRu* 42 (1977): 279–359. Major studies include K. Beyschlag, *Simon Magus und die christliche Gnosis*, WUNT 16 (Tübingen: J. C. B. Mohr [Paul Siebeck], 1975); and G. Lüdemann, *Untersuchungen zur simonianischen Gnosis* (Göttingen: Vandenhoeck & Ruprecht, 1975). Cf. also R. Bergmeier, "Die Gestalt des Simon Magus in Act 8 und in der simonianischen Gnosis—Aporien einer Gesamtdeutung," *ZNW* 77 (1986): 267–75. The Acts 8:9–13 reference to acclamations of Simon as "the power of God which is called great" cannot be taken as clear indication that Simon was the object of a cultus; cf. Meeks, "Simon Magus," 139.

Chapter 4
Principal Angels

1. For surveys of ancient Jewish angelology, L. Hackspill, "L'angelologie juive à l'époque neo-testamentaire," *RB* 11 (1902): 527–50; J.-B. Frey, "L'angelologie juive au temps de Jésus-Christ," *RSPT* (1911): 75–110; J. Barbel, *Christos Angelos* (Bonn: Peter Hanstein, 1964 [1941]), 1–33; H. B. Kuhn, "The Angelology of the Non-Canonical Jewish Apocalypses"; B. Tsakonas, "The Angelology According to the Later Jewish Literature," *Theologica* 34 (1963): 136–51; Schäfer, *Rivalität*, 9–74; Carr, *Angels and Principalities*, 25–40; Bietenhard, *Die himmlische Welt*, 101–42; Noll, "Angelology in the Qumran Texts." For specialized discussion of angels in rabbinic sources, see Urbach, "The Celestial Retinue," in *The Sages*, 1:135–83, and Schäfer, *Rivalität*. For the Old Testament, see W. H. Heidt, *The Angelology of the Old Testament* (Washington, D.C.: Catholic University of America, 1949); Stier, *Gott und sein Engel*; and R. Yates, "Angels in the Old Testament," *ITQ* 38 (1971): 164–67.

2. A glance at a concordance will confirm my observation. Note that these data are often overlooked in surveys of postexilic Jewish angelology. For surveys of NT data, see, e.g., H. Schlier, *Principalities and Powers in the New Testament* (QD 1/3; Freiburg: Verlag Herder; London: Thomas Nelson & Sons, 1961); idem, "The Angels According to the New Testament," in *The Relevance of the New Testament*

(London: Burns & Oates; New York: Herder & Herder, 1967), 172-92; G. B. Caird, *Principalities and Powers: A Study in Pauline Theology* (Oxford: Clarendon Press, 1956); W. Wink, *Naming the Powers: The Language of Power in the New Testament* (Philadelphia: Fortress Press, 1984).

3. E.g., note the lengthy description of such a heavenly ascent in *2 Enoch* 1—9. For further references, see A. F. Segal, "Heavenly Ascent in Hellenistic Judaism, Early Christianity, and Their Environment," *ANRW* 2. 23/2:1333-94.

4. The earliest stage of this principal angel conception may be the references to the "angel of the Lord" in some of the narrative sections of the OT (e.g., Gen. 16:7-14). On this figure, see Stier, *Gott und sein Engel*.

5. Lueken, *Michael*, esp. 133-66.

6. Lueken's case for Jewish worship of angels rests upon misinterpretation of texts I have discussed in chap. 2. His methodological errors include the use of rabbinic and patristic materials too simplistically to describe pre-Christian Jewish angelology. He was theologically tendentious at times, as reflected in his comparison of Judaism and Christianity on p. 166.

7. Barbel, *Christos Angelos*. The 1964 edition contains an additional chapter (pp. 335-52) discussing literature subsequent to 1941; my references are to the 1964 edition. See also A. Bakker ("Christ an Angel? A Study of Early Christian Docetism," *ZNW* 32 [1933]: 255-65), who depends too heavily upon Harris's "Testimony Book" hypothesis to be of much value (see J. R. Harris, *Testimonies*, 2 vols. [Cambridge: Cambridge Univ. Press, 1916, 1920]).

8. M. Werner, *Die Entstehung des christlichen Dogmas* (Bern: Paul Haupt, 1941; 2d ed., 1954). Werner prepared an edition for translation by S. G. F. Brandon: *The Formation of Christian Dogma* (New York: Harper & Brothers, 1957); I refer to a reprint (Boston: Beacon Press, 1965).

9. Ibid., vii.

10. Ibid., 120-30. One consequence of Werner's thesis was that he saw the Christology of Arius as the much more authentic preservation of the earliest teaching than what became orthodox Christian teaching concerning the person of Christ (ibid., 131-61).

11. E.g., his attempt to make the NT use of *kyrios* evidence that the exalted Jesus was understood as an angelic being has justifiably been ignored. Cf. ibid., 123-25.

12. W. Michaelis, *Zur Engelchristologie im Urchristentum: Abbau der Konstruktion Martin Werners* (Basel: Heinrich Majer, 1942). On the influence of Michaelis, see, e.g., J. Daniélou, *The Theology of Jewish Christianity* (Philadelphia: Westminster Press; London: Darton, Longman & Todd, 1964 [1958]), 118 n. 3. On Werner's views in the light of subsequent study, see Barbel, *Christos Angelos*, 341-44, 347-50.

13. G. Kretschmer, *Studien zur frühchristlichen Trinitätstheologie* (Tübingen: J. C. B. Mohr [Paul Siebeck], 1956).

14. Daniélou, *The Theology of Jewish Christianity*.

15. Similarly, see the approach of R. N. Longenecker, *The Christology of Early Jewish Christianity* (London: SCM Press, 1970); esp. 26-32 on "Angelomorphic

Christology"; and idem, "Some Distinctive Early Christological Motifs," *NTS* 14 (1967/68): 529-45.

16. Dunn, *Christology in the Making*, 149-59.

17. Ibid., e.g., 149, 154, 158; cf. also 162.

18. Segal, *Two Powers in Heaven*, 208.

19. Rowland, *The Open Heaven*, 94-113, esp. 112-13; idem, "A Man Clothed in Linen: Daniel 10.6ff. and Jewish Angelology," *JSNT* 24 (1985): 99-110; idem, "Apocalyptic Visions and the Exaltation of Christ in the Letter to the Colossians," *JSNT* 19 (1983): 73-83; idem, "The Vision of the Risen Christ in Rev. i.13ff: The Debt of an Early Christology to an Aspect of Jewish Angelology," *JTS* 31 (1980): 1-11.

20. See, e.g., Fossum (*The Name of God*, 315-17) on Col. 1:15-20; see also idem, "Jewish-Christian Christology and Jewish Mysticism," *VC* 37 (1983): 260-87; idem, "Kyrios Jesus as the Angel of the Lord in Jude 5-7," *NTS* 33 (1987): 226-43.

21. See also Hengel, *The Son of God*, 46-48; Balz, *Methodische Probleme der neutestamentlichen Christologie*, 87ff.

22. C. C. Rowland, "The Influence of the First Chapter of Ezekiel on Jewish and Early Christian Literature" (Ph.D. thesis, Cambridge University, 1974).

23. See, e.g., W. Zimmerli, *Ezekiel 1*, Hermeneia (Philadelphia: Fortress Press, 1979), 236.

24. Ibid., 236.

25. On pp. 85-87 I discuss the suggestion that Ezek. 8:2-4 shows a bifurcation of God and his "glory" (*kābôd*).

26. Rowland, "The Vision of the Risen Christ," esp. 1-4.

27. It is also possible that Ezekiel and Daniel both show applications of a body of traditional descriptions for heavenly beings and that resemblances between passages in the two books should not be pressed very far as indications of conscious borrowing. Rowland's claim of "a close connection with the first chapter of Ezekiel" is something of an overstatement. Cf. Rowland, "The Vision of the Risen Christ," 3.

28. For details, see Rowland, "The Vision of the Risen Christ."

29. Is the "Prince of the host" of Dan. 8:11 God or a particularly important angel prince? If the latter, is this prince Michael, who is called "the great prince" in 12:1?

30. E.g., M. Black, "The Throne-Theophany Prophetic Commission and the 'Son of Man,'" in *Jews, Greeks and Christians: Religious Cultures in Late Antiquity*, ed. R. G. Hamerton-Kelly and R. Scroggs (Leiden: E. J. Brill, 1976), 57-73; and M. Casey, *Son of Man*, esp. 7-50.

31. On the interpretation of the "Son of man" figure in ancient Jewish and Christian sources, see M. Casey, *Son of Man*. See also W. Bittner, "Gott-Menschensohn-Davidsohn. Eine Untersuchung zur Traditionsgeschichte von Daniel 7,13f.," *Freiburger Zeitschrift für Philosophie und Theologie* 32 (1985): 343-72, who emphasizes the royal-Davidic connections of the "son of man" figure of Dan. 7:13-14.

32. For the references to *2 Enoch*, see *OTP*, 1:91–221.

33. E. P. Sanders, "Testament of Abraham," *OTP*, 1:882.

34. I cite the translation by G. Vermes, *The Dead Sea Scrolls in English*, 145–46. For the Hebrew text, see E. Lohse, *Die Texte aus Qumran*, 3d ed. (Munich: Kösel-Verlag, 1981), 219. The connection of the exaltation of Michael among the heavenly beings ("gods"—'*elim*) with the exaltation of Israel among "all flesh" can be compared with the connection of the exaltation of the "one like a son of man" (before God) in Dan. 7:13–14 and the exaltation of the elect on earth in Dan. 7:26–27. This similarity in turn may supply further reason for taking the figure in Dan. 7:13–14 to be a heavenly being, perhaps Michael.

35. For a full discussion of Michael in the Qumran texts, see Noll, "Angelology in the Qumran Texts," esp. 171–215.

36. For the wider history of interest in Michael in Judaism and Christianity, see J. P. Rohland, *Der Erzengel Michael: Arzt und Herr* (Leiden: E. J. Brill, 1977).

37. See Kobelski, *Melchizedek*. He thoroughly discusses the Qumran references to Melchizedek, with reference to the secondary literature. See the translation of *11Q Melchizedek* in Vermes, *The Dead Sea Scrolls in English*, 265–68. Vermes, Kobelski, and other scholars conclude that Melchizedek and Michael were alternate names for the same being in the Qumran community (e.g., Kobelski, *Melchizedek*, 139). Also valuable is Noll, "Angelology in the Qumran Texts," 57–71.

38. Melchizedek probably also appeared in the even more fragmentary Qumran text known as *4QAmram*, but the text is too damaged to be absolutely certain of this (so, e.g., Kobelski, *Melchizedek*, 24–36). Also note the possible references to Melchizedek in the Angel Liturgy of Qumran, as discussed by Newsom, *Songs of the Sabbath Sacrifice*, 133–34.

39. The translation is from Kobelski, *Melchizedek*, 7–9.

40. "While Melchizedek retains the traditional aspects of Michael, at the same time he rises for judgment in the divine council and perhaps atones for the people. No other Qumran text reconciles monotheism with dualism in this way" (Noll, "Angelology in the Qumran Texts," 211).

41. I follow the English translation and versification of this text in *OTP*, 1:681–705; see also the translation in *AOT*, 363–91.

42. The name of the figure varies in the Slavonic manuscripts, but it is generally agreed that the restoration accepted here is correct.

43. *Apoc. Abr.* 10:17 refers to Michael, portrayed as God's chief angel in some other texts, as joining with Yahoel in blessing Abraham and his posterity but does not clarify the respective status of the two angels.

44. The unnamed angel who appears to Asenath in *Joseph and Asenath* also holds a "royal staff," indicating that he has been given authority by God to exercise rule on God's behalf (14:9). Similarly, the enthroned figure seen by Moses in the *Exagoge* of Ezekiel the Tragedian holds a scepter and also is crowned (lines 68–82).

45. See the translation in *OTP*, 1:497–515 and in *AOT*, 915–25. I cite the text according to the divisions in *OTP*. See also the comments of R. Bauckham, "The

Apocalypses in the New Pseudepigrapha," *JSNT* 26 (1986): 100–103. Cf. also *4 Ezra* 4:36–39 and *2 Bar.* 75:1. In both references the angel is apparently Eremiel (though the name is rendered slightly differently), and the seers seem to address this figure in quite exalted terms.

46. See the translation in *OTP*, 2:177–247. On the date and provenance, see ibid., 187–88. See also *AOT*, 465–503.

47. So C. Burchard, *OTP*, 2:225 (n. p).

48. Ibid., 2:225 (n. k).

49. Recall that Philo's references to the Logos (see chap. 2 in this book) include the use of the term "angel" as a title for this figure. Whatever the Logos was for Philo, his use of "angel" as a title for a figure described as God's chief agent or vizier shows that principal angel speculation was known to this Alexandrian Jew also.

50. Citations of *2 Enoch* are from *OTP*, 1:93–221.

51. See also the early Christian document *The Ascension of Isaiah*, where Christ and the Holy Spirit join in worshiping God (9:40–42). But the distinctive Christian devotional treatment of Christ is reflected in 8:18 and 9:27–35, where Christ receives worship along with God.

52. Noll, "Angelology in the Qumran Texts." Note esp. his discussion of angels in the hymns and liturgical texts of the sect (pp. 72–129). On the fellowship of the elect and angels, see also pp. 184–99.

53. See the Qumran liturgical texts in Vermes, *The Dead Sea Scrolls in English*, 149–213. On the Angel Liturgy texts, see Newsom, *Songs of the Sabbath Sacrifice*.

54. Fossum, *The Name of God*.

55. Ibid., esp. 307–21.

56. Note that it is not entirely clear what Philo means by saying that the Logos can be called the "name of God" (*onoma theou*). He may reflect his notion that the Logos is referred to in the Bible when *theos* ("god") is said to have been manifested or "seen." Fossum seems to take it for granted that the phrase means that the Logos is the personification of the tetragrammaton, YHWH, but this is debatable.

57. Fossum, *The Name of God*, 310 (in the discussion of Metatron), and his summary, 333.

58. Ibid., 333.

59. Fossum (ibid., 276 n. 52) seems to imply that there is a tradition of God's principal angel receiving worship in the talmudic passage *b. Ber.* 7a, where Rabbi Ishmael is (fictionally) said to have entered the Holy of Holies of the Jerusalem temple, there encountering "Akatriel Yah, the Lord of Hosts, sitting on a high and sublime throne." This figure then said to him, "Ishmael, my son, give me your praise." But in this text and *3 Enoch* 15B:4, "Akatriel Yah" is clearly a name for God. Only in later Jewish texts does the name seem to be used of an angel, and in these later texts the figure is not an object of worship. See Scholem, *Jewish Gnosticism, Merkabah Mysticism and Talmudic Tradition*, 51–55; and P. S. Alexander's comments in *OTP*, 1:304.

60. Rowland, "The Vision of the Risen Christ"; idem, *The Open Heaven*,

94–113. My criticism of Rowland draws upon my essay "The Binitarian Shape of Early Christian Devotion and Ancient Jewish Monotheism," in *Society of Biblical Literature 1985 Seminar Papers*, ed. K. H. Richards (Atlanta: Scholars Press, 1985), 377–91.

61. Rowland, *The Open Heaven*, 103.
62. Ibid., 96.
63. Ibid., 97.
64. Ibid., 100.
65. Ibid., 101–3.
66. Cf. ibid., 96.
67. In a letter to me (30 August 1986) Fossum cites Ezek. 3:23 as evidence of a separation of a human-shaped *kābôd* from the divine throne. But it seems to me that the text does not give any indication of a permanent splitting off of God's glory.
68. Rowland, *The Open Heaven*, 101–3.
69. Fossum, *The Name of God*, 318–21.
70. Ibid., 318. This view is also taken by Segal, *Two Powers in Heaven*, 196.
71. Nor is the probable allusion to Exod. 23: 20–21 necessarily evidence that Yahoel is presented as the "Angel of the Lord," who is nearly indistinguishable from God himself in certain OT passages. Exodus 23:20–21 does not seem to be a reference to this figure. See the discussion in Stier, *Gott und sein Engel*, 63–71.
72. Fossum, *The Name of God*, 319–20; Rowland, *The Open Heaven*, 102–3.
73. Ibid., 103.
74. Ibid., 102–3; Fossum, *The Name of God*, 320.
75. The phrase is Rowland's (*The Open Heaven*, 103). Fossum (*The Name of God*, 320) states only that "possibly the throne is empty."
76. Note also I. Chernus, "Visions of God in Merkabah Mysticism," *JSS* 13 (1983): 123–46. He challenges the view of Scholem, Quispel, and others that early Jewish mystics distinguished between God and some visible personification of his glory. But cf. Fossum, *The Name of God*, 178–79 n. 311.
77. Segal, *Two Powers in Heaven*, esp. 33–155.
78. Ibid., 187.
79. Ibid., 200–201. After noting the limitations in our knowledge of first-century Judaism, Segal qualifies: "So we cannot be sure than any of the systems would have been called heresy in the first century or even if there was a central power interested to define it. But we cannot altogether dismiss the possibility that some apocalyptic groups posited an independent power as early as the first century or that other groups, among them the predecessors of the rabbis, would have called them heretics" (p. 201).

Chapter 5
The Early Christian Mutation

1. Meeks, *The Prophet-King*. See my discussion of Meeks's work in chap. 3.
2. Dunn, *Christology in the Making*.

3. N. A. Dahl, *The Crucified Messiah and Other Essays* (Minneapolis: Augsburg Publishing House, 1974), 10-36.

4. Hengel (*The Son of God*, 58) warns about taking earliest Christology as "a simple reproduction of earlier Jewish speculations about hypostases and mediators."

5. See Hengel, *The Son of God*, 59-66; and Kramer, *Christ, Lord, Son of God*, 108-11.

6. Hengel, *The Son of God*, 60.

7. Hay, *Glory at the Right Hand*, 61.

8. On the backgrounds of Phil. 2:5-11, see esp. R. P. Martin, *Carmen Christi*, rev. ed. (Grand Rapids: Baker Book House, 1984); and Deichgräber, *Gotteshymnus und Christushymnus*, 118-33. Note also T. Nagata, "Philippians 2:5-11: A Case Study in the Contextual Shaping of Early Christology" (Ph.D. thesis, Princeton Theological Seminary, 1981). On the function of the passage in its present context, see L. W. Hurtado, "Jesus as Lordly Example in Philippians 2:5-11," in *From Jesus to Paul: Studies in Honour of Francis Wright Beare*, ed. P. Richardson and J. Hurd (Waterloo, Ont.: Wilfrid Laurier Univ. Press, 1984), 113-26.

9. Kramer (*Christ, Lord, Son of God*, 65-71) makes an unpersuasive attempt to locate the hymn's origin in a pre-Pauline "Hellenistic Gentile" church.

10. Opinion is divided over whether the hymn thought to lie behind the passage derives from a Palestinian or Diaspora Jewish-Christian setting. Deichgräber (p. 130) opts for the latter, but G. G. Stroumsa connects the hymn with "the very first stratum of Palestinian Christianity" ("Form(s) of God: Some Notes on Metatron and Christ," *HTR* 76 [1983]: 282); and the best-known case for this position was stated by E. Lohmeyer, *Kyrios Jesus. Eine Untersuchung zu Phil 2, 5-11* (Heidelberg: Winter, 1928). See also the summary of recent work in Martin, *Carmen Christi*, xxv-xxxiii.

11. The treatment of the term *Yahweh* in some early copies of the Greek OT is interesting but not decisive. We cannot seriously suppose that readers of these manuscripts in Greek-speaking synagogues pronounced such scribal devices as *pipi* at those points in the text where scribes used them to indicate the divine name. Philo and Josephus indicate that *Kyrios* was a normal Greek *qere* or oral equivalent. See Fitzmyer, *A Wandering Aramean*, 119-23.

12. In addition to the commentaries on 1 Corinthians, see C. H. Giblin, "Three Monotheistic Texts in Paul," *CBQ* 37 (1975): 527-47; Thüsing, *Per Christum in Deum*, 225-58; Dunn, *Christology in the Making*, 179-83; and Horsley, "The Background of the Confessional Formula in 1 Kor. 8:6," 130-34.

13. Thus, use of the phrase "one god" (*heis theos*) and similar prepositional formulae ("from whom," etc.) in pagan writers of the time is of limited relevance. These writers do not share Paul's essentially Jewish view that belief in "one God" demands the rejection of all others. Cf. Conzelmann, *1 Corinthians*, 139-45; W. A. Meeks, *The First Urban Christians* (New Haven: Yale Univ. Press, 1983), 91, 228 n. 93, for references to pagan writers. See Horsley, "The Background of the Confessional Formula in 1 Kor. 8:6," for emphasis on the pre-Pauline, Jewish

adaptation of Greek philosophical formulae.

14. The Shema is of course a pre-Christian Jewish confession, constructed from Deut. 6:4-9; 11:13-21; and Num. 15:37-41. The Greek wording of Deut. 6:4 is especially relevant—*kyrios ho theos hēmōn kyrios heis estin* ("The Lord our God is one Lord," or "The Lord our God, the Lord is one"). Dunn (*Christology in the Making*, 180) says that Paul here "splits the *Shema*...between God the Father and Christ the Lord in a way that has no earlier parallel."

15. On *eidōlon*, see F. Büchsel, *TDNT*, 2:375-81.

16. E.g., Philo refers to "Wisdom, by whose agency the universe was brought to completion" in *Det*. 54 (cf. *Fug*. 109).

17. Thus W. A. Elwell, "The Deity of Christ in the Writings of Paul," in *Current Issues in Biblical and Patristic Interpretation*, ed. Hawthorne, 297-308, reads the data to fit later apologetic concerns in claiming that "no distinction is made whatsoever" in Paul between Christ and God (p. 305).

18. See C. H. Talbert, *What Is a Gospel? The Genre of the Canonical Gospels* (Philadelphia: Fortress Press, 1977), 25-52. He discusses pagan ideas of deified heroes (using his essay "The Concept of Immortals in Mediterranean Antiquity," *JBL* 94 [1975]: 419-36); but cf. Aune, "The Problem of the Genre of the Gospels," esp. 18-38. Talbert's position has to do with the way the Gospels are structured and does not really concern the much earlier and more fundamental conception of the exalted Jesus as chief agent of the one God. See also Nock, *Essays on Religion and the Ancient World*, 2:928-39.

19. As has been shown by Holladay, even Philo, who refers to Moses as made "god," gives clear evidence that he meant it only figuratively. On this matter, see chap. 3 of this book. Cf. also Acts 12:21-23; 14:11-15, which echo the same Jewish attitude.

20. Though "mutation" carries a certain pejorative connotation in some colloquial usage, I intend no such meaning here. I draw upon the use of the term in the biological sciences, where it describes a sudden and significant development in a species.

21. J. Wach, *Sociology of Religion* (Chicago: Univ. of Chicago Press, 1944), 25. The quote represents Wach's definition of "cult," the more formal and corporate functions by which religious devotion is offered by a group. I find his definition too loose for "cult" and much more serviceable in defining the wider sphere of religion devotion. On the other hand, R. Bultmann's definition of "cult" as requiring a holy place and time, priests, sacramental actions, etc., is too narrow to allow for the diversity in organized religion (*Theology of the New Testament*, 2 vols. [New York: Charles Scribner's Sons, 1951, 1955], 1:121).

22. See D. E. Aune, *The Cultic Setting of Realized Eschatology in Early Christianity*, NovTSup 28 (Leiden: E. J. Brill, 1972), 9-11.

23. See Wainwright on "The Worship of Jesus Christ," in *The Trinity in the New Testament*, 93-104. He briefly discusses doxologies directed to Christ, prayer to Christ, OT quotations transferred from Yahweh to Christ, and Greek equivalents of the word "worship."

24. Bousset, *Kyrios Christos*, 119-52; Bultmann, *Theology of the New Testament*, 1:42-53.

25. A. Deissmann, *Light from the Ancient East* (Grand Rapids: Baker Book House, 1965 [1927]), 382 n. 2; idem, *Paul: A Study in Social and Religious History* (New York: Harper & Row, 1957), 113-32; J. Weiss, *Earliest Christianity*, 2 vols. (New York: Harper & Row, 1959), 1:37-38.

26. See Aune, *The Cultic Setting*, 5: "Perhaps the single most important historical development within the early church was the rise of the cultic worship of the exalted Jesus within the primitive Palestinian church." Cf. Bultmann, *Theology of the New Testament* (1:51): "In any case, the earliest Church did not cultically worship Jesus, even if it should have called him Lord; the Kyrios-cult originated on Hellenistic soil." There are numerous general studies of early Christian worship, but they do not usually focus on devotion to Jesus sufficiently to be of much direct value in the present discussion. See, e.g., C. C. Richardson, "Worship in NT Times, Christian," *IDB*, 4:883-94; O. Cullmann, *Early Christian Worship*, SBT 10 (London: SCM Press, 1953); G. Delling, *Worship in the New Testament* (Philadelphia: Westminster Press, 1962); F. Hahn, *The Worship of the Early Church* (Philadelphia: Fortress Press, 1973); R. P. Martin, *Worship in the Early Church* (Grand Rapids: Wm. B. Eerdmans, 1974); C. F. D. Moule, *Worship in the New Testament* (London: Lutterworth Press, 1961).

27. For an overview of early evidence concerning hymns sung to Christ, see Martin, *Carmen Christi*, 1-13. On NT hymns to Christ, see J. T. Sanders, *The New Testament Christological Hymns*, SNTSMS 15 (Cambridge: Cambridge Univ. Press, 1971); Deichgräber, *Gotteshymnus und Christushymnus*; K. Wengst, *Christologische Formeln und Lieder des Urchristentums* (Gütersloh: Gerd Mohn, 1972); Hengel, "Hymns and Christology," in *Between Jesus and Paul*, 78-96.

28. The hymnic passages in the nativity story in Luke should be mentioned, although there has been disagreement as to whether these are early Christian compositions or were inherited from pre-Christian circles of pious Jews. See R. E. Brown, *The Birth of the Messiah* (Garden City, N.Y.: Doubleday & Co., 1977), for discussion of the infancy accounts in Matthew and Luke.

29. Deichgräber, *Gotteshymnus und Christushymnus*, 60-61, 207-8.

30. This is emphasized persuasively in Hengel, *Between Jesus and Paul*, 78-96; and see Martin, "Some Reflections on New Testament Hymns," in *Christ the Lord*, ed. Rowden, 37-49.

31. J. D. G. Dunn, *Jesus and the Spirit* (London: SCM Press; Philadelphia: Westminster Press, 1975), esp. 157-96.

32. Cf. Bousset, *Kyrios Christos*, 119-52. The same point was made by Wainwright, *The Trinity in the New Testament*, 87.

33. The Qumran Hymn Scroll *(1QH)* is devoted wholly to the praise of God. The Angel Liturgy does not make the angels the object of praise but testifies to the Qumran belief in the union of heavenly and earthly worship and is concerned with describing the liturgy offered in heaven by the angels. See also K. E. Grözinger, *Musik und Gesang in der Theologie der frühen jüdischen Literatur* (Tübingen:

J. C. B. Mohr [Paul Siebeck], 1982), for a wide-ranging discussion of the Jewish liturgical background.

34. Cf. Col. 3:16–17. The textual witnesses are here divided between the variants "to God" and "to the Lord," but the former is usually preferred on the assumption that the latter variant arose as a harmonization with Eph. 5:19, which shows no variation in its reading "to the Lord."

35. See other doxologies to Christ in 2 Pet. 3:18 and probably 2 Tim. 4:18. See Wainwright, *The Trinity in the New Testament*, 93–96.

36. On Revelation, see E. Schüssler Fiorenza, *The Book of Revelation: Justice and Judgment* (Philadelphia: Fortress Press, 1985).

37. See Wainwright, *The Trinity in the New Testament*, 97–101. See also A. Hamman, "La prière chrétienne et la prière païenne, formes et différences," *ANRW* 2. 23/2:1190–1247; and H. Schönweiss et al., *NIDNTT* 2:855–86.

38. In Acts 4:24 God is addressed by a different term, *despotēs*. Does this show the writer attempting to distinguish God from the *kyrios* Jesus? But 4:29 continues the prayer by addressing God as *kyrios*, showing that there was not a consistent reservation of the term for the exalted Jesus.

39. Here and elsewhere, it is sufficient to cite as Pauline evidence only those writings accepted by all as genuine.

40. Bultmann, *Theology of the New Testament*, 1:128.

41. See Dunn, *Jesus and the Spirit*, 199–300; E. Schweizer, *Church Order in the New Testament* (London: SCM Press, 1961).

42. Wainwright, *The Trinity in the New Testament*, 99–100.

43. On *maranatha*, see O. Cullmann, *The Christology of the New Testament*, rev. ed. (Philadelphia: Westminster Press; London: SCM Press, 1963), 195–237, though some of his linguistic data is dated. J. A. Fitzmyer ("The Semitic Background of the New Testament *Kyrios*-Title," 115–42) gives a thorough treatment of the linguistic evidence and issues, together with full citation of important literature. See also K. G. Kuhn, *"maranatha," TDNT*, 4:466–72; and D. Flusser, "Paganism in Palestine," 1078–79; but Flusser's view that the cry cannot come from the early Christian community is not convincing.

44. See Bultmann, *Theology of the New Testament*, 1:52; and the review of the various attempts by Bousset and Bultmann to avoid the force of the *maranatha* expression (in Cullmann, *The Christology of the New Testament*, 214).

45. Fitzmyer (*A Wandering Aramean*, 123–27) offers a careful assessment of the Aramaic evidence for the usage of *marêh*.

46. On early Jewish liturgical prayer, see S. Talmon, "The Emergence of Institutionalized Prayer in Israel in the Light of the Qumran Literature," in *Qumran: Sa piété, sa théologie et son milieu*, ed. M. Delcor (Leuven: Leuven Univ. Press, 1978), 265–84. For a general description of ancient Jewish worship, see, e.g., A. Cronback, "Worship in NT Times, Jewish," *IDB*, 4:894–903.

47. Sometimes the "name" is "Jesus Christ," or "the Lord Jesus," or "Jesus Christ our Lord," or "our Lord Jesus Christ." Cf., e.g., Acts 2:38; 8:16; 1 Cor. 1:2, 10; etc. On the use of the "name," see Kramer, *Christ, Lord, Son of God*, 75–80.

48. For a judicious discussion, see Hartman, "Baptism 'Into the Name of Jesus,' " 21–48. For a general treatment of the rite, see, e.g., G. R. Beasley-Murray, *Baptism in the New Testament*, rev. ed. (Grand Rapids: Wm. B. Eerdmans, 1962).

49. Among other reasons for assuming an early and Semitic-language setting for the origin of the practice and its link with the name of Jesus, there is the variation in the Greek phrasing of the formula, "in" (*en*), "into" (*eis*), "upon" (*epi*), which suggests various attempts to translate something like the Semitic expression *le shem*. See Hartman, "Baptism 'Into the Name of Jesus,' " 24–28, for examples of such expressions in Jewish texts.

50. Hartman, "Baptism 'Into the Name of Jesus,' " 26.

51. Ibid., 27.

52. Ibid., 35–37.

53. See H. Räisänen, "Galatians 2:16 and Paul's Break with Judaism," *NTS* 31 (1985): 543–53.

54. See also Kramer, *Christ, Lord, Son of God*, 77–78.

55. It bears noting that the OT expression seems to refer to a cultic action such as sacrifice to *Yahweh*. Thus Christian adaptation of the expression as a way of describing cultic invocation of Christ is all the more clearly an innovation in Jewish devotion.

56. Kramer, *Christ, Lord, Son of God*, 79. Cf. P. Vielhauer, *Aufsätze zum Neuen Testament* (Munich: Chr. Kaiser, 1965), 141–98.

57. Kramer, *Christ, Lord, Son of God*, 79.

58. See Conzelmann, *1 Corinthians*, 23; but Conzelmann's claim that "calling upon" the risen Lord is not to be seen as including prayer to him (n. 38) is refuted by our evidence indicating that Christ was regularly addressed in the worship gatherings of Christians as well as in their personal lives. Such appeals did not of course detract from prayer being understood as characteristically offered to God. Nevertheless the practice of appealing to Christ as well as to God *regularly and in corporate worship gatherings* is a significant adaptation of monotheistic devotion and is as close to being prayer as any practice could be within a tradition still committed to belief in "one God."

59. See also Col. 4:17, where Christians are exhorted to "do everything in the name of the Lord Jesus," confirming the observations made here. If Colossians is genuinely from Paul, the reference is even more significant as indication of the early date of such ideas.

60. Thüsing, *Erhöhungsvorstellung und Parusieerwartung in der ältesten nachösterlichen Christologie*.

61. Aune, *The Cultic Setting*. Aune acknowledges as important further confirmation the work of H.-W. Kuhn, *Enderwartung und gegenwärtiges Heil. Untersuchungen zu den Gemeindeliedern von Qumran* (Göttingen: Vandenhoeck & Ruprecht, 1966).

62. On this practice, see, e.g., H. Lietzmann, *Mass and Lord's Supper*, with "Introduction and Further Inquiry" by R. D. Richardson (Leiden: E. J. Brill, 1979).

63. See Conzelmann, *1 Corinthians*, 195–96 for references. The Hebrew terms are *kibbel min* ("receive") and *masar le* ("hand on").

64. Thus, though Conzelmann (*1 Corinthians*, 201–2) thinks that v. 26 begins "Paul's own exposition," nevertheless he grants that "it, too, leans upon traditional terminology."

65. For a critique of the focus on christological titles, see L. E. Keck, "Toward the Renewal of New Testament Christology," *NTS* 32 (1986): 362–77.

66. Cf. D. E. Aune, *Prophecy in Early Christianity and the Ancient Mediterranean World* (Grand Rapids: Wm. B. Eerdmans, 1983), 257. He regards "Jesus is Lord" as a prophetic utterance, specifically a "recognition oracle." But, if so, this "oracle" is almost indistinguishable in form from the "non-prophetic" confession cited by Paul in Rom. 10:9.

67. Early Christian prophecy has also been the subject of much recent publication and cannot be treated in all its contours here. Most recently, see Aune, *Prophecy in Early Christianity*, who also gives full citation of other literature; and D. Hill, *New Testament Prophecy* (Richmond: John Knox Press, 1979).

68. M. E. Boring ("How May We Identify Oracles of Christian Prophets in the Synoptic Tradition? Mark 3:28–29 as a Test Case," *JBL* 91 [1972]: 501–21) holds that prophecy was always first-person address of the risen Christ; but D. Hill ("Prophecy and Prophets in the Revelation of St. John," *NTS* 18 [1971–72]: 401–18) argues that this was done only exceptionally, and that Revelation is a very unusual case of Christian prophecy in this respect. Cf. Aune, *Prophecy in Early Christianity*, 233–35.

69. Aune, *Prophecy in Early Christianity*, 416 n. 13.

70. For a classic discussion of the process of innovation, see H. G. Barnett, *Innovation: The Basis of Cultural Change* (New York: McGraw-Hill Book Co., 1953).

71. On Jesus' ministry, see E. P. Sanders, *Jesus and Judaism.* Cf. Rowland, *Christian Origins*, 122–87.

72. The classic defense of this view is H. E. Tödt, *The Son of Man in the Synoptic Tradition* (Philadelphia: Westminster Press; London: SCM Press, 1965). I am, however, not alone in finding his case unpersuasive. Cf., e.g., Lindars, *Jesus Son of Man.*

73. Rowland (*Christian Origins*, 187–93) offers a judicious discussion of the Easter experiences. On the resurrection appearances, see esp. J. E. Alsup, *The Post-Resurrection Appearance Stories of the Gospel Tradition* (London: SPCK, 1975).

74. For a vigorous defense of the historical value of Acts, see M. Hengel, *Acts and the History of Earliest Christianity* (Philadelphia: Fortress Press; London: SCM Press, 1979).

75. See Kim, *The Origin of Paul's Gospel*, esp. 223–33, for discussion of Paul's vision of Christ, and 3–31 for his treatment of possible Pauline allusions to the Damascus road experience.

76. See A. F. Segal, "Paul and Ecstasy," in *Society of Biblical Literature 1986*

Seminar Papers, ed. Richards, 555–80. He sets Paul's experiences in the context of ancient Jewish mystical experiences. See also J. O. Tabor, *Things Unutterable: Paul's Ascent to Paradise in Its Greco-Roman, Judaic, and Early Christian Contexts* (Lanham, Md.: University Press of America, 1986). Cf. B. R. Gaventa, *From Darkness to Light: Aspects of Conversion in the New Testament* (Philadelphia: Fortress Press, 1986), who doubts that Gal. 1:11–17 refers to "a vision or miraculous encounter."

77. Gaventa (*From Darkness to Light*, 39) analyzes conversion experiences in three types: alternation, pendulum-like conversion, and transformation. She classifies Paul's experience in the last category.

78. On *doxa* ("glory"), see G. von Rad, *TDNT*, 2:233–52.

79. See Kim (*The Origin of Paul's Gospel*, 5–13) for more detailed discussion and references to other literature.

80. Ibid., 8.

81. Rowland, "The Vision of the Risen Christ."

82. Aune (*The Cultic Setting*) discusses the cultic gathering as the setting for mystical experiences. See now Newsom's judgment that the Angel Liturgy of Qumran was used to incite mystical experiences of heavenly things in gatherings of the sect (*Songs of the Sabbath Sacrifice*, 17–21).

83. Note that John says his vision happened "on the Lord's day" (Rev. 1:10). Perhaps this indicates that such religious experiences were expected in the gatherings of Christians, especially on this special day of worship. Cf. 1 Cor. 14:26, where Paul includes "revelation" (*apokalypsis*) as one familiar type of experience in early Christian worship gatherings.

84. The English texts of the creeds associated with Nicaea appear in H. Bettenson, *Documents of the Christian Church*, 2d ed. (London: Oxford Univ. Press, 1963), 34–37. For discussion of the Council, see J. N. D. Kelly, *Early Christian Doctrines*, 2d ed. (New York: Harper & Row, 1960), 223–51; and W. H. C. Frend, *The Rise of Christianity* (Philadelphia: Fortress Press, 1984).

85. Hengel, *Between Jesus and Paul*, 30–47.

86. For an introduction to Pentecostalism, see, e.g., W. J. Hollenweger, *The Pentecostals* (Minneapolis: Augsburg Publishing House, 1972).

87. R. Bauckham (*Jude, 2 Peter*, Word Biblical Commentary 50 [Waco: Word Books, 1983], 97) argues that creative reinterpretation of OT texts about God as references to Jesus began in Palestinian Jewish Christianity. See now D. Juel, *Messianic Exegesis* (Philadelphia: Fortress Press, 1987).

88. I borrow the term "constraints" from A. E. Harvey, *Jesus and the Constraints of History* (Philadelphia: Westminster Press; London: SPCK, 1982); see esp. chap. 7, "The Son of God: The Constraint of Monotheism." I must dissent, however, from Harvey's simplistic understanding of early christological convictions and practices, on account of his preoccupation with such questions as whether Jesus is ever called *theos* in the NT.

89. See J. D. G. Dunn, "Was Christianity a Monotheistic Faith from the Beginning?" *SJT* 35 (1980): 303–36. He is correct in insisting that early Christol-

ogy was not intended as a departure from the traditional concern for one God. In my view, however, Dunn resolves the problem of early Christology too easily, because he fails to do justice to the evidence presented here that shows the place of the exalted Christ in early Christian devotional life.

90. See R. T. France, "The Worship of Jesus: A Neglected Factor in Christological Debate?" in *Christ the Lord*, ed. Rowdon, 17–36.

91. See J. Weiss, *Earliest Christianity*, 1:37, who recognized that the earliest disciples prayed to the exalted Jesus and described the early emergence of cultic devotion to Jesus as "the most significant step of all in the history of the origins of Christianity."

Conclusions

1. R. Stark's influential studies are a good introduction to the study of the growth of religious movements. See, e.g., "The Rise of a New World Faith," *RRR* 26 (1984): 18–27; idem, "How New Religions Succeed: A Theoretical Model," in *The Future of New Religious Movements*, ed. D. Bromley and P. E. Hammond (Macon: Mercer Univ. Press, 1986); idem, "Jewish Conversion and the Rise of Christianity: Rethinking the Received Wisdom," in *Society of Biblical Literature 1986 Seminar Papers*, ed. Richards, 314–29.

2. For an introductory discussion, see R. Stark, "A Taxonomy of Religious Experience," *JSSR* 5 (1965): 97–116. See also, e.g., A. Hardy, *The Spiritual Nature of Man: A Study of Contemporary Religious Experience* (Oxford: Clarendon Press, 1979).

3. Barnett (*Innovation*) includes examples of religious innovations in framing a general theory of cultural innovation.

4. See, e.g., J. Daniélou, *Gospel Message and Hellenistic Culture* (London: Darton, Longman & Todd; Philadelphia: Westminster Press, 1973); and E. Osborn, *The Beginning of Christian Philosophy* (Cambridge: Cambridge Univ. Press, 1981).

Index of Ancient Sources

OLD TESTAMENT

Genesis
1:1—56
1:27—45
5:18-24—51, 54
5:24—52, 53, 148 n.5
12:8—108
13:4—108
16:7-14—75, 156 n.4
21:23—108
22:11-18—75
26:25—108
32:1-2—71
32:24-30—64
37:9-10—59

Exodus
1—15—57
4:16—56, 60
7:1—20, 56, 60, 61, 62,
   152 n.43, 153 nn.44, 49
14:19-20—75
20:4—31
23:20-21—20, 32, 45, 49,
   50, 55, 75, 80, 87, 90,
   140 n.45, 160 n.71

Numbers
15:37-41—162 n.14

Deuteronomy
5:31—60, 61
6:4-9—162 n.14
6:4—162 n.14
11:13-21—162 n.14
13—114
16:1—147 n.22
30:11-12—42
33:3—150 n.26
34:6—61

Joshua
5:13-15—20, 78, 90
5:14—71

Job
5:1—150 n.26
15:7-8—42
28:12-28—42
38:7—59

Psalms
2:7—95
8—123
8:5—56
20:1—47
45:6—54
54:6—47
82—81
82:1—56, 79
99:6—108
103:20—29
105:1—108
110—101, 123
110:1-2—152 n.37
110:1—94, 121
143:13—47
147:4—152 n.37

Proverbs
1:7—42
1:20-33—42
1:29—42
2:1-6—42
3:13-18—42
8:1-9:12—42
8:22-31—42, 44, 47
18:10—47

Isaiah
30:27—47
40—55—54

40:26—152 n.37
41:28—138 n.21
42:6—53
43:10—138 n.21
44:2—138 n.21
44:6—120, 138 n.21
44:24—138 n.21
45:5-8—138 n.21
45:12—138 n.21
45:18—138 n.21
45:21—138 n.21
45:23—97, 127
48:12—120
49:6—53
49:8—79
55:10-11—47
61:1-3—79

Jeremiah
10:6—47

Ezekiel
1:24—120
1:26-28—75, 76, 80, 86,
   87, 88, 89, 137 n.7
3:23—160 n.67
8:2-4—75-76, 86, 87
10:4—87
10:18-19—87
11:22—87

Daniel
7:9-14—54, 75, 77, 149
   n.13
7:9-10—88
7:9—80, 88, 120, 149 n.13
7:13-14—54, 66, 77, 149
   nn.13, 15; 152 n.37, 157
   n.31, 158 n.34
7:13—120, 149 n.13
7:14—77

7:26-27—158 n.34
7:27—66, 77
8:11—157 n.29
8:15-26—76
8:16—23
9:21—76
9:25—79
10—12—76
10:2-9—75, 76
10:5-9—87, 88
10:5-6—80
10:13-21—76
10:13-14—77
10:13—23, 76, 77
10:21—76, 77
12:1-4—78
12:1—23, 76, 79, 90, 140
   n.44, 157 n.29
12:13—76

Joel
2:26—47, 108-9
2:32—109

Malachi
1:11—47

NEW TESTAMENT

Matthew
10:32—112
22:30—154 n.62
23:2—152 n.39
28:16-20—117

Mark
8:38—115
12:24—154 n.62
14:22-25—111
15:26—116

Luke
20:36—154 n.62
22:14-20—111
24:25-27—117
24:36-49—117

John
1:1-18—101
1:1-4—41
1:1-3—21, 104
9:22—112

Acts
1:1-11—118
1:21—104
1:24—104
2:33-36—94
2:33—94
2:34-36—104
2:36—95
2:38—112, 164 n.47
3:1-6—110

4:24—164 n.38
4:27—113
4:29—164 n.38
4:30—113
4:36—134 n.24
5:42—112
6:1—134 n.24
6:8-9—134 n.24
6:11-14—130 n.4
7:55-56—118, 121
7:59-60—104
8:9-13—155 n.72
8:16—164 n.47
9:14—108
9:21—108
9:22—112
10:36—112
11:27—114
12:21-23—162 n.19
14:11-16—162 n.19
19:13-16—30
21:10-11—114
22:16—108, 109

Romans
1:1-4—95
1:3-4—4, 95, 96, 112
1:7—105
1:8-10—104
3:23-26—21
4:24-25—21
8:15-16—106
8:15—4
10:9-13—109, 112
10:9-10—4, 12
10:9—112, 166 n.66
10:13—108
15:30-33—104
16:7—5
16:20—105

1 Corinthians
1:2—108, 109, 164 n.47
1:3—105
1:4—104
1:10—164 n.47
1:30—21
2:8—119
5:1-5—109
5:4—110
5:5—109
6:11—109
8:1-13—130 n.2
8:1-6—97
8:5-6—1
8:5—130 n.2
8:6—2, 21, 97
9:1—118
10:14-21—129 n.1
11—14—105
11:20—111
11:23-26—4, 98, 111

11:23—111
11:26—106, 111
12:1-3—112
12:3—4, 12
14:23-33—105
14:26—101, 122, 167 n.83
15:1-8—4
15:8—118
15:9—2, 5
15:20-28—21, 96
15:24—96
15:25-26—96
15:25—96
15:27-28—96
15:27—96
15:28—96
16:22—4, 106
16:23—105

2 Corinthians
1:2—105
1:3-4—104
3:4-4:6—119
3:7-9—119
3:10-11—119
4:4-6—119
4:4—119
4:6—119
5:10—21
11:23—130 n.4
12:1—118
12:2-10—104
12:8—104
12:9-10—105
13:14—105

Galatians
1:3-4—105
1:11-2:21—132 n.15
1:11-17—4, 167 n.76
1:12—118
1:13-14—2
1:13—5
1:15-16—118
1:16—2, 118
1:17-23—5
1:18—132 n.15
1:23—130 n.4
3:19—34
4:1-11—34
4:6—4, 106
4:9-10—34
5:11—130 n.4
6:12—130 n.4
6:18—105

Ephesians
2:14-16—101
4:6—103
5:14—101
5:18-20—101
5:19—102-3, 164 n.34

Philippians
1:2—105
1:3-5—104
2:5-11—4, 96-97, 101, 102, 161 n.8
2:5-8—104
2:9-11—4, 21, 96-97, 104, 112, 121, 127
3:2-21—130 n.4
3:3—130 n.4
3:7-10—130 n.4
3:14—130 n.4
3:20-21—118, 130 n.4

Colossians
1:15-20—4, 41, 74, 101
1:15-17—104
1:20—104
2:8-23—34
2:8—24, 34
2:16-18—32
2:16—32, 141 n.50
2:18—24, 32, 33, 141 nn.57-58
2:20—34
3:16-17—101, 164 n.34
4:17—165 n.59

1 Thessalonians
1:2-3—104
1:9-10—95
1:10—21
2:16—130 n.4
3:11-13—105
5:28—105

1 Timothy
2:5—29
3:16—101

2 Timothy
4:18—164 n.35

Philemon
3—105
4—104
25—105

Hebrews
1—2—73, 74
1—24
1:1-14—20
1:1-4—41
1:2—21
1:3—21, 101, 104
1:10—21
1:13—21
2:5—21

1 Peter
3:18-22—101
3:22—74

2 Peter
3:18—164 n.35

1 John
4:2-3—112
4:15—112

Revelation
1:5-6—103
1:10—167 n.83
1:12—3:22—119, 120
1:12-20—76
1:12-16—119, 120
1:13—120
1:14—120
1:15—120
1:17—3:22—113
1:17—120
1:18—120
2—3—119, 120
4—89
4:8—101
4:11—101
5—122
5:1-14—4
5:5-12—122
5:8-10—103
5:9-10—101, 104
5:13-14—101, 103
7:9-12—103
7:15-17—101
11:15—101
13:4-18—103
14:6-7—103
14:9-12—103
15:3-4—101
19:1-8—101
19:10—24, 28, 30, 103
19:20-21—103
22:8-9—28, 30, 103
22:8—24
22:20—106

APOCRYPHA AND PSEUDEPIGRAPHA

Apocalypse of Abraham
1—8—79
9—32—79
9—79
10:1-14—20
10:3-10—85, 87
10:3-4—79
10:4-17—83
10:8-17—80, 87
10:17—80, 158 n.43
11—88
11:1-4—80, 83, 88, 137 n.7
16:1-4—83
16:3-4—89

17—19—88
17:1-21—83
17:1—89
18:1-12—80
18:1-5—88
18:1-4—89
18:13-14—89
19:1—89
19:1-5—89

Apocalypse of Zephaniah
6:11-15—80, 84
6:14-15—28
6:15—30, 84

Ascension of Isaiah
6:8—150 n.26
7:21-23—28
7:21-22—30
7:21—24
8:5—24
8:18—159 n.51
9:27-35—159 n.51
9:40-42—159 n.51
10:6—150 n.26

Baruch
3:9—4:4—42
3:29-30—42

2 Baruch
1:2—26
3:1—26
4:1—26
5:1-2—26
6:5-9—26
15:1—26
17:1—26
48:1-24—26
48:2-9—26
48:10—26
48:11-24—26
48:11—26
48:18—26
48:25-41—26
48:42—52:7—26
55:3—74:4—26
75:1—159 n.45

3 Baruch
11:6—78

Biblical Antiquities of Pseudo-Philo
11:14—57
13:8-9—57
18:5—152 n.38

1 Enoch
——52

1:9—150 n.26
9:1—77
9:3—27, 150 n.26
10:1—77
14—36—59
25:3—152 n.37
37—71—53, 54, 149 nn.8, 11
40:5-7—31
40:6—27
40:9-10—77
45:3—53, 59
46—54
46:1-8—20
46:1-3—54
46:2—149 n.13
46:3—53
46:4-8—53
47:1-2—27
47:2—31
48:2-7—57
48:2-3—53
48:4-10—20
48:4-7—53
48:4—53
48:6—53
49:2-4—53
49:4—149 n.7
51:3-5—20, 53
51:3—53, 59, 149 n.12
51:4-5—154 n.62
52:4-9—20, 53
55:4—53, 59, 149 n.7
60:3—150 n.20
61:4-9—53
61:8-9—20
61:8—53, 59
62:2-16—53
62:2—53, 149 n.12
62:3—53
62:5-6—53
62:7-16—20
62:7—53
62:9—53
62:14—53
63:11—53
69:27-29—53
69:27—149 n.7
70:27—53
71—56
71:1—54
71:2—54
71:5—54
71:7-9—54
71:10-13—54
71:11—55
71:14-17—54
71:14—149 n.7, 150 n.16
71:15—149 n.16
71:16—149 n.16
72—82—59
104:1—27, 31

2 Enoch
——52
1—9—156 n.3
9—83
10:1-7—52
11:37-38—52
13:57—52
13:74—52
20—21—83
22:5-10—5
22:5-6—55
22:6—78
22:8-10—55
24:1-3—55
30:8—47, 146 n.21
30:11-12—146 n.21
33:4-10—83
33:10—78
71:28—78
72:5—78

3 Enoch
——53
4:2-3—55
4:8-9—55
9—55
10—12—55
10:1—55
10:3-6—55
12:1—55
12:3-4—55
12:5—55
15B:4—159 n.59

Exagōgē of Ezekiel
——57-59, 151 nn.29-30; 152 n.38, 158 n.44

4 Ezra
4:36-39—159 n.45
6:1-6—138 n.21

Joseph and Asenath
1—9—81
10—13—81
11:3-14—84
11:4—84
11:16-18—84
11:16-17—84
12:5-9—84
12:12-13—84
13:11—84
14—17—81
14:4-7—78
14:8—81, 84
14:9-10—81, 84
14:9—81, 158 n.44
15:7-8—47
15:11-12—81
15:12—84

Jubilees
1:27—151 n.28
4:17-26—52
4:17—52
4:18-19—52
4:21—52, 59
4:23-24—52
4:25—52
10:17—52
21:10—52
30:20—24

Life of Adam and Eve
14:1-2—90

4 Maccabees
4:10-14—28
4:13—28

Paraleipomena of Jeremiah
3:4-14—28
3:4—28

Prayer of Joseph
——64-65

Sirach
4:11-19—42
24:2—42, 44, 49
24:4—44
24:5-6—44
24:8—42
24:9—42
24:10-12—44
24:19-22—42
24:23—42
42:17—150 n.26
44—49—51
44:16—148 n.5
45:2—56, 62, 153 n.44
45:4—57
45:5—57
47:11—54

Testament of Abraham
1:4-5—90
1:4—20, 78
2:1—20
2:2-12—78
11:6—148 n.7
13:21-27—52, 148 n.7

Testament (Assumption) of Moses
1:14—57
3:12—57
10:2-3—140 n.44
10:9—66
11:16-19—57

Testament of Solomon
2:5—28

2:7—28
14:8—28
15:7—28
18—29
18:1-40—28

Testaments of the
Twelve Patriarchs

Testament of Asher
6:6—24

Testament of Benjamin
9:1—52

Testament of Dan
5:6—52
6:1-2—24
6:2—27, 29
6:3-11—29
6:10—29

Testament of Judah
18:1—52

Testament of Levi
3:5-7—27
5:5-7—24
5:5—28, 29
5:6—27
10:5—52
14:1—52

Testament of Naphtali
4:1—52

Testament of Simeon
5:4—52

Testament of Zebulon
3:4—52, 148 n.6

Tobit
3:1-6—27
3:16—27
3:17—27
4:11-15—27
5:4—23
8:5-7—27
8:15-17—27
12:12—24
12:15—27, 77
13:1-18—27

Wisdom of Solomon
2:12—148 n.29
2:15-16—148 n.29
2:18—95
3:1-8—148 n.29
4:10-15—148 n.5
6—10—48
6:1-11—43

6:12—11:1—42
6:12—10:21—23
6:22—43
7:1-22—43
7:22—9:18—43
7:22—20, 42, 44
7:24-26—50
7:25-26—42, 44
7:29-30—44
8:1—20, 42, 44
8:2—44
8:4—20, 42, 44, 50
9:2—42
9:4—42, 44, 50
9:9-11—44
9:9—20
9:10—44, 50
9:11—20, 50
10—11—137 n.6
10:1-2—43
10:5—43
10:6-8—43
10:9-12—43
10:13-14—43
10:15—12:11—43
12:12—19:22—43
18:15-16—47

PHILO OF ALEXANDRIA
De Agricultura
51—49, 50

De Cherubim
27—146 n.12

De Confusione Linguarum
63—50
146—45, 46, 50, 85
168-175—45, 147 n.28

De Fuga et Inventione
94-105—45
94-99—45
100-102—45
101-102—46
101—50, 148 n.30
103-105—45
108-118—50
109—162 n.16

De Gigantibus
49—61

In Flaccum
——153 n.54

De Legatione ad Gaium
——153 n.54

Legum Allegoriae
1.40-41—153 n.47
3.115—147 n.28

De Migratione Abrahami
84—153 n.47
102—50
174—49

De Mutatione Nominum
19—62, 153 n.47
24-26—62
125-129—61, 153 n.47
127-128—62

De Opificio Mundi
24-25—148 n.30
72-75—85
148—154 n.56

De Posteritate Caini
27-31—61
28-30—62
28—21

De Specialibus Legibus
1.13-31—155 n.69
3.111—147 n.28
4.92—147 n.28
4.123—147 n.28
4.168—147 n.28

Quaestiones et Solutiones
in Exodum
2.6—153 n.47
2.13—45, 49
2.29—62
2.46—62
2.62—146 n.12
2.68—146 n.13

Quaestiones et Solutiones
in Genesin
2.51—146 n.12
2.62—45
2.75—147 n.28
4.2—146 n.12
4.8—61
4.110-111—20, 45
4.110—50

Quod Deterius Potiori
insidiari solet
54—162 n.16
160-162—153 n.47
161-162—62

Quod Omnis Probus
Liber sit
42-44—153 n.47
43—62

De Sacrificiis Abelis
et Caini
5—150 n.26
8-9—153 n.47

8—61
9-10—62
9—61
10—61
28—61

De Somniis
1.75—50
1.164-165—67, 155 n.70
2.183—50
2.187-189—153 n.47

De Vita Mosis
1.155-159—21, 60
1.155—60
1.156—60
1.158-159—60
1.158—60, 61, 153 n.47
1.159—61
2.99—146 n.12

QUMRAN TEXTS

Angel Liturgy
——85, 142 n.58, 158
  n.38, 159 n.53, 163
  n.33, 167 n.82

4Q Amram
——158 n.38

11Q Melchizedek
——18, 20, 95, 140 n.44,
  158 n.37
2:4-25—79
2:9-11—79

1Q Milchamah (War
Scroll)
——163 n.33
13:10—78
17:6-8—78

JOSEPHUS

Jewish Antiquities
8.2.5—140 n.48

RABBINIC TEXTS

Babylonian Talmud

  Aboda Zara
42b—30

  Berakot
7a—159 n.59

  Sanhedrin
38b—30, 32

Mekilta
Exod. 20:4—141 n.51
Exod. 20:20—141 n.51

Midrash Bereshit Rabbah
1:1—44
1:4—44

Mishnah Hullin
2:8—30

Tosephta Hullin
2:18—30

TARGUMS

Pseudo-Jonathan
Exod. 20:20—141 n.51

EARLY CHRISTIAN
LITERATURE

Apology of Aristides
14—33, 34

Clement of Alexandria,
The Strommata
6.5.39-41—138 n.21
6.5.39—33

Didache
10:6—106

Epistle to Diognetus
3—4—34

Eusebius, *Praeparatio
Evangelica*
9.28.2-4—151 n.29
9.29.5-16—151 n.29

Justin Martyr, *Dialogue
with Trypho*
——141 n.54
56:4—140 n.47
56:10—140 n.47
61:1—140 n.47

Kerygma Petrou
——33, 34, 138 n.21

Origen, *Commentary on
John*
2.31—154 n.57
13.17—33, 138 n.21

Origen, *Contra Celsum*
1.26—138 n.21, 142 n.61
5.6—138 n.21, 142
  nn.61-62

Origen, *Philocalia*
22.15—154 n.57

Index of Authors

Alexander, P. S., 150 nn.18–19; 159 n.59
Alsup, J. E., 166 n.73
Anderson, F. I., 150 n.21
Aune, D. E., 110, 114, 131 n.6, 162
nn.18, 22; 163 n.26, 165 n.61, 166
nn.66–69; 167 n.82

Bakker, A., 156 n.7
Balz, H. R., 136 n.40, 157 n.21
Barbel, J., 72, 155 n.1, 156 nn.7, 12
Barnett, H. G., 166 n.70, 168 n.3
Barrett, C. K., 130 n.2
Bauckham, R., 38, 144 n.81, 158 n.45,
167 n.87
Beasley-Murray, G. R., 165 n.48
Benoit, A., 133 n.23
Bergmeier, R., 155 n.72
Bettenson, H., 167 n.84
Beyschlag, K., 155 n.72
Bianchi, U., 135 n.31
Bietenhard, H., 25, 138 n.25, 139 n.28,
147 n.22, 155 n.1
Billerbeck, P., 36, 142 n.70
Bittner, W., 157 n.31
Black, M., 149 nn.8, 11–12, 14; 150 n.20,
157 n.30
Borgen, P., 145 n.11
Boring, M. E., 166 n.68
Bousset, W., 22, 23, 24, 25, 27, 35, 36, 41,
100, 106, 131 nn.7, 11; 132 n.15, 134
n.30, 135 nn.34–35; 137 nn.11, 13–17;
138 nn.18–22; 139 n.31, 142 n.68, 143
nn.71–72, 76; 145 n.4, 163 nn.24, 32
Bowman, J., 144 n.85
Box, G. H., 143 n.76
Brandon, S. G. F., 156 n.8
Brown, R. E., 163 n.28
Büchsel, F., 162 n.15
Bultmann, R., 100, 105, 106, 162 n.21,
163 nn.24, 26; 164 nn.40, 44
Burchard, C., 81, 159 nn.47–48

Caird, G. B., 156 n.2
Carr, W., 141 n.58, 155 n.1
Casey, P. M., 131 n.7, 135 n.37, 149 n.11,
150 n.22, 154 n.68, 157 nn.30–31
Charles, R. H., 149 n.16
Charlesworth, J. H., 139 nn.30, 33; 140
n.43, 147 n.24, 148 n.4, 149 nn.8–9;
150 n.17, 151 n.29
Chernus, I., 160 n.76
Coggins, R. J., 144 n.83
Collins, J. J., 133 n.23, 154 n.64
Collins, M. F., 137 n.8, 144 n.85
Colpe, C., 134 n.31, 149 n.11
Colson, F. H., 152 n.42
Conzelmann, H., 130 n.2, 161 n.13, 165
n.58, 166 nn.63–64
Crenshaw, J. L., 145 n.5
Cronback, A., 164 n.46
Cullmann, O., 163 n.26, 164 nn.43–44

Dahl, N. A., 136 n.42, 146 n.12, 161 n.3
Daniélou, J., 73, 156 nn.12, 14; 168 n.4
Daube, D., 136 n.42
Davies, W. D., 133 n.20, 136 n.42
Day, J., 144 n.83
Deichgräber, R., 132 n.12, 161 nn.8, 10;
163 nn.27, 29
Deissmann, A., 28, 101, 135 n.32, 140
n.42, 163 n.25
de Jonge, M., 140 n.45
Delcor, M., 164 n.46
Delling, G., 163 n.26
Denis, A.-M., 151 n.29, 154 n.57
Dey, L. K. K., 145 n.11
Duling, D. C., 141 n.48
Dunn, J. D. G., 6, 46, 73–74, 93, 133
n.18, 136 n.39, 145 nn.2, 11; 146 n.18,
147 n.26, 157 nn.16–17; 160 n.2, 161
n.12, 162 n.14, 163 n.31, 164 n.41, 167
n.89

Elwell, W. A., 162 n.17

Emerton, J. A., 144 n.83
Epp, E. J., 145 n.3
Ernst, J., 136 n.40
Evans, C. A., 141 n.58

Fiorenza, E. S., 46–47, 145 n.9, 146 n.19, 150 n.23, 164 n.36
Fitzmyer, J. A., 132 n.11, 133 n.22, 161 n.11, 164 nn.43, 45
Flusser, D., 133 n.23, 164 n.43
Fossum, J. E., 19, 22, 37, 38, 39, 47, 74, 85, 86, 87, 88, 134 n.26, 136 n.2, 144 nn.79–80, 82; 146 nn.17, 21; 157 n.20, 159 nn.54–59; 160 nn.67, 69–70, 72, 74–76
France, R. T., 131 n.6, 168 n.90
Francis, F. O., 32, 33, 141 n.58
Frend, W. H. C., 167 n.84
Frey, J.-B., 155 n.1

Gager, J. G., 150 n.24
Gaventa, B. R., 167 nn.76–77
Giblin, C. H., 161 n.12
Gibson, A., 143 n.77, 146 n.16, 147 n.23
Goldberg, A. M., 143 n.73, 146 n.14
Goodenough, E. R., 28, 49, 62, 66–67, 140 nn.36, 41–42; 145 n.11, 147 nn.25, 28; 151 n.31, 152 n.41, 153 nn.46, 50, 52–53; 154 nn.65–67
Goodman, M., 134 n.23
Granfield, P., 144 n.79
Grant, R. M., 130 n.1, 131 n.6, 133 n.17
Greenfield, J. C., 150 n.19
Grelot, P., 65, 148 n.3, 149 n.10, 154 nn.63–64
Gressmann, H., 137 n.11
Grillmeier, A., 135 n.36
Grözinger, K. E., 163 n.33
Gruenwald, I., 150 n.19

Hackspill, L., 155 n.1
Hahn, F., 135 n.38, 163 n.26
Halperin, D. J., 151 n.28
Hamerton-Kelly, R. G., 136 n.41, 145 n.1, 157 n.30
Hamman, A., 164 n.37
Hardy, A., 168 n.2
Harris, J. R., 156 n.7
Hartman, L., 108, 132 n.13, 149 n.14, 165 nn.48–52
Harvey, A. E., 167 n.88
Hawthorne, G. F., 145 n.3
Hay, D. M., 96, 137 n.10, 161 n.7
Hayward, R., 143 n.73
Hegermann, H., 145 n.1
Heidt, W. H., 155 n.1
Heitmüller, W., 134 n.30
Hengel, M., 95, 130 n.4, 131 n.9, 132 nn.11–12; 133 n.23, 134 n.24, 136 n.38, 138 n.17, 141 n.57, 144 n.84, 147 n.27, 157 n.21, 161 nn.4–6; 163 nn.27, 30; 166 n.74, 167 n.85

Hennecke, E., 138 n.21
Herford, R. T., 141 n.54
Hilgert, E., 145 n.11
Hill, D., 166 nn.67–68
Holladay, C. R., 6, 58, 62, 133 n.18, 151 nn.29, 33–35; 152 nn.41, 43; 153 nn.46, 48–49, 51; 155 n.68, 162 n.19
Hollenweger, W. J., 167 n.86
Holmberg, B., 131 n.10
Hooker, M. D., 131 n.7, 149 n.15
Horbury, W., 131 n.4
Horsley, R. A., 130 n.2, 161 nn.12–13
Hultgren, A. J., 130 n.4
Hunter, A. M., 131 n.10
Hurd, J., 161 n.8
Hurtado, L. W., 131 n.7, 132 n.14, 134 n.29, 160 n.60, 161 n.8
Hyatt, J. P., 144 n.79

Isser, S. J., 144 n.83, 155 n.71

Jacobson, H., 57, 59, 151 nn.29, 32; 152 nn.33–34, 36–37, 39–40
James, M. R., 151 n.28
Johnson, N. B., 139 n.32
Juel, D., 167 n.87
Jungman, J. A., 144 n.79

Keck, L. E., 166 n.65
Kee, H. C., 134 n.30
Kelly, J. N. D., 167 n.84
Kim, S., 119, 130 n.4, 166 n.75, 167 nn.79–80
Kippenberg, H. G., 144 n.83
Kleinknecht, H., 130 n.1
Klijn, A. F. J., 133 n.16
Knibb, M. A., 150 nn.17, 20
Kobelski, P. J., 137 n.5, 140 n.44, 158 nn.37–39
Kraabel, A. T., 133 n.23
Kraeling, E. G., 144 n.83
Kramer, W., 109, 136 n.38, 161 nn.5, 9; 164 n.47, 165 nn.54, 56–57
Kretschmar, G., 73, 156 n.13
Kuhn, H. B., 25, 138 nn.23, 26; 139 n.28, 155 n.1
Kuhn, H.-W., 165 n.61
Kuhn, K. G., 164 n.43
Kümmel, W. G., 134 n.30

Lieberman, S., 133 n.22, 150 n.19
Lietzmann, H., 165 n.62
Lightstone, J. N., 139 n.33
Lindars, B., 135 n.37, 149 n.11, 166 n.72
Livingstone, E. A., 152 n.41
Lohmeyer, E., 161 n.10
Lohse, E., 158 n.34
Longenecker, R. N., 156 n.15
Lüdemann, G., 155 n.72
Lueken, W., 72, 139 n.35, 140 n.40, 141 n.51, 142 n.64, 156 nn.5–6
Lyons, J., 135 n.32

Macdonald, J., 144 n.85
Mack, B. L., 145 nn.1, 11; 152 n.41
McMullen, R., 129 n.1, 131 n.6
Manns, F., 133 n.16
Marböck, J., 145 n.5
Marcus, R., 143 n.77, 146 n.20, 147 n.21, 152 n.42
Marshall, I. H., 133 n.21, 136 n.39
Martin, R. P., 132 n.12, 161 nn.8, 10; 163 nn.26-27, 30
Mearns, C. L., 150 n.17
Meeks, W. A., 56, 58, 59, 63, 65, 93, 137 n.8, 141 n.58, 150 nn.23-24; 151 nn.28-29, 31, 33; 152 nn.35, 41; 153 nn.45, 49, 53-55; 154 nn.63, 67; 155 nn.70, 72; 160 n.1, 161 n.13
Metzger, B. M., 135 n.31
Meyers, E. M., 133 n.23
Michaelis, W., 73, 156 n.12
Moore, G. F., 36, 136 n.1, 137 n.16, 139 n.31, 142 n.69, 146 n.14
Moule, C. F. D., 163 n.26
Munck, J., 131 n.10

Nagata, T., 161 n.8
Neusner, J., 133 n.16, 150 n.24, 154 n.57
Newsom, C., 142 n.58, 158 n.38, 159 n.53, 167 n.82
Nickelsburg, G. W. E., 139 n.29, 154 n.64
Nilsson, M. P., 130 n.1
Nock, A. D., 133 n.17, 140 n.36, 154 n.67, 162 n.18
Noll, S. F., 24, 25, 84, 138 n.24, 155 n.1, 158 nn.35, 37, 40; 159 n.52

Odeberg, H., 150 n.19
Oesterley, W. O. E., 143 n.76, 151 n.27
Olyan, S., 143 nn.75-76; 144 n.83
Osborn, E., 168 n.4

Pearson, B. A., 145 nn.1, 2
Pfeifer, G., 36, 143 nn.74-75; 146 n.14, 147 nn.25, 27
Pfleiderer, O., 134 n.30
Philonenko, M., 133 n.23
Pummer, R., 144 n.85, 155 n.72

Quispel, G., 144 n.79, 160 n.76

Räisänen, H., 142 n.66, 165 n.53
Reinharz, J., 141 n.49
Reinink, G. J., 133 n.16
Reitzenstein, R., 134 nn.30-31
Richards, K. H., 134 n.29, 142 n.67
Richardson, C. C., 163 n.26
Richardson, P., 161 n.8
Richardson, R. D., 165 n.62
Richardson, W., 152 n.41
Ringgren, H., 47, 143 n.76, 145 nn.5-6, 8; 146 n.17, 146-47 n.21
Rohland, J. P., 158 n.36
Rost, L., 150 n.25

Rowdon, H. H., 132 n.12
Rowland, C. C., 74, 86-87, 88, 133 n.19, 144 n.78, 149 n.15, 157 nn.19, 22, 26-28; 159 n.60, 160 nn.61-66, 68, 72-75; 166 nn.71, 73; 167 n.81
Rudolf, K., 134 n.31, 155 n.72
Russell, D. S., 148 n.1

Safrai, S., 133 n.23
Sanders, E. P., 10, 78, 130 n.4, 133 n.20, 135 n.33, 137 n.12, 139 n.31, 142 n.66, 158 n.33, 166 n.71
Sanders, J. T., 145 n.7, 163 n.27
Sandmel, S., 131 n.8, 135 n.32, 145 n.11
Schäfer, P., 24, 25, 30, 31, 32, 138 n.23, 140 n.37, 141 nn.51-53; 155 n.1
Schenke, H. M., 134 n.31
Schiffman, L. H., 141 nn.49, 53; 142 n.58
Schimanowski, G., 136 n.41
Schlier, H., 155 n.2
Schneemelcher, W., 138 n.21
Schoeps, H. J., 133 n.20
Scholem, G. G., 150 n.19, 159 n.59, 160 n.76
Schönweiss, H., 164 n.37
Schulz, S., 132 n.11
Schweitzer, A., 72
Schweizer, E., 142 n.59, 164 n.41
Scroggs, R., 157 n.30
Segal, A. F., 19, 32, 74, 91, 130 n.3, 133 n.19, 134 nn.26-27; 136 nn.2-3; 141 nn.54-55; 146 n.12, 148 n.2, 156 n.3, 157 n.18, 160 nn.70, 77-79; 166 n.76
Silverman, M. H., 144 n.83
Simon, M., 30, 34, 133 n.16, 134 n.25, 139 n.34, 140 n.42, 141 nn.50, 57; 142 nn.60, 64-65
Smend, R., 151 n.27
Smith, J. Z., 64, 154 nn.57-61
Smith, M., 142 n.67, 154 n.67
Snell, B., 151 n.29
Sparks, H. F. D., 139 n.30
Stanton, G. N., 131 n.4
Stark, R., 168 nn.1-2
Stern, M., 133 n.23
Stier, F., 140 n.39, 155 n.1, 156 n.4, 160 n.71
Stone, M., 139 n.29
Strack, H. L., 36, 142 n.70
Strange, J. F., 133 n.23
Stroumsa, G. G., 161 n.10
Suter, D. W., 149 n.8
Swetschinski, D., 141 n.49

Tabor, J. O., 167 n.76
Talbert, C. H., 162 n.18
Talmon, S., 164 n.46
Teixidor, J., 129 n.1, 131 n.6
Trakatellis, D. C., 140 n.47
Thüsing, W., 110, 136 n.40, 161 n.12, 165 n.60
Tödt, H. E., 166 n.72

Tsakonas, B., 155 n.1

Urbach, E. E., 141 n.54, 143 n.73, 145
   n.10, 146 nn.12, 14; 147 n.22, 155 n.1

van der Horst, P. W., 58, 59, 151 nn.29,
   31; 152 nn.33, 40; 154 n.68
VanderKam, J. C., 148 nn.3-4, 149 n.10
Vattioni, F., 151 n.27
Vermasseren, J., 135 n.31
Vermes, G., 142 n.58, 158 nn.34, 37; 159
   n.53
Vielhauer, P., 165 n.56
Vincent, A., 144 n.83
Vogel, C., 133 n.23
von Rad, G., 145 n.5, 167 n.78

Wach, J., 162 n.21
Wainwright, A. W., 105, 132 n.14, 162
   n.23, 163 n.32, 164 nn.35, 37, 42
Wedderburn, J. M., 135 n.31
Weiss, H.-F., 145 n.1, 147 n.25

Weiss, J., 101, 163 n.25, 168 n.91
Wengst, K., 163 n.27
Wenham, D., 131 n.6
Werner, M., 72, 73, 74, 156 nn.8-11
Whitaker, G. H., 152 n.42
Wicks, H. J., 26, 139 n.29
Wiens, D. H., 135 n.31
Wilckens, U., 145 n.1
Wilken, R. L., 145 n.1
Williams, A. L., 140 nn.43, 46; 141
   nn.49, 56; 142 nn.60, 63
Williamson, R., 152 n.41, 154 n.68
Wilson, S. G., 131 n.7
Wink, W., 156 n.2
Wolfson, H. A., 145 n.11
Wrede, W., 134 n.30

Yamauchi, E., 134 n.31
Yates, R., 142 n.58, 155 n.1

Zimmerli, W., 76, 157 nn.23-24